"Leilah Nadir's insightful, searching story about her Iraqi roots, family, exile, and survival, told in absorbing and moving language, reveals the great civilization now under assault."
— George Elliot Clarke, Poet Laureate of Toronto

"*The Orange Trees of Baghdad* is a stunning book, the best I've read in the past year. Leilah Nadir takes us on her quest to meet the members of her family whose lives have been uprooted by war. In the process, we are drawn into the heart of the world's most ancient civilization. In the haunting, dreamlike pages of this book, we discover that as Baghdad is destroyed, the roots of our own deepest past are being torn asunder. Hypnotically readable."
— James Laxer, author of *The Border* and *The Acadians*

"To understand the suffering of Iraqis through the scattered leaves of exile, read Leilah Nadir's beautiful memoir *The Orange Trees of Baghdad*. In it she tells in detail the history of her country through that of her family. A rich, generous autobiography that takes us to the heart of the Iraqi soul."
— Martine Gozlan, *Marianne* magazine

"Masterfully constructed and profoundly moving, *The Orange Trees of Baghdad* is an intimate and unforgettable account of one woman's quest to connect with her Iraqi heritage, and a stunning portrait of war's ravages on a once-majestic country and its people. This soul-stirring journey of personal and political discovery is a must-read for anyone interested in the tragic reality of Iraq since the Gulf War."
— Carol Shaben, author of *Into the Abyss*, winner of the 2013 Edna Staebler Award for Creative Non-Fiction

THE ORANGE TREES OF
BAGHDAD

In Search of My Lost Family

Leilah Nadir

READ LEAF

Published in 2014 by Read Leaf
www.readleaf.net

Text copyright © 2007, 2014 by Leilah Nadir
Photography copyright © 2007, 2014 by Farah Nosh

CIP Data available from Library and Archives Canada

ISBN 978-1-927018-35-4

We gratefully acknowledge for their financial support of our
publishing program the Canada Council for the Arts, the BC Arts
Council, and the Government of Canada through the Canada
Book Fund (CBF).

Printed in the USA

10 9 8 7 6 5 4 3 2 1

Text design and formatting: Marijke Friesen

For my father and mother
my aunties
and my ancestors

CONTENTS

"Step by step, and you shall get to Baghdad."
—Turkish Proverb

NADIR FAMILY TREE

IRAQ

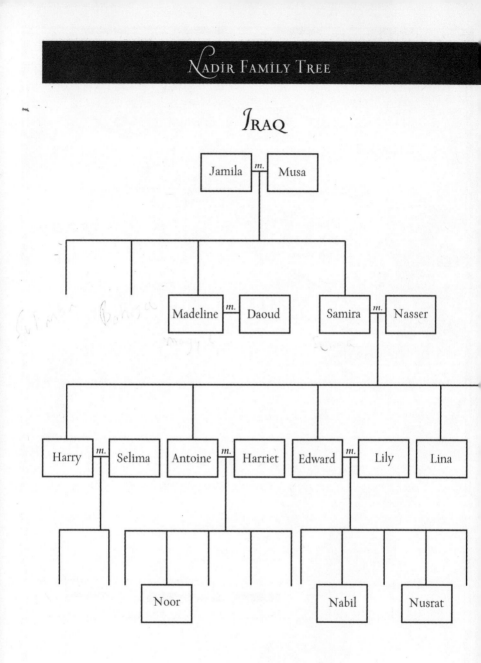

Syria

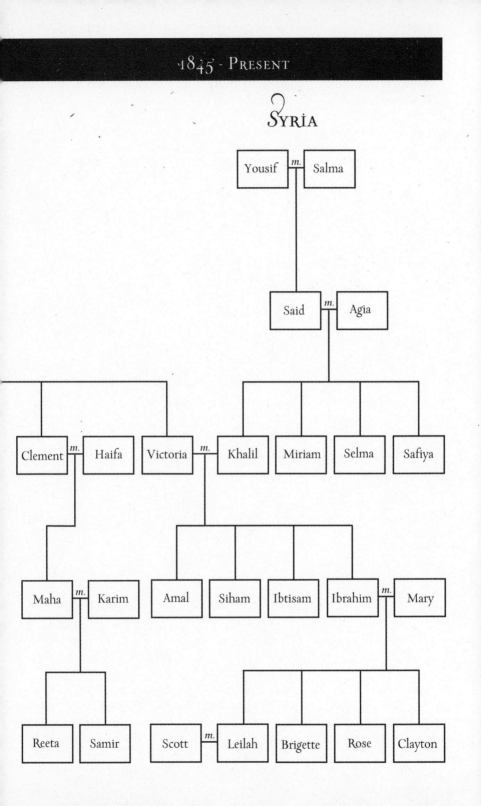

Author's Note

Due to the volatility of politics in Iraq, and because many people still fear reprisals for speaking publicly, I have changed most of the names in this book. The characters and events are real, although minor details may have been altered for the sake of security.

To protect my family's privacy, I display few of our photographs in this book.

AN ORANGE TREE IN A BAGHDAD GARDEN

PHOTO CREDIT: FARAH NOSH

INTRODUCTION
The Mother Tongue

Old Salih the boatman . . . knew all the superstitions of the river: the Jinn, the Divs, the invocations to Elias who hovers on its shores at sunset. He knew the names of the stars: the Children of the Coffin, who follow the North Star to its eternal funeral; and Sirius and Betelgeux, the lovers, who are Majnun and Leila and meet, said he, together in the heavens on one night in the year. —Freya Stark, *Baghdad Sketches*, 1938

"I remember our garden in Baghdad. Rose bushes lined the walls and orange trees hung over the blossoms and dark leaves. A date palm stretched high over all the foliage, intermingled with a few fronds from the palms in the large garden that backed onto ours. We had a pomegranate tree that bore small fruit that my younger sister liked to eat. We grew mint and parsley for salads and my mother even nurtured a loofah plant that she harvested for household sponges. A grapevine crept over a trellis on the patio behind the house, giving us shade in the heat of summer. The grapevine reminded my father of his home village in Syria, but the vine didn't produce grapes. The climate wasn't right for them to ripen. But my mother wrapped fresh dolma in the leaves."

This is not my recollection. The picture is hidden inside my father's memory. Like all our mythical origins, his beginnings are in a garden.

I feel Iraq in my bones, though I have never been there. I have never lazed in the shade of the date palm on a stiflingly hot day or underneath the grape leaves hanging on the vine in the evening. I haven't smelled jasmine or orange blossom scenting a Baghdad night. I've never tasted mango pickle with *masgouf*—the speciality fish dish of Baghdad—at an open-air restaurant on the banks of the Tigris. My father Ibrahim has done none of these things either since he left Iraq at age sixteen in 1960 to go to college in England. Around the world, there are approximately five million exiles from a country of twenty-five million; about one in five Iraqis does not live in Iraq. Most of them, like my father, are afraid to go back, even in peacetime. So we never have.

Yet the garden still exists, my father's childhood house still stands. The orange trees are still there. I sense the garden only through my family's stories; words and pictures about its smells, the searing heat, the light, the butterflies, the storks, eating the Baghdadi delicacy of buffalo cream there. Baghdad is an outdoor city, and family meals were often eaten in the garden or as picnics on the lawn, or cooked on charcoal barbecues on the terrace. I imagine Iraq spreading and rippling out in circles with the house and garden in the halo at the centre. I see the last thirty years passing as the house stands, aging gracefully, then I see family members leaving it, emigrating, dying, and those that remain being slowly ground down by war and poverty.

My paternal grandparents Victoria and Khalil, Iraqi Christians, built the house over fifty years ago. They'd been living at my great-grandmother Samira's house since they got married and were still there despite having had three children: my father and his sisters, Siham and Ibtisam. Amal, the youngest, hadn't been born yet. Victoria and Khalil designed and supervised the building of the family house themselves; people didn't move frequently in the Middle East in those days so they planned to live in it for the rest of their lives and hand it on to their children one day.

When my father was six, he, his parents, and his two sisters moved into their new home. From that day on it was always full of people. Victoria's sister Lina and her mother, Samira, had moved to a street nearby, and their place backed on to Victoria's aunt Madeline's house; Lina, Samira and Madeline were always dropping by for coffee. Victoria and Khalil's home was also the family hub that her unmarried brothers gravitated towards. Amal, the youngest of my father's three sisters, was born in the house. Siham remembers the excitement when Amal first cried out, and how when Siham first saw her still naked, she felt sorry for her little sister because she didn't have any clothes.

I have only seen black-and-white photographs, but it is an elegant, flat-roofed house made of brick and stucco in a streamlined fifties style, with an iron gate entrance and a high wall surrounding the front and back gardens. The house has two levels of walled roofs designed for privacy and joined by a staircase, one for the parents and a lower one with a rounded wall for the children. Baghdadis sleep in cot beds on the roof on summer nights because it is uncomfortably hot inside. Summer lasts for a third of the year, so they need to slumber under the stars for months. The photographs show the house at every angle, complete with the empty lot next door, where a peasant family from the countryside looking for work in the city built their mud-and-straw huts and tended their buffalo. The woman baked bread in a special clay oven, a tanour (like a tandoori oven), and sold it. My father and his sisters watched from the roof while the neighbours made up their beds of reeds in the evening. My grandfather Khalil bought bread and fresh buffalo milk and cream directly from them each day.

Once my father's family moved in, they obtained their furniture and carpets over many years, slowly easing into the house. My father tells me that buying a carpet was like acquiring a work of art because you had to live with it for a very long time. The carpets were bought from Persians on pilgrimage to the Shia shrines in Kerbala and Najaf; they would come to Iraq by donkey every year, selling carpets in the streets to fund their pilgrimage from Iran and back. They'd bring one or two carpets each, likely handmade by their own relatives. A large carpet often took six months to weave. The carpet sellers weren't just street hawkers. They sold intricate, fine-quality carpets, and one sale would suffice to fund their entire journey. My father remembers the neighbourhood women gathering to watch the bargaining spectacle, which was like street theatre. He stood by as his mother haggled for the first carpet for their new house. At first, after showing her the carpet with great fanfare, extolling its unique beauty and high quality, the seller named his price. My grandmother immediately retorted with a low sum, about thirty percent of what the seller asked, knowing she would be refused. Predictably, the seller clicked his tongue in disgust and started to roll up the carpet, while my grandmother strolled back towards the house. The seller shouted out another price, slightly lower than his original, just before she reached the door. She hesitated, turned around and asked to look at it again. The neighbourhood women got involved in the discussion, pointing out defects and merits, before my grandmother named a slightly better price than her original offer. This process took many hours until finally a deal was made. The haggling was a psychological drama, the seller needing the money to support his family for many months, Victoria wanting to get the best price she could for a carpet she'd have for years to come. The carpets were used every winter when the desert cooled, then cleaned and rolled up in the spring to leave the tiles bare for the heat of summer.

❈

I was born in Canada to a British mother and an Iraqi father. I am the oldest of four children, three girls and a boy, the youngest. My sister Brigette and I were born in Canada, in 1973 and 1971, respectively, but we spent our childhoods in England when we moved to London for my father's work. My youngest sister Rose, and brother, Clayton, were born in England, in 1978 and 1982, respectively, but then our family moved back to Canada for good in 1982.

My curiosity with Iraq began with my name, Leilah, which in Arabic means "night," "dark as night," or "dark-haired." Nadir means "rare." But Leilah has other more ancient and literary roots. The most famous Arab book in the Western world, *One Thousand and One Nights*, mentions my name twice in Arabic, "Alf Layla Wa Layla," literally "One Night and a Thousand Nights." And whenever I introduce myself to an Arab or an Iranian, the first thing they always say is, "Ahh, Layla and Qays, like Romeo and Juliet."

Layla and Qays is one of the earliest Arab legends and is said to be based on a true story. It began as an oral tale handed down among Bedouin tribes in the seventh century, and was later retold in countless adaptations, the most famous by the Persian poet Nizami, who brought many versions together in one epic poem. The details vary depending on who is telling them, but the essence remains the same. Qays (also known by his nickname, Majnun) became infatuated to the point of madness with a woman of the same Bedouin tribe named Layla, who reciprocated his love but was obliged to marry another man to satisfy her father. Qays passed the rest of his days wandering half-naked among the hills and valleys of his native land, singing about the beauty of his beloved and yearning for a sight of her. Only when her name was mentioned would he return to his normal self.

But when I asked my mother why she gave me this particular Arabic name, she told me that the first time she heard it was when she saw Leila Khaled on television in 1969. Leila was a young Palestinian refugee who hijacked a TWA plane from Rome to Athens to protest against the largest American airline flying to Israel. The flight was diverted to Damascus, but first it flew over Haifa, Leila's birthplace, where her family had been driven from in 1948. The hijacking helped put the Palestinian issue into the international consciousness and made Leila Khaled the poster girl for Palestinian freedom fighters. I was shocked and asked my mother how she could have named me after such a notorious woman. She reminded me that she was only twenty-two at the time and Leila was only seventeen, and seemed so young, beautiful and brave. My mother was inspired by this woman's fierce courage to stand up against injustice. These days it is hard to imagine an English mother naming her first-born after a hijacker.

Despite my name, I was a typical English schoolgirl. I wore a uniform to school including a tie and a maroon felt hat in the winter or a straw boater in the summer. We lived on a quiet, tree-lined street full of large houses and wild, spacious gardens in a leafy suburb of Surrey. From my perspective as a young girl, Iraq was only an abstract world out of which emerged a travelling circus composed of my Iraqi grandparents, aunts, great-aunts and uncles. Once every few years they drove from Iraq through Turkey to Greece and across Europe to England.

My grandfather loved travelling and was a rare Iraqi in that he thought nothing of driving to London for weeks to visit his son. He'd come with his family in car convoys like desert caravans, stopping in Istanbul, Rome, Vienna and Paris before crossing the channel to England by ferry. My father's parents, sisters and Aunt Lina came together, and on one occasion, his great-aunt Madeline and her husband, Daoud, accompanied them. My mother could never believe how they fit everything and everyone into the small cars. They came in a Volkswagen Beetle, but somehow managed to cram in endless numbers of suitcases and arrive in London with creamy pistachios, olives, nougat with nuts, boxes of dates and an Iraqi speciality called *kletcha*, crescent-moon pastries filled with dates, and of course baklava. Each time, my father reminded them that he could get nearly everything in London, but they didn't care. It was Iraqi hospitality to come laden with gifts.

There were also presents of gold for my mother, and food, spices and, most importantly, olive oil for my father, which came from Safita, Syria, from my great-grandfather's olive groves. This was the most valuable gift because such high-quality olive oil couldn't be found in London. The oil came in large glass bottles in woven grass baskets; to my father it was the best olive oil you could get. It was delicious and so fresh—the colour of liquid gold with only a hint of green. My father transferred the oil into another container so his parents could take the bottles back to Baghdad to reuse them.

Without realizing what they were doing, my father's relatives immediately transformed the English house usually run by my mother into an Iraqi home run by all the women. They took over our house, bringing the exotic right into the familiar; they came with their own pungent smells, spicy dishes, gold filigree jewellery, incomprehensible language, moaning music and strange belly dancing. To me, Iraq was my new family: hearing Arabic conversation peppered with English, eating Arabic food, listening to Arabic music—Farouz, Umm Kalthoum—and learning how to dance to it.

I can see the house in the village in Surrey where I grew up, and can still feel them there moving up and down the stairs, in and out of rooms: my great-aunt Madeline who was a retired midwife; Daoud, who had owned a printing press and had been a journalist and publisher; my great-aunt Lina who worked in Customs; my grandmother Victoria and my grandfather Khalil who were both schoolteachers. My father's three sisters, Amal, Ibtisam and Siham, who now live in London, were all in their early twenties and were beautiful with their unfamiliar, shiny black hair and smooth olive skin.

The world was turned upside down; my father spoke a language I didn't understand. I was embraced by countless fleshy arms, seated aloft on laps cushioning my small legs, kissed and tickled, submerged in love. I sat awestruck through entire conversations in Arabic, where I only recognized my own name, "Leilah." My aunts teased and tortured my sister and I, little dark-haired English schoolgirls, randomly inserting our names into their conversations so we would tug at their sleeves with a physical need to know what they were saying about us. My mother called my father "*habib*," which means "beloved." It was one of the only Arabic words she knew. My father used "*Yullah*," instead of "Hurry up." I only understood a smattering of Arabic: "*la*" for "no," "*aye*" for "yes;" the rest was a mystery of guttural sounds and deep laughs. My father never taught me Arabic; they say "mother tongue" for a reason—mine came from my mother. Raised in England, we girls spoke to both our parents in English; since my mother couldn't speak Arabic, we didn't hear it in our house. So my father, now among his Iraqi family, was suddenly sweetly foreign to me. And I loved it.

Iraq came to me next through food. Our large polished dining-room table, usually empty except at Christmas and Easter and the odd Sunday lunch, creaked under a feast of yellow rice chicken biryani, dolma (stuffed vine leaves), green bean, tomato and lamb casseroles, chicken curry, *bamiya*, tabbouleh, hummus, baba ganouj, pita bread and *fattoush*. The hot dishes steamed their fragrance into the damp English air. Iraqi food is a mixture of all the countries that surround it; there are Lebanese, Syrian, Indian, Persian and Turkish dishes, so we had curries, sweet-and-sour dishes, Mediterranean-style *mezze* and grilled meats. My Iraqi family bustled around talking loudly, passionately, and their animated gestures, more sweeping than my mother's, seemed to make them dance around the table.

In my memories, my grandfather Khalil is a glass of chestnut-tinted cardamom tea. Into a tiny hourglass-shaped cup with a gold-decorated glass saucer, he drops three sugar cubes, almost spilling the tea over the rim, and sips. I watch him stir it with a tiny silver spoon that tinkles against the glass as the sugar spins white and syrupy and settles in a round heap at the bottom. He has thick silver and black hair, despite being in his sixties, and a small moustache, brown skin and black eyes. His frame is small and he is neatly dressed. He speaks to me in English because he is an English teacher in Baghdad.

Victoria, my grandmother, is rosewater- and pistachio-flavoured Turkish delight. My mother took a photograph of her standing in front of a blooming bed of English rose bushes in our garden; yellow, red, pink, white, fuchsia, burgundy. She smiles slightly, shy with her dark hair piled on her head, her stout body covered in a flowery print dress. She had her own rose garden behind her house in Baghdad. She was a silent presence, and I realize now that it was because she couldn't speak much English. She was large, pillowy, with big brown eyes and thick black hair, even then. We cuddled and kissed but couldn't communicate with words. She'd feed me pieces of Turkish delight, soft gelatine that tasted unlike any sweet I'd ever eaten. The chewy, fragrant squares gave off puffs of white sugar when I bit into them that drifted into the air around me, making it magical to eat.

Her sister, my great-auntie Lina, is a laughing face with an attractive gap in her front teeth. Fifteen years younger than my grandmother and single throughout her life, she had a youthful spirit. Her voice, deep and warm, caresses my ears. Since she had no children of her own, she doted on us like a mother. Her cuddles were powerful, fierce with a love that had only a short time to make its imprint. On her last visit to London, she brought a carpet for my brother, Clayton, to celebrate his birth. It depicts the great ancient king Nebuchadnezzar riding a chariot into battle on a dark blue background with red decoration.

My grandmother's aunt, my great-great-auntie Madeline (Maddie), is the remarkable beauty in the family. She is her night-black eyes and cheeks like polished stone, her wavy thick hair and her fashionable clothes. She grew wealthy from being a midwife to rich Iraqis. Childless, too, she was glamorous and exotic because she left Iraq on her own when she was only sixteen to study midwifery in India at a school run by nuns. She knew English from those days and was the first family member to travel to Europe, in the 1950s.

Her husband, my great-great-uncle Daoud, is the chocolate uncle. Each time he saw us he gave my sister and I a massive plastic bag full of chocolate: large dark bars in gold paper, milk-chocolate buttons, slabs of nutty chocolate. It was more than my sister and I could carry, and we spent hours dividing the stash fairly between us.

I found out later that he was a leftist in the democratic party and a journalist, and had spent three years as a political prisoner in Iraq not long before he visited us.

My father is warm pita bread dipped in *lebne* (strained yogurt) dribbled in olive oil, which he ate each morning before work. He alternated each bite with a sip of sweet tea, just like his father, though he drank his with milk and sugar in a mug instead of black in a chiming glass. He is also Saturday afternoon standing quietly in the kitchen stirring an Iraqi *bamiya*—tomato, okra and lamb casserole—or an Indian-style potato and chicken curry. The weekdays were English food cooked by my mother, but the weekends were often Arabic food, tabbouleh (chopping the parsley took hours), grilled chicken with garlic sauce, kebabs, saffron rice with raisins, almonds and pine nuts.

My mother is the tinkle of the six jangling gold bangles from Iraq that she wears on her right arm and has not removed in forty years since she first put them on. They were a wedding present from my father's family, the traditional gold jewellery given to a bride in Iraq. When I was a girl, they were an alarm, always announcing her arrival into a room before she got there. One day, she took me into her bedroom and opened her jewellery box and showed me all the gold necklaces, bracelets and rings that my father's family had given her over the years of their visits. There was a gold-and-black winged bull of Assyria on a gold chain from her mother-in-law, a bracelet that was linked with small blocks of gold that looked to my eyes like tiny chocolate bars from Auntie Madeline, and gold-and-turquoise necklaces, rings and bracelets.

I remember her unlacing a small velvet bag and showing me the tiny pearl-and-gold bracelet that my grandparents had given to me when I was born. It was a miniature replica of a bracelet-and-necklace set they had presented to my mother. Already it was far too small for me because it was made for a baby, but my mother fastened on my wrist another gold bracelet engraved with my name. The gold was so pure that it was soft and bent easily. Even though I never wore the petite pearl bracelet, it hung in my mind and I waited patiently for the day when my arm would be big enough to wear my mother's bracelet.

A year after their visit, when I was eight, Iraq became associated with a faraway place, rather than just a people. A foreign-looking package arrived from Iraq. My grandmother had sent me a traditional Arab costume, a black head scarf and an embroidered dress she'd made out of scratchy pink-and-silver material. The fabric was scented with the peculiar musky smell of another country that had been preserved in its packaging. The dress fit perfectly, and I wore it on a float that was part of a multicultural parade in the local village. I sat cross-legged in my costume, waving an Iraqi flag at the English townspeople. I felt different compared to all the other times I'd played dress-up. My dark brown eyes and brown hair looked right underneath the black scarf. My features that hadn't looked pale enough in my maroon English school uniform suddenly felt like they had a place. On the float, waving behind this other self, I caught a glimpse of what it was to be an outsider, and of what England looked like from a small distance behind a head scarf.

In 1982 my family moved from London to Canada, and I didn't see my Iraqi grandparents or great-aunts and -uncles anymore or have any direct contact with them, never even hearing their voices on the telephone. The vitality of that half of my bloodline went dormant, silent, and I was left with my ghostly memories. But I always thought that I would see them again someday. I didn't realize then that I'd already said my goodbyes.

IBRAHIM

AMAL IN THE GARDEN OF OUR HOUSE IN BAGHDAD

CHAPTER ONE
The Orange Orchard

Ten minutes was all it took to keep the Pentagon's promise . . . of "shock and awe," as the trappings of Saddam Hussein's regime were obliterated. The onslaught began at 9.02pm Baghdad time and by 9.12pm the mass of concrete hulks and lavish palaces that had symbolised Saddam's thirty-year rule . . . were turned into burning pyres. . . . From the east side of the river, it was like watching a gigantic video game. As soon as one building was hit, low-flying jets struck again . . . They set off great jets of fire as easily as the flick of a cigarette lighter . . . trails of red anti-aircraft fire from the Iraqi defences twinkled in the sky, as insubstantial as fairy lights. . . . —"30 Years of Saddam Razed," The Guardian, March 22, 2003*

I am alone at home in Vancouver watching Baghdad burning on television. It is March 22, 2003. Fires rage all over the city, and the black night is illuminated by those bonfires. A few nights ago, I woke from a vivid dream of walking in those streets, along the walls of Saddam's palace enclosures near where I know my family house is, touching the sand-coloured stone. I felt such relief to be in Baghdad, despite my fear. Now it is all burning; great blazes of yellow light destroying the city. For the first time I can see a live feed of the Baghdad of my father's childhood, which he hasn't seen himself for more than forty years. I pick up the phone and call my father. His choked words echo in my mind: "There are people in all those buildings. Those aren't empty buildings. Just think of that."

I imagine all the people I know who are trapped and cowering under the threat of those bombs landing on their houses: my great-aunt Lina, my cousins Karim and Maha, their children Reeta and Samir, my other uncles and aunts on my father's side who I have never met. I think of all their extended families and of my friend Farah Nosh, an Iraqi-Canadian photojournalist who is covering the war for the *New York Times* and other international publications.

Three days earlier, the front page of *The Globe and Mail* newspaper ran a photograph of Baghdad at sunset. The peaceful city is a beautiful golden sandy hue and pale green date palms line the Tigris River. Staring into it, I felt cheated. I was finally seeing Baghdad, but it was about to be destroyed.

The next day, *The Globe and Mail* front page headline ran, "First strike on Baghdad targets Iraqi leadership." The war had started. Cruise missiles and stealth F-117 warplanes launched "decapitation strikes" to kill Saddam Hussein at dawn.

In all the months of buildup to the war, I hadn't believed the United States would attack Iraq again. When the invasion proved imminent and inevitable, a week before war was declared, I'd called my aunts, Amal, Siham and Ibtisam, in London and asked them if they thought Saddam Hussein had weapons of mass destruction.

"How can he have weapons?" Amal said in her lilting Iraqi accent. "The country has nothing, no medicine, no food, no money, never mind weapons! How can people believe this?"

Amal lived through the Iran–Iraq War until 1988 and was on holiday in London in August 1990, when Iraq invaded Kuwait. The Gulf War started five months later, and she and her two sisters have lived in London together ever since.

"I've just been on the phone with Auntie Lina in Baghdad. Of course, we are more frightened than they are," she said.

"We have lived through war before," Lina had told Amal. Unmarried Lina, now seventy, had been like a mother to my aunts, visiting them every day when they were children and moving in with them when Amal was a teenager in Baghdad. "We know what it is to be bombed. In a way, the bombing has never stopped."

They were frightened, Lina said, but since they didn't have satellite television they didn't know just how much weaponry was targeting their country. Iraqi state television was galvanizing the weary people to believe that the war would be won by Iraq. And Amal didn't contradict this message. She didn't tell Lina that our newspapers were speculating that the US–UK war plan was to launch more missiles in the first day of bombarding Baghdad than they had done in the first sixty days of the Gulf War, and that the Pentagon planned to strike Baghdad with three thousand precision-guided bombs and missiles in the first two days.

My middle-class relatives in Baghdad were reduced to stockpiling their yearly rations of flour, sugar and rice, which amounted to one sack of each and a small amount of tea.

"We are already dieting," my great-aunt joked.

There were no perishable items, of course, because the fridge and stove wouldn't work as soon as the electrical plant was bombed. The neighbours were digging a well. During the Gulf War, the water supply was hit immediately ("Why?" my great-aunt asked). But the well water was contaminated, and she'd have to boil it before they could drink it. She was planning to cook on a portable stove until her one canister of gas ran out.

Amal asked Auntie Lina what she would do when that canister was finished.

"I will look out at the Seville orange trees in the garden," Lina replied.

Lina was planning to stay at our family house for the duration of the war, however long it took. She was going to look after it, just as she had done during the Gulf War and since, because her own house was rented out. She didn't want to leave our house empty for fear of looting. She saw herself as the guardian of our home and garden until our family could come back to claim it. It was if she was expecting us one day.

When my father lived in Iraq as a boy, in the months of February and March the *narinj* trees produced small juicy oranges as bitter as lemons. It is a different species of orange than the one we know and eat. Even in Spain, this species is merely ornamental, but in Iraq the fruit of the tree is used for cooking. My grandfather Khalil would cut down the oranges when they were ripe.

"The juice was excellent for making many delicious dishes and salads," my great-aunt told Amal. "Do you remember? Your brother and his cousins used to collect them, your mother would squeeze them and heat the juice, which we'd keep for the winter—a hundred jars of orange juice," she said, "and we'd make marmalade with the peel."

During the Gulf War, the trees lost all their leaves.

"Maybe it was the lack of water or they were poisoned," Lina speculated.

After the war, the trees produced deformed fruit that was inedible.

"The orange trees are dying," Lina told Amal.

If the war lasted too long and the gas ran out, my great-aunt said that they planned to chop the trees down and burn them for fuel.

"What else can we do?" she said, her voice rising.

When Amal and I discussed it afterwards we agreed that we couldn't tell how serious she was.

On the eve of the 2003 invasion of Iraq, through this short conversation, my great-aunt was resurrected for me. Through the sanction years, after the Gulf War until the 2003 invasion, no one had talked much about her. Since I had left London, she hadn't been alive to me. And now I pictured her daily life, her real concerns and her kindness in protecting our family home while preparing for yet another siege and bombardment. Just as I'd found her, I was going to lose her again.

We couldn't drop bombs on my seventy-year-old aunt. I felt that anyone hearing her story would realize this. In a desperate rush, I wrote an article entitled "Living Through a War in Baghdad" and sent it to *The Globe and Mail*, praying the newspaper would publish it. But by the time the article was published, it was March 20, and the

US and UK were dropping their "targeted" bombs on Saddam Hussein and "collaterally" on the people of Iraq.

The next day, I got up and went to work as usual, numb from shock. I called my aunts, and they'd managed to speak to Auntie Lina one more time. Thankfully, the phone line still worked. They urged her to go and live with our other family members and not worry about the house. They didn't want her to be alone. Lina said that all the neighbours were staying in, hiding in their homes. She was determined to stay in our house. They didn't have a bomb shelter to go to anyway. The house is between an oil refinery with a human shield on it, which they thought was good, and one of Saddam's palaces, which they thought was bad—very bad. My aunts asked why Lina didn't leave Iraq. She said no one was taking Iraqis. Some neighbours who had tried to get out via Syria had been turned back; the border was sealed. The people have to stay in Iraq now and face whatever comes.

The last thing my great-aunt said, now sick with fear, was, "Why are they doing this to us?"

VICTORIA AND TWENTY-
MONTH-OLD IBRAHIM

THE FAMILY ON THE TIGRIS RIVER,
GOING TO AL JAZZRA (THE ISLAND)

CHAPTER TWO

The Father Country

Every year around this time I would look for the one or two white storks that used to nest on the dome of the old church in Bab Al-Mu'azzam. I wonder if they have made it to Baghdad this year? I doubt it. . . . On the second day of the [2003] war, American B-52 bombers were taking off from Fairfield Airbase in England and heading toward the skies over Baghdad. Someone on Fox News described them as "beautiful birds," and [US Secretary of Defense Donald] Rumsfeld spoke of "the humanity which went into the making of these weapons." If they don't perish first, the storks will try to return next year. —Sinan Antoon, "Of Bridges and Birds," Al-Ahram Weekly, April 17–23, 2003

With the war raging, I wasn't sleeping, and I found it difficult to go through the rituals of my daily life. I realized that my mother's culture was terrorizing my father's. The present was invading the past. This had already happened in my lifetime during the 1991 Gulf War, but then the international agreement to go to war and the complicit silence of the Western media had shielded us from the reality of the devastation wrought on Iraqi society. This time I was thirty-two, twelve years older, and I knew that there was something deeply wrong with what was happening.

My siblings and I would not exist if the British hadn't created Iraq from the defeated provinces of the Ottoman Empire after World War I. Battles and empire produced our family, and so we are the fruits of war. When I look in the mirror, I try to guess which of my features I inherited from my Iraqi father and which from my English mother. But the same clash of cultures that created me is also part of what makes it impossible for me to visit my ancestral home. Now, as I watch this war, it's as if one part of me is invading the other. I feel like this war is between two cultures whose blood flows in me, and it makes the experience entirely different. To look at me is to look at both the aggressor and the victim. I am both the enemy and the ally.

And my father was the enemy once again. Despite being close to him, I knew little about his relationship to Iraq or his extended family. His past had been submerged inside him, and he had kept it from us for reasons we didn't understand.

The outline of his story is simple. The Iraqi government granted him a scholarship to go to England, but he was expected to return and bring his knowledge back home. Instead, my father fell in love with my English mother, and my grandfather paid back the scholarship to the government. As the Iraqi regime was so ruthless, my father never knew what would happen if he went back, so he never risked returning to his homeland. He might have been forced to stay at the whim of the regime, or be drafted into the army or be forced to work at the Iraq Petroleum Company as an engineer or some other job that he didn't want.

In retrospect the story should have seemed strange, vacant of details, but I never questioned it. My father is not loquacious, especially when the subject of conversation turns to himself, his past or his emotions. A good listener, he is an observer and thinker who rarely says anything superfluous and who, when he does speak, usually says something unusual, ironic or surprising. So it was not strange to us, his children, that he never spoke much about his homeland.

At fifty-nine years old, his hair is still black with few silvery strands, his thick black eyebrows make him look very serious, but his dark eyes are gentle. He looks like an Arab, but from living for so many years in Northern countries, his olive skin is pale and burns when first exposed to the summer sun.

A successful engineer and businessman, he has a scientific, rational approach to life. He is very reliable, loves math and famously, as his colleagues sometimes tease, "never makes mistakes." He isn't superstitious, a conspiracy theorist or a reactive thinker; he loves games of strategy like bridge and chess and laughs off mysticism and miracles. Perhaps because he married an Englishwoman, he didn't socialize much with other Iraqis or live out an Arabic life in Canada. He assimilated willingly and easily, and was happy in the West.

After 9/11, the public discussions about whether the US should invade Iraq began to heat up. In all the confusion and conflicting arguments I'd asked my father if he thought that Iraqis would be happy to see Saddam removed. He shook his head. Then I said, "Will you be happy to see him gone? I mean, you couldn't ever go to Iraq because of him." Then I stumbled; it was hard to say, "You couldn't even go to your parents' funerals, even see them before they died because of his regime. You must want to see him gone." He shrugged; he still didn't want to betray his feelings. He'd never stood at their graves. I thought he wasn't going to answer me, but he did.

"No one hates Saddam Hussein as much as I do, no one would be happier than me to see him gone," he'd replied angrily. "But this war is illegal, immoral! It would be unjustified, it is a pre-emptive war. It would be seen in the Middle East as an unprovoked invasion by the West, against international law, confirming everyone's worst fears about Western imperialism. It would not be acceptable. You can't just decide that you don't like your neighbour and go into his house and murder him. You can't take the law into your own hands. Innocent people will die and then how can the world ever turn to a country ruled by a despot and tell them that such actions are unacceptable? It would be hypocrisy."

My father believed that the goodwill the world had shown the United States after September 11, 2001, gave them an opportunity to show restraint, to get the world on their side and to begin the new millennium peacefully.

The first protest my father had ever attended was against the US invasion of Iraq. He was skeptical.

"I can't believe I'm protesting the removal of Saddam—that just shows you how bad Bush's policies are! It's ridiculous," he'd said, shaking his head. "If George Bush can't win a popularity contest with Saddam Hussein, he must be pretty bad." He'd then added sardonically, "I'm sure Bush is going to be really scared by all this peaceful protest." But he marched anyway.

All the years of the Iran–Iraq War, the Gulf War and the sanctions, when I think about it now, must have been agonizing for him. But he never complained or expressed bitter anger. In fact, I'd never heard him complain about anything in his life. His parents, two of his sisters (during the Iran–Iraq War), his aunts and uncles, his childhood friends and countless cousins were all left behind in Baghdad, while he was living in the safety and prosperity of Canada, bringing up a family of four children. His pain was deeply hidden from us all.

All my life I'd never perceived my father as an immigrant and so whenever there was a war in Iraq, I was startled to be reminded that he came from an enemy land. I became more and more fascinated by him. Once, I asked him if he had an Iraqi passport, like dual citizenship. He'd laughed, saying, "You can't get rid of an Iraqi passport," but he never mentioned going back.

On March 29, 2003, I decided to go to London with my father to visit his sisters, who had been living in England since the 1991 Gulf War. On the plane, I picked up *The Globe and Mail* and began to read an article by Paul William Roberts, one of the few journalists who was reporting from Baghdad, unembedded. The article, "Rocking the Cradle," is both a lament for the city of Baghdad and an introduction to Iraqi history and culture. It was also the first article I'd read that offered the Western reader a sense of what Iraqi civilians felt about the war. He described the aftermath of what the Pentagon was calling shock-and-awe bombardment: "As I write, Baghdad lies in ruins around me. Not the ruins it was in last week, last year, a decade or even thirty decades ago. These are new ruins, and they've pushed Baghdad into the critical mass of ruin; more of it is now ruined than isn't. No longer a city with ruins, it's a ruined city in which even the intact buildings partake of desolation, silence and despair. It is empty, abandoned, but the people have not yet gone."

I read aloud the summary of five millennia of Iraqi history to my father, and when I got to the word "Nebuchadnezzar" he corrected my pronunciation, adding a guttural growl and an Arabic accent. It was like when he pronounced Aladdin *Alah-ah-din* with an emphasis on the "ah." It reminded me of when he spoke the language to our relatives on the phone, or when I saw him read a letter in Arabic or write in Arabic script. It reminded me that my father had an alternate existence that I was not privy to, a family that I did not know.

My father had only seen his parents a handful of times since he'd left home at age sixteen, and they had never had the opportunity to develop a relationship with us, their only grandchildren. His sisters had never married. Despite desiring to know Iraq, I'd never thought of how different my life might have been if Iraq had not been such an isolated country, but now I wondered what it would have been like to visit my family in their own home in Baghdad. Maybe I'd speak Arabic in the Iraqi Christian dialect, maybe I'd know how to cook Iraqi food, I'd know about the poetry, the music, the culture, the history.

The Iran–Iraq War made it impossible for my family to visit Baghdad, and like all Iraqis, my relatives were forbidden to leave the country during wartime. For my grandfather Khalil this was especially hard because he had always loved travelling. From his days as a young man hiking in Syria and Lebanon, to his travels through Europe in the 1970s, he had always wanted to see more of the world. For a Syrian or an Iraqi of his generation, he was intrepid. Until his death, Khalil had to make do with travel within the borders of Iraq to satiate his nomadic appetite, with trips to Babylon, the desert and the Tigris and Euphrates Rivers.

By the 1980s, Saddam Hussein's totalitarian dictatorship made it extremely risky to ask questions on the telephone about our relatives' true circumstances, which could put them in danger for perceived criticism of the regime. Iraq had an elaborate network of *mukharabat* (secret police), and no one knew who they could trust, so people never spoke about politics openly, even to their friends and neighbours. Even though we were not a political family and should not have been at risk, the ruthless brutality of the regime made it impossible for my father to visit his mother when she was ill, or to attend her funeral when she died in 1983.

By the time I started university in Montreal in 1988, Iraq was the dark place of war, suffering and isolation we think of today. The Iran–Iraq War ended in the summer of 1988, though I knew almost nothing about it at the time. Iranians accepted the UN–brokered ceasefire, largely because they realized they were not just at war with Iraq, but also with the Western powers Iraq was developing increasingly close relationships with, especially the United States, which had naval forces in the Persian Gulf that were effectively supporting Saddam Hussein. I didn't know that the front resembled the trench warfare of World War I in all its indiscriminate horror and use of chemical weapons, or that the West was complicit in arming Iraq. The "victory" was hollow though, because the toll on Iraq was tremendous: a quarter million Iraqis were dead, including the victims of the government's brutal campaign against the Kurds; sixty thousand more were prisoners of the Iranians, and Iraq had run up a debt of eighty billion dollars.

In August 1989, the Berlin Wall fell, marking the end of the cold war and the beginning of the dissolution of the Soviet Union. That same year my grandfather became suddenly ill. My father wasn't told how serious Khalil's condition was, because his relatives wanted to protect him from feeling obliged to risk going to Baghdad to see Khalil. When my grandfather died, my father couldn't attend the funeral once again.

When the travel restrictions were finally lifted in 1990, my two aunts Amal and Ibtisam came to London to visit their sister, Siham. On August 2, Iraq invaded Kuwait, completing the occupation in just twenty-four hours. Amal and Ibtisam were given emergency amnesty to stay in England until the crisis was over. They are still in London seventeen years later, their limbo extended indefinitely.

Iraqi and Kuwaiti assets were frozen, and the UN Security Council imposed a total economic and trade embargo on Iraq. Saudi Arabia asked for US military assistance, and the US committed itself to the unconditional withdrawal of Iraq from Kuwait. Within six months half a million American troops were stationed in Saudi Arabia. On January 16, 1991, the US-led coalition of twenty-eight other UN members began a fierce aerial bombardment of Iraq followed by a brief land war to push Iraqi forces out of Kuwait. A ceasefire was signed on February 28, 1991; by then, Kuwait had been liberated. Encouraged by the American president's appeal to the Iraqi people to rise up and overthrow Saddam Hussein, there were rebellions in the North by the Kurds and in the South by the Shia. But no American help materialized, and it soon became clear that the United States, fearing the possible fragmentation of Iraq, preferred to allow Saddam Hussein to maintain his hold on the country.

Though the "Gulf War" had ended, strict UN sanctions—the harshest ever imposed on a country—were left in place, ostensibly to prevent Iraq's development of putative weapons of mass destruction and missile capabilities. But the sanctions only strengthened Saddam Hussein's regime, while crippling the economy and civil life and making international communication even more difficult. So what little we did hear from our relatives was always, all of it, bad.

Through all of this, I always had a mysteriously strong urge to visit Iraq and meet my remaining relatives. Even though I could never see my grandparents again, I could see the house where my father grew up and discover for myself the sights of ancient Mesopotamia and biblical Iraq. I'd been taken with the people of the south since I'd first read Wilfred Thesiger's book *The Marsh Arabs* on his travels among this ancient people who have lived, until recent decades, in the same manner since Sumerian times, and the books by the English traveller Freya Stark had increased my fascination with Baghdad. I'd felt proprietary towards the country; it was somehow mine because of my heritage, and I felt proud of it and wanted to know it. But there was always something stopping me. I was eight when Saddam Hussein took power, and since then my family has always advised me to wait, without any explanation, saying, "Not now, wait until the situation gets better, when it isn't so risky, so unsafe." That day has not yet come.

※

As the plane destined for London rushed forward into the night, propelling us into the future of the next day, my father finally started telling me the story of his past. The flight attendant was pushing her trolley in the aisle, and my father pulled down the tray in front of him. The neutrality of the airplane, high above land and its borders, seemed to allow my father to talk more freely than usual. He started at his beginning, as far back as he knew.

"Well, I spent the first years of my life living in my grandmother Samira's house because there was no such thing as a mortgage in Iraq, and so my parents couldn't afford to have their own house right away, they had to save for it," he said. "I don't remember much about that time. I think she lived in Old Baghdad, though.

"My mother didn't cut my hair until I was three. I don't know why, but she must have been superstitious. Sometimes Arab women believe that they can fool bad spirits, and so they disguise their sons as young girls to confuse the evil demons so they won't hurt their children. Warding off the evil eye. In my baby photos I look like a girl. I think before I was born she must have prayed for a healthy baby, a son even, and when I was safely in this world she had to fulfill her part of the bargain and not cut my hair. Who knows, who knows? I never got to ask her. Ask my sisters. Maybe they know," he said.

His grandparents on his mother's side, Nasser and Samira, were originally from Mosul in northern Iraq, then home to a large Christian population. Northern Iraq is still full of Christian villages, some of which date back to the beginnings of Christianity. Samira and Nasser were born at the end of the nineteenth century in circumstances that were almost unimaginable even for my father. At the time, Iraq was divided into three provinces that had been ruled by the Ottoman Empire since 1638. Despite having Arabic names themselves, they made the curious decision to give their six children English or European names: Victoria, Harry, Antoine, Edward, Clement and Lina. Victoria, my father's mother, was the eldest.

"I am not sure why they did that, but the timing is interesting," said my father.

The British conquered Iraq in March 1917, eighty-six years to the month before the Americans in March 2003.

"I don't know much about my grandfather, Nasser, but the one thing I'm sure of is that he was a translator for the occupying British army." He paused for a moment, deep in thought. "But my mother was born in 1914, just before World War I, so the dates don't add up to her parents naming her for patriotic reasons. I'd love to know if giving babies English names was fashionable at the time."

By the beginning of World War I in 1914, many Iraqis were quite happy that the Allies, led by the British, had come to oust the Ottoman Turks who had been ruling and oppressing them for centuries. Initially, many Iraqis co-operated with the British. The British conquest and this naming of children with English names laid down the foundations for, and foreshadowed, the possibility of my current half-English and half-Iraqi family.

"So, were Nasser and Samira Chaldean Christians?" I asked, as I'd heard of Iraqi Christians being called Chaldean.

"No, no. It's different," my father said. "We're Syrian Catholics. We're Suriyan, not Assyrian or *Athuri*."

"So that's obviously different from Roman Catholic?" I couldn't understand how Syrian Christians could be Catholics, and my father didn't really know either.

My father had never even hinted that the kind of Christianity he'd grown up with in Iraq was any different from what my mother had grown up with in England. My mother had once said that despite their different cultural backgrounds, she felt that she and Ibrahim had had similar upbringings because of their Catholicism. I'd assumed it was the same Catholicism.

Later on, I found out that Christianity had existed in Iraq since the second century AD, when Jews who had converted to Christianity arrived there and began to convert the Mesopotamians. Our family is considered Suriyani, more specifically Syrian Catholic, the branch of the Syrian Orthodox Church that united with the Roman Catholic Church in 1782. Syrian Catholics have maintained many Eastern rites, and the liturgy is still performed in the ancient Syriac language, a dialect of Aramaic, the language that Jesus himself presumably spoke. Syriac replaced Aramaic, and the language became synonymous with Eastern Christians.

At church when they were young, my father and aunts heard the sacred liturgy in Syriac while the homily was in Arabic. An Iraqi man I once met in Paris took one look at me and said, "You have a Chaldean face." This comment wasn't quite accurate because Chaldeans are a separate branch of Iraqi Catholicism, but I took it to mean that I look like an Iraqi Christian.

"Why don't you know more about your religion?" I asked my father.

"I never questioned it." He shrugged, moving on. "There is little family lore about Nasser because he died young of pneumonia. Forty-two, I think he was. By then the family had moved to Old Baghdad with its shadowy bazaars selling silks and spices, indigo and velvet. The lanes were so narrow that a heavily loaded donkey could block the whole space, making it impossible to pass. Wooden lattice-work balconies hung out into the lanes, and old houses were hidden behind doors in the walls of the streets. My mother was just eighteen, and to think, she was the eldest. She had a place at medical school, which she had to give up to become a teacher so she could help support the family." When I press him about why he knows so little about his own grandfather, even anecdotes, he answers, "Life was hard then, you know. People had to struggle, people didn't have the luxury to talk about family history or stories about the past, even the middle classes like us. You just got on with life, with surviving. Besides, we were too young to be asking questions about our ancestors; we just didn't think about it."

"Perhaps your grandfather was already a translator for the British before World War I, since there was a British presence in the area due to their interests in India and Iraq, which was on the trade route," I speculated.

"Maybe, maybe," he said, nodding. "I'll have to check the history. You see, there must have been a reason why he knew English well enough to be a translator by 1917. Maybe World War I explains it, but I just don't know. In 1917, Britain occupied Baghdad, and after the dissolution of the Ottoman Empire in 1918 the mandate for Iraq was given to the British, and King Faisal was enthroned the next year as king of Iraq."

"Is there a photograph of Nasser at least?" I asked.

"I think there might be a wedding photo of Nasser and Samira, but it is at home, in Baghdad. I remember Nasser had a huge black twirly moustache that came to two hard points at either tip. I can't remember what they were wearing in the photo, but I think it was Western-style wedding attire," he said.

Now I had a picture of Samira's life, living in a house in Old Baghdad as a young widow with six children to bring up. Despite the hardship, she managed to send four of her children to university. She made her living as a midwife. Harry became a schoolteacher, and Antoine studied law. Surprising to me, the girls studied and worked as well. Victoria became a teacher; she had to study quickly and get a job as soon as possible to help contribute to the family when my great-grandfather died. Lina took economics at university and worked her way up to a high position in Customs and Excise. Clement, the youngest, was wild and handsome and loved partying and staying out late. Eventually, he got married and opened an automotive spare-parts company.

"The Iraqi government always put on so many import restrictions, so Clement never actually had much to sell. It was a controlled economy, remember. Of course, people always find a way of getting around these things, but he never did a huge amount of business. He's Maha's father. He's still alive."

"Maha, who's that?" I ask.

"She is my cousin. She lives in Baghdad with her husband, Karim, and their children. She is very close to Auntie Lina as well," he explained.

We sat side by side, our dinner eaten, and the dim lights made it easier for my father to freely reminisce.

My father thinks his parents met through Victoria's brother, Edward. By 1939, Khalil had moved to Iraq to start his professional life as a teacher after finishing his degree at the American University in Beirut. He'd already taught in Kirkuk, in northern Iraq, but now he'd moved to Baghdad and gave private lessons in English. Edward was one of Khalil's students. Edward was bright in some subjects, but students had to pass all of their exams in the same year in order to go on to the next year. And Uncle Edward passed everything for two years running, except English. In his third year, he had to write the national final exam that all Iraqi students had to sit, and somehow the exam papers were leaked and some students got hold of them. Edward took them to Khalil's house. "Khalil gave Edward the answers," my father explains, "but he still got only fifty percent.

English was just too hard for him. The way my father told it, laughing at the absurdity, he just couldn't believe that even when Edward knew the answers in advance, he still almost failed English! But my father must have been madly in love with Victoria, so that's why he gave Edward the answers, I suspect, to impress her. He was a very honest man. Usually, he abhorred any mention of cheating, never mind cheating itself."

In 1939, King Ghazi (who had succeeded Faisal in 1933) was killed in a car accident and was succeeded by his infant son, Faisal II, under the regency of Prince 'Abd al-Ilah who had been educated in England like his cousin, King Hussein of Jordan. They were Hashemites (a dynasty from the Hejaz region of Arabia), not Iraqis. Britain had given them Jordan and Iraq to thank them for their help in defeating the Turks in World War I. In April 1941, a military coup d'état by Rashid 'Ali al-Kailani caused the regent to flee Baghdad. But the government of Rashid collapsed two months later when British troops marched on Baghdad, and the regent was reinstalled, propped up by the British.

I've seen my grandparents' wedding photograph, taken in a studio in Baghdad on the day they were married, August 8, 1943. They are dressed in Western-style wedding clothes: Victoria in a long white silk dress with a tiara of orange blossoms and a very long veil that trails down her back, and Khalil in a black suit with a white bowtie. They are standing arm in arm flanked by two bridesmaids, Victoria's aunt Madeline and her teenage sister, Lina. Both Victoria and Khalil are wearing white gloves, and Victoria holds a bouquet of lilies. They were in their thirties when they got married. At first they lived with Victoria's mother, Samira, in Old Baghdad, where my father was born a year later in 1944, just as World War II was ending.

My father doesn't remember living in that first house, but he recollects visiting relatives in the back streets of the old city when he was a bit older. His first memories are of riding his tricycle on the roof of his grandmother's house in a new suburb near the Tigris

River, which she moved into when the city started to spread out in the late forties and early fifties. Her house backed onto her sister Madeline's, and the two gardens were connected by a gate. Nine people lived there with Samira: my father, his parents, his two sisters, his three uncles and Aunt Lina. His childhood memories are happy ones. The house was alive with people. He remembers his uncles, handsome young men who were in their early twenties at the time. They didn't do much. They went to work in the day and in the evenings played backgammon or went out to cafés and friends' houses to socialize and philosophize. My father was doted on by his fierce grandmother, a great matriarch with an extremely powerful personality. Auntie Lina and her three brothers always had friends dropping by, so there was continual laughter, eating and drinking tea. He was never alone.

To add to the activity, Samira was a very busy midwife and a nurse, and her patients came to the house for a host of minor medical needs: injections, penicillin, and once in a while even a night birth. People from all walks of life came to the house to see Samira, but there was a variable charging system depending on whether the patient was rich or poor. Most of the visitors were poor, and house calls were reserved for rich families, especially when the women were having their babies.

Samira's sister Madeline was also a midwife, but she didn't, or couldn't, have children of her own. She married Daoud—the "chocolate uncle" my sister and I remember—for romantic love, which was unusual and glamorous at the time. In Iraq in the early twentieth century, marriages generally occurred between families who already knew each other. Older female family members would play matchmaker, searching out eligible partners for their young relatives. Once introduced, it was up to the man and woman to fall in love or decide to marry. In Madeline's case, the families did not know each other and so no matchmaking occurred. She was said to be very beautiful with her dark hair and large coffee-black eyes, but she chose an intellectual from a poorer background rather than a rich husband. Aunt Madeline and Daoud even honeymooned in Alexandria in Egypt, which was an exceptional and exotic destination at the time.

"My grandmother disliked Uncle Daoud and couldn't understand why Madeline had married him," my father said. "He was a bit arrogant, spoke English and was an Athuri. She thought he was too full of himself."

Unlike my father's own uncles, Uncle Daoud was political. He was a printer and a publisher who owned and ran his own printing press. He also imported printing presses and copying machines, mimeographs called Roneos. They were a cheap way to make a few copies, and many political pamphlets were printed in this way. He was also a journalist who sometimes worked as a correspondent for Western wire services during the 1940s and 1950s. Daoud was on the left and was anti-monarchy; he wanted a more socialist country that wasn't tied to Britain, and even ran in the Iraqi elections as a social democrat in the 1950s, but was never elected.

"So what was the political scene like in those days?" I asked.

"It was the appearance of democracy, but the British were behind the puppet government. The structure was similar to the relationship between the British monarchy and Parliament, but the Iraqi monarchy made sure that the elections resulted in a friendly, co-operative prime minister. Nuri al-Said was prime minister for as long as I can remember until the revolution in 1958. Parliament was just a rubber-stamp body. There were regular elections, but they were rigged. In comparison to what happened after the revolution, though, it was a mild dictatorship. We even had double-decker buses in Baghdad," he recalled.

"I thought Iraq had never had elections before?"

"Oh, we've had democracy before. There were many elections under the monarchy, but they were all manipulated. Even under Saddam there were elections! So what if he got 99 per cent of the vote! Having elections is what makes elections, right, not whether they are fair or not," he said sarcastically. "That's why Daoud was never elected. He never even got three votes! When Auntie Siham was a little girl, she used to campaign for him at the bus stops, handing out his political leaflets to people as they got on or off the bus. But, of course, nothing ever came of it."

My father then said, "Have I ever told you that Iraqi joke about the old man?"

"No."

"Well, an old man goes to vote. He comes out of the voting booth, and starts going home. Suddenly, he remembers something and goes back to the polling station. He says to the officials, 'I'm sorry, I think I made a mistake on my ballot and did not vote for our great leader Saddam Hussein.' The officials laugh and say, 'Don't worry, don't worry, we already made the correction for you. We *knew* who you really meant to vote for.'"

In the end, Daoud was jailed in the early 1970s, when he was sixty.

"They found one of his printing presses in an anti-government cell, an organization that was publishing a pamphlet or something antagonistic to the government. Daoud sold the printer to these men who were in the cell, so he was put in prison. I think he was in prison for three years, maybe less. I think Madeline pulled strings and more or less got him out. She was a respected midwife and had lots of contacts. People felt that because she helped bring their children into the world, they had a kind of obligation to her. So if she wants to see you, and you are a minister or something, you would give her your time. The government probably eventually realized Daoud was a harmless old man and let him go. He was probably tortured in prison though," my father said casually.

"But I met him in London. When was that?" I asked.

"I think it must have been just after he'd been released from prison. He was very quiet and remote, and got on well with my father all their lives. He never spoke about what had happened to him in jail, but he ceased to be political after that," he concluded.

It was hard to put into perspective my memories of my kind great-great uncle and the idea of him being imprisoned and tortured in an Iraqi jail. My father was used to this idea, so he was already thinking about something else.

"But back to my grandmother," he said. His memories, now jolted, seemed to be coming back quickly, as one story after another streamed out of him. "So both sisters were midwives and made a good living."

Madeline was also part owner of a cinema close to Martyrs Square in the centre of Baghdad, so the family went to the movies for free and sat in the special box seats.

"I spent much of my boyhood going to old movies with Auntie Madeline. She was very glamorous, dressed beautifully and was quite rich," he said. "She even had a fur coat, which was very unusual in those days . . . maybe it came from India. Even though she was my grandmother's sister, she was only four years older than my own mother. So she seemed quite young to me, comparatively. And maybe because she'd never had children too. She took me to the cinema on Sundays because I went to Baghdad College, which was a Christian school, and we had Sundays off rather than Fridays like everyone else. All my friends were at school, and my father was working. Madeline wasn't working much as she was getting older, and so she used to take me to church and then to the cinema afterwards. I only remember seeing English movies; they were subtitled, but I could understand them mostly. We saw fifties Hollywood movies like *Ben Hur* or ones starring Elizabeth Taylor."

By 1951, Victoria and Khalil had built their own house on a street near Samira's. The family moved in just before Amal, the youngest daughter, was born. This is the house that is still spoken of as "our house." My grandparents lived there until they died, and Aunts Amal and Ibtisam lived there until the Gulf War.

"When Amal was born, I recall coming home from school and being told, 'You have a new sister.' Of course, Madeline and Samira delivered her, and Lina was there too. Always a household full of women." My father shook his head, rolling his eyes. "I think that's why we were not a very political family, not many men and lots of strong women. So by and large we were left alone by the regime."

At the time of Amal's birth, tragedy befell one of Khalil's sisters, Miriam, whom he had left behind in Syria. Her newborn daughter had died suddenly, and her husband died very shortly afterwards. So she moved to Baghdad to be with her brother's family, enlarging the household further.

"What happened to them?" I asked.

"I don't know. You'll have to ask my sisters. No one really knew how they died."

I looked unconvinced.

"Well, they didn't tell us anyway. But their deaths were the result of natural causes; I think no one liked to talk about sad things." He went on. "Because my mother and father both worked all day, Miriam really raised Amal. She doted on Amal and loved her like a mother, and Amal was like her daughter, except she could do nothing wrong. She probably spoiled her. It didn't seem strange at the time, but when you think of it now, she must have been channelling her grief. Years later, Miriam married a family friend and left the house, but she was a fixture there while we were growing up."

"So what was growing up in Iraq like?" I asked.

"Just ordinary," he said. "I went to school, and we had mass every day." He seemed sleepy now—it was the middle of the night—but I was wide awake on his stories.

I didn't want him to stop talking. It felt as if his childhood had been somehow hidden away, even from him. My mother was always passing on her family history. There was an oral tradition in her house, and she told stories of everyone in her family. Without knowing it, I'd absorbed her past, memorized her family history. But this was all new and tantalizing.

"How did you learn English?" I asked.

"My Baba."

Khalil had taught his son English as soon as he started speaking, and communicated with him in both languages. So Ibrahim was, in essence, brought up bilingual. In primary school, he learned English as well. By the time Ibrahim was eleven and attending an all-boys' Jesuit college, his English was quite good. All his foreign teachers were American priests, but the boys also had local Iraqi teachers. The curriculum was bilingual and all the subjects, including math and science, were taught twice, once in each language. He remembered Arabic literature and English literature class.

"We learnt Arabic poetry and some modern literature and Shakespeare," he said. "*Julius Caesar, Romeo and Juliet*, and our teacher even read out the entire play of *Othello* once. He tried to explain the poetry to us. I don't know if we got it. I think we read the play in both Arabic and English."

They learned Iraqi history as well.

"We were taught about Islam and how it spread, the first Islamic Empire and the Caliphate that was established around Damascus and then moved to Baghdad when the city was founded in AD 763 by the Abbasid Caliph Mansur who called it Medinat al-Salam, 'the city of peace.' We read *One Thousand and One Nights*, and learned how Baghdad already had universities, science and art, literature and poetry, by AD 800 under the famous Caliph Harun al-Rashid. It was the greatest city on earth back then. But I hated history. It's such a dry subject if it isn't taught properly.

"Of course, we loved the summer holidays," my father mused aloud. "The summers in Baghdad are so hot that if you go out at the height of the heat of the day, it can practically kill you. Temperatures rise to 50 degrees Celsius. We'd hang around at home, or go to the outdoor swimming pool, which was a ten-minute bike ride from my house. I learned how to swim there. I remember only boys being allowed to go, but I think there was a special time for the girls to swim. We never swam in the Tigris, my parents forbade it. But, in the spring, the Tigris floods, and then by summer it has gone down a bit and so there are all these sandy islands in the middle. My uncle Clement camped in a little temporary structure made of straw matting and cane, called a *jerdah*, on one of the islands when he was in his twenties. He'd spend the summer there, which is three or four months long in Baghdad, sleeping out overnight. He spent more time there than he did at home. It was called colloquially, Al Jazzra, the island. He slept, washed and ate there; he'd sit by the river and catch fish, swim. It was refreshing in the intense heat. But once in a while he'd row us all over in a little rowboat for picnics in the evenings, which I loved. The whole family would come—aunts, uncles, cousins, friends—and we'd cook *masgouf*, a method of barbecuing fish on wooden stakes around an open fire, and the women brought a picnic in an icebox and tea and coffee and sweets. It was a popular summer pastime in Baghdad."

But by far, the best summers were when Khalil took my father and his eldest daughter, Siham, to Lebanon and Syria, for a month at a time. First, they'd go to cosmopolitan Beirut and stay with Khalil's sister, Selma, in her flat near the Corniche and La Rocha, the arched rocks that are Beirut's signature sight. They'd walk on the Corniche at sunset eating corn on the cob.

"You could see the whole sun going into the sea," my father reminisced. "I found it beautiful, it was something you didn't see at home. Aunt Selma lived near the American University in Beirut where my father had studied. So we'd go there and meet his old friends and get a drink in a café nearby. Then, as a treat for being well-behaved, he'd take us on the tram to another neighbourhood and buy us ice cream."

When my father was seven, he went with his father to a village in northern Lebanon near Tripoli where Khalil's best friend, Ibrahim, lived. (My father was named after this man, who was more like a brother to Khalil.)

When Khalil was a boy, Syria and Lebanon were one province of the Ottoman Empire. After World War I, the French took control, and separated Lebanon and Syria two years later. Khalil's hometown, Safita (now in Syria), was not far from Tripoli (now in Lebanon). Khalil had been sent to boarding school in Tripoli where he'd met Ibrahim. Neither had brothers, and they became inseparable.

"I remember a café in the village square, really just a concrete floor and a straw awning for shade, near a creek," my father described. "There was beautiful, picturesque Mediterranean mountain scenery all around us. I was bored in the village; there was nothing for a young boy to do. So we'd go to the café, and one of the old men there taught me how to play chess. That's how I learned chess and became quite good playing those old guys."

A few times Khalil took Siham and Ibrahim to Safita. The town is built on three hills and around the white tower of the Chastel Blanc, the remains of a Crusader fortress, built by the Knights of the Templar in 1188. At the turn of the century, when my grandfather lived there, Safita had a population of a few thousand, almost all of whom were Christians.

I remembered my own visit to Safita in 1992 when I was only twenty-one. I arrived by bus, and the road climbed, undulating over hill after hill covered in olive groves, revealing scenes evocative of Greece or the south of France. The pink-and-white town appeared to be huddling around the ancient square tower. In the old town centre, the cobbled streets and houses are made of white, yellow and black stone. Most houses are roofed in red tile and have terraces.

I tried to track down my remaining relatives and find my grandfather's house. I found myself in this unfamiliar town in a strange country, searching for some shred of my ancestral connection; I didn't really know what I was looking for, but some strong urge had brought me there. But I didn't speak Arabic, and no one I encountered spoke English. In the old days there were no addresses, so I couldn't just find my grandfather's house for myself. My father had said I should go to the church and see if the priest recognized our last name, so I did. But the day I went there and knocked on the huge wooden door of the Chapel St. Michael on the ground floor of the Chastel Blanc tower, it was closed. I was disappointed because I'd heard that you could climb the tower, and that, on a clear day, you could see as far as Tripoli and the Mediterranean Sea.

I'd seen a few photographs of my grandfather's father, Said, who'd been the mayor of Safita for some years. According to the family stories, he was a serious, trustworthy man. In the only formal portrait we have, he is around sixty and wearing a suit and tie, with a suit vest underneath. His hair and eyebrows are black, but his toothbrush moustache is white. His old stone house was covered with grapevines and had olive trees growing all around it. It was high on one of the hills that had a direct view of the tower. He was an extremely pious man who knew the Bible by heart, and he treated the poor the way it was prescribed in the Bible. Every year, he let the poor come to take from his olive harvest.

"The Bible is our culture," he'd say.

During World War I, Khalil's two eldest sisters used to go into the surrounding countryside and give food to their relatives who were fighting the Ottomans, and so living in camps and unable to come into the towns.

My father still has the family Bible in Arabic from Safita. It belonged to his great-grandfather Yousif who was born in 1845 and had his name printed in Arabic in gold letters on the black cover. Inside, my grandfather Khalil had mapped out the family tree. He'd also written in English that his grandfather's sight had become weak, and he couldn't read. When he saw this Bible he'd cry, lamenting his bad luck for not being able to read it. So Khalil kept it in its original form so that "his descendants would keep as a memory the pure soul of this man who lived his life without harming anybody and without coveting anything. This is the first Bible of the family." The inscription reminded me of the day I visited Safita. I remember how the bell rang out from the tower, and echoed far away down the hills and olive groves below, when I was finally leaving to go back to Damascus.

Khalil always cherished Safita, but he loved Beirut best and wanted to retire there. All through his life he visited his friends and family in Syria and Lebanon as often as he could. One of my father's earliest memories is of his father not returning home to Baghdad from one of these trips.

"The taxis crossed the desert at night," he told me. "They usually leave Damascus around 4:00 p.m. in the afternoon and get in to Baghdad early in the morning. It's better to travel at night in the summer because of the heat. But this time, Khalil didn't arrive at the usual time. And in the late 1940s, there were no phones, no way of knowing what had happened to him. He just didn't arrive for hours and hours. My mother was getting really worried. Finally, late in the evening, he walked into the house. The taxi had got lost in the desert. In those days, the road to Damascus wasn't paved; it was just a hard mud track. Most drivers just knew the way, and there was lots of traffic. The taxis had two drivers, as it was a long overnight drive, and usually four passengers, one in front with the drivers and three in the back seat. But the young driver wasn't experienced enough at reading the stars to guide him at night. At daybreak, when the older driver woke up and saw that they weren't anywhere near Baghdad, he took the wheel and steered them in the right direction. The young driver hadn't even known he was lost; he'd just been driving what he thought was straight ahead, but had been going around and around in circles." He laughed.

"That reminds me of another story from when I was about thirteen," my father continued. "The whole family—Lina, Victoria, Khalil, and Siham and I—were on a bus coming back from Damascus to Baghdad. It was the first time we'd been to Safita for the summer all together. The bus broke down in the middle of the night, in the heart of the desert. I remember the stars were so bright and thick, like millions of droplets of light reflecting on water . . . you never see them like that in cities.

"My father was panicking all night, worried sick about being stuck, lost, broken down, conjuring up all the worst case scenarios, so he'd stayed awake waiting for someone to come by. If we were lost in the desert, he thought we might not find our way home. In the morning, we realized we'd broken down right by the start of the newly paved road. We weren't lost at all. The bus was fixed and we got going again. We arrived at the border and Customs, where we had to show our passports and declare our goods. But remember, by then, Auntie Lina was very senior in the Customs ministry, and she told the officials who she was. They were very impressed and didn't search our luggage, but gave us tea instead.

"Lina chatted to the guards and discovered there had been a wanted communist on the bus. The Secret Police had been tracking the bus. We saw the communist being hauled off by the police and we felt very sorry for him. The officials laughed when Lina told them how worried we'd been. They said, with typical Iraqi black humour, 'You didn't need to worry about being lost, we were watching you and we knew exactly where you were all the time. . . . '" My father laughed at the joke, despite having told it.

"I wish you'd known my father," he said. "I think you are like him. Reading and travelling . . . like you he loved books, theology, philosophy, ancient history, and like you all he really wanted to do was travel. He used to believe in meaningful connections between things, coincidences that always came in threes."

"What do you think he would have thought about this war?"

"I remember he came to London when you were still a girl, and I gave him Orwell's *Animal Farm* to read. He loved it, saying, 'This is exactly what happened in Iraq every time there was a coup or revolution. Exactly.' Maybe he'd think the same was happening now. Who knows? He hated hypocrisy. He used to ask my sisters how they could watch the lies on television in Iraq, just sit and watch. They said, 'We know they are lying, so we ignore it.' But he hated that."

In the 1940s and 1950s, Iraq was a relatively prosperous country because it had oil revenues, and its internal food supply made it self-sufficient. "Iraq was very feudal; the various tribes owned and worked the land, and produced a lot of food," my father continued.

I reminded him I'd never seen Baghdad; I didn't even know what the city looked like, what it smelled like.

"The river is the biggest feature, and it is a very dry, sandy city," he explained. "But people irrigated the city, and so there are trees and gardens. Without irrigation, nothing would grow. You could tell where the irrigation stopped on the edge of the city, as the greenery stopped too. When I first flew from Baghdad to Beirut, I saw how dramatic it was, nothing grows in that desert."

Unfortunately, anti-British sentiment worsened when Israel was established in 1948. Iraq wanted Palestine to remain for the Palestinians, and the country became increasingly anti-Jewish as the loyalties of the 117,000-strong Iraqi-Jewish community were questioned and restrictions were imposed on them. They were accused of serving both the British authorities in Iraq and the Zionist project in Palestine, because the British Mandate in Palestine that had led to the creation of Israel and the British Mandate in Iraq had been established at the same time. Finally, Nuri al-Said threatened to expel the entire Iraqi-Jewish community if Palestinian refugees were not allowed to return to their homes. In 1950, a new law allowed Jews to renounce their Iraqi citizenship and leave Iraq forever, and most of the remaining Iraqi Jews left, for Israel or the West. Until then, Iraqi Jews had lived in Iraq for more than two thousand five hundred years. Abraham, the father of the Jewish people, was from northern Mesopotamia. When the Babylonians conquered Judah in 587 BC, they took some Jews as captives, who continued to practise their religion even in Babylon.

"I remember in the mid-1950s going with my mother to another lady's house, and she was crying because she had to sell everything and go to Israel. It was so sad, and my mother felt sorry for her. The woman didn't want to leave Iraq, but she was an Iraqi Jew so she was forced to go," my father said.

One of the other issues that generated anti-British sentiment was oil. In the mid-1950s, the Iraq Petroleum Company (IPC) was the only oil company in Iraq. It was jointly owned by British Petroleum (BP), Shell, Compagnie Française Petrole (Total), Exxon, Mobil and a private investor called Gulbenkian. IPC was a stand-alone company with shares, and BP was the operator. Iraq only received a royalty from the oil.

"It was peanuts," my father said. "But in the mid-1950s, the rate increased a lot. The Iraqi government suddenly had lots of money and so civil servants, like my parents, who were teachers, got big raises. But Iraq was still under a puppet government. IPC was still active, with offices all over, but it was run by foreigners, so Iraqis didn't get very high up. I remember making friends with an American boy whose father worked at the Dora refinery. I think he was the first American I met, and I bought his bike when he and his family went back to the States."

"But what happened to the British? When did they finally leave Iraq?"

"We had a revolution in 1958. I was staying over at my grandmother's house that day. Some of my best friends lived on her street, so I often slept at her place. When I woke up we heard gunfire, and we listened to the radio. I remember my grandmother saying, 'The radio sounds funny.' The propaganda had changed, you see. Suddenly the message was 'Down with the British,' not the pro-monarchy party line that had been repeated before. A curfew was imposed, and we were forbidden to go into the streets. It was a military coup and an army officer, Abd al-Karim Qasim, had taken power. They occupied all Baghdad's strategic buildings including the radio station. It was horrific. They shot King Faisal, the regent and the royal family when they emerged from the palace. Nuri al-Said's house was surrounded. He managed to escape, but was captured the next day and shot in the street. Of course, as a young boy, this was all very exciting. I wanted to go and see the palace, but thank God my father forbade me. Really, apart from those murders, it was actually a bloodless revolution, since it didn't cause widespread anarchy and killing."

Not long afterwards, another curfew was announced when my father was at his great-aunt's house playing cards with his mother, Madeline and his sisters. Curfews became common as the political situation in Iraq was highly unstable. He wasn't allowed to play outside, so he was left with the women.

"My uncles wouldn't play backgammon with me, and they wouldn't play with Madeline either," he said. "So we played together. I learned quickly and would play her for money and beat her. Just for pennies. When you think about it, it was strange she played backgammon as well. That was exotic too; women didn't play usually."

The house was only a block away from his own home, and the women suddenly needed something and sent the fourteen-year-old boy home to get it. My father ran out as quickly as possible, but a young guard, dressed in the uniform of the Bedouin regiment, pointed at him and told him to stop. He asked my father what he was doing breaking the curfew, and my father explained he was only going a few houses down to do an errand.

"He dragged me back to the house where all the women were. Suddenly, they all started shouting at the guard and giving him hell. It was like walking into a hornet's nest. They demanded to know what he thought I was going to do in those small steps between the two houses." My father was giggling. "That poor guard, he was scared. He just wanted to get out of there, away from all those women, as quickly as he could. He didn't bother me anymore after that."

Most people were happy with the revolution, and Qasim was popular because he worked to improve normal people's lives after a long period of self-interested rule by a small monarchist elite. British influence disappeared in Iraqi politics, and Qasim passed Law 80 in

1961, which seized 99 per cent of Iraqi land from the British-owned IPC concessionary area (the exclusive geographical area that the IPC was allowed to operate in to produce oil and gas). He also enacted Law 30, an aggregation law that seized estates from the three thousand wealthy landowners who owned half of Iraq's cultivable land, and distributed them to landless peasants or small landowners. The size of the middle class increased as a result of Qasim's policies. In retrospect, my father realized how profoundly this revolution affected his life, because he happened to graduate in 1959, the year after the coup.

"When you think of it," he said, "only for a couple of years out of the last fifty, government scholarships to study abroad were given to students on the basis of merit rather than influence. I was in the top two hundred students in Iraq in my year, so I was sent to Britain. I was very lucky."

Two people were responsible for encouraging my father to study outside of Iraq. His father wanted him to win a scholarship and go to a Western country either in Europe or North America to get a good education. Adventurous Aunt Madeline also influenced my father. She had flown to London in 1956 with a female relative and returned with outlandish stories of the Underground, Buckingham Palace, Big Ben and the Houses of Parliament. My father took his exams, hoping to get a scholarship to Britain. In June 1960, the family travelled to Beirut for the holidays, while Khalil went on a British Council–sponsored trip to England for teachers. It was the first time he had been to Europe. We have a photograph of Khalil standing in the open air on the tarmac at the Baghdad airport with the Iraqi Airlines plane behind him. He's smiling, looking happy and carefree, despite his smart double-breasted suit and tie, and he's surrounded by dark-haired women and men in white suits, laughing, probably the other teachers going on the trip.

Auntie Lina had stayed in our home in Baghdad while the rest of the family vacationed in Beirut. She received Ibrahim's marks when they were delivered to the house. They were good, so he flew back alone from Beirut to interview for the scholarship. At the Ministry of Education he was quizzed by a panel. The students were ranked by marks, and the top ones were given a choice of which country they wanted to study in. The top two hundred could go to Britain. They asked my father where he wanted to go in England, and he said London. He wanted to study civil engineering, but all the spots were taken, so he decided on a whim to take petroleum engineering. They told him that he had won a scholarship, and that he'd be going to England that autumn.

"When I came out of the interview I was really happy. But my grandmother didn't like the idea; she didn't want me to go. She said, 'I'll never see you again.' Everyone knew that when you sent a young man away to the West, he didn't tend to come back home to live. But the rest of the family was excited, and they had a huge party for me with a typically massive spread of Arabic food. My parents gave me a watch as a going-away present."

Like any young man embarking on a new adventure, Ibrahim was thinking about his future and not what he was leaving behind. He never dreamed he'd never return to his home city. But his grandmother was right; my father never saw her again.

TRAFALGAR SQUARE FROM THE STEPS OF THE NATIONAL GALLERY
LONDON, ENGLAND, EARLY 1960S

Chapter Three

The Motherland

. . . our armies do not come into your cities and lands as conquerors or enemies, but as liberators. Since the days of Hugalu, your citizens have been subject to the tyranny of strangers . . . and your fathers and yourselves have groaned in bondage. Your sons have been carried off to wars not of your seeking, your wealth has been stripped from you by unjust men and squandered in different places. It is the wish not only of my King and his peoples, but it is also the wish of the great Nations with whom he is in alliance, that you should prosper even as in the past when your lands were fertile . . .
—British Lieutenant-General Sir Frederick Stanley Maude, Commanding the British Forces in Iraq, "Proclamation to the People of Baghdad," March 1917

In October 1960, my sixteen-year-old father, along with the top two hundred students in the country that year, took a chartered Iraqi Airlines flight to swinging-sixties London with a refuelling stop in Vienna.

"We were flying to London, but in the opposite direction to this flight," my father thought aloud. "Funny, I've never made the reverse trip, Baghdad to London, but I've done this flight from Canada countless times. Flying was so exciting for me then; it was only the second time I'd flown alone."

He'd just turned sixteen a few months earlier, so he was at the time a slender boy, with a head of impossibly thick black hair on top of a smooth nut-brown face. A few friends from Baghdad College (which was actually a high school) had also made the cut, and so the atmosphere on the airplane was like a boys' school holiday, full of loud jostly energy and the excitement of being unfettered from family and country. The cultural attaché from the Iraqi Embassy met them at the airport, and they were put up in a British Council hostel and given a three-day "indoctrination," as my father put it, into British life.

He sent a short, expensive telegram to his parents reporting that he'd arrived safely. After that, his parents had to wait for more than two weeks to receive any further news from him. They had no idea where he was in England, how he was living, eating or sleeping, and his mother brooded about him all the time and couldn't sleep during those weeks. She was worried about him alone in a new country, with not a single relative or friend and not one familiar face.

Ibrahim already knew all about British culture from his father, the basics of how to dress, how to introduce yourself and make small talk. But there were many terrified students from small Iraqi villages who were very clever but had never lived in a city before and had no idea how they were going to manage in England. All the students were a year or two older than Ibrahim because he'd started elementary school a year early, but his English was better than most of theirs. During those first three days, he was overwhelmed by London; he loved it. It was crowded, vibrant and exciting; he was fascinated by the Underground and the escalators, and the grey streets lined with fashionable shops and the European architecture were new and refreshingly unfamiliar. Couples kissed in the streets, which felt almost pornographic to a young Iraqi who wasn't allowed to have a girlfriend or be alone with a young woman who wasn't a relative. Here, people flaunted their affairs in public.

Soon the students realized that hardly anyone was going to be staying in London. All the Baghdad College boys were to be split up. My father found out he was being sent to a small city in Yorkshire in the north of England with two Kurdish students, Shirzad and Ahmed. The British Council helped them open bank accounts, gave them references and a train ticket, and on a miserable rainy October day, they were dropped off at King's Cross station in northeast central London to catch the train to Yorkshire. There were no cell phones or credit cards, and international calls were prohibitively expensive, so Ibrahim was on his own, fending for himself for the first time in his life without the buffer of his large, doting family.

When the students got off the train, they saw that their new home was even darker and drearier than London. The grey skies stripped all colour from the town, while the rain poured down with a force they had never before experienced. For Ibrahim, raised on romantic notions of Britain and the West, it felt like the most horrible place in the world. He was almost offended by the relentless rain that made him feel so damp and uncomfortable. To this day, he hates rain. As soon as a few drops touch his head, he immediately ducks for cover. He can't understand how people can accept going out in it, even with an umbrella.

My father and his new friend, Shirzad, were staying together with a landlady and her family in a typical English semi-detached row house. There were three bedrooms and a bath upstairs, and two rooms and a kitchen downstairs. Ibrahim found the house small and cramped, and the front room where they first sat was alien to him with its dark wallpaper, little mantelpiece ornaments, English-landscape etchings and the flowery china teacups and teapot. His landlady was a widow who lived with her invalid elderly mother and her tall twenty-one-year-old daughter. Her son had just joined the army, which is why they had a spare room for boarders. Ibrahim and Shirzad shared one room, the daughter was in another, and the widow and her mother in a third. Ibrahim was allowed to use the front room as a sitting-study area; there was a gas heater with a grill on top to keep him warm. And he needed it because he was often freezing, suffering a damp seeping cold he'd never felt before.

"I'd never bathed in a tub," he recalled. "At home in Baghdad we had a Turkish bath. It was like a sauna room with running boiling water that you poured over yourself to wash. Here, I had to sit in the water that I was making dirty, which didn't seem hygienic, and I wondered how I was going to wash my hair. I was told off for not cleaning the tub after. The soap scum formed a ring because of the hard water. But what did I know?"

The widow gave the boys breakfast and dinner, and they had a hot lunch at school. Breakfast was often bacon, which the Muslims ate even though they weren't supposed to. The evening meal was usually light—cheese sandwiches, a boiled egg and a piece of cake.

Ibrahim was enrolled in the local College of Technology to study for his A-level exams in physics, chemistry and maths in preparation to get into university. The college was co-ed, but he was doing sciences, so there was only one girl in his class. It was peculiar to have girls in the same school; he was envious of the Kurdish students studying politics, who had many girls in their classes.

The local people had very strong accents that made their English almost incomprehensible, and his teacher was Welsh, so Ibrahim could barely understand him during his classes. He found it hard to study in his first year because of the culture shock and his intense loneliness.

After about six months in the widow's house, the unbearably tasteless food drove the boys away. Ibrahim moved into a one-room bachelor apartment in a rougher part of town. It was in a big semi-detached house split into several apartments.

"I have no idea how I could afford it," my father recalls.

Now he was a sixteen-year-old boy, who had not even finished high school, living alone in another country with complete freedom to do and live as he liked. But instead of going 'wild,' he went domestic. What he liked was Iraqi food, and if he wanted to eat it, he had to learn to cook it himself. He asked his parents and grandmother to send him recipes. On his one-ring burner, he learned, through trial and error, to prepare simple casseroles with tomatoes and okra or green beans and rice. He played chess with his friends

and listened to records since he didn't have his own TV. Heartbroken
with homesickness, he wrote long letters to his parents, but it never
occurred to him that he could go back home.

"People didn't think like that in those days," he explained. "You
just got on with life. There weren't any other options. How would
I even get home? Plane tickets were very expensive in those days."

Not long afterwards, three of his close friends from Baghdad
College, Selime, Nasser and Yaseen, who'd been sent to a nearby town,
finally worked out where Ibrahim had ended up, and one day they
turned up at his apartment completely unannounced. He'd known
Selime since the day he was born, and Nasser was a school friend.
The boys shuttled back and forth between the two towns visiting
each other, and suddenly Ibrahim was having more fun. The loneliness
started to ease, and he began to enjoy and adjust to English life.

He went to the pub and drank beer even though initially he didn't
like the taste, because he knew that you had to have a beer if you
went out in England. All social activities revolved around a pint
or two and eventually he acquired a liking for it. He met girls and
socialized with them; a welcome novelty. No one he met had ever
heard of Iraq, although they knew about "Arabia," but everyone was
relatively welcoming. Some of the Iraqis complained about discrimi-
nation, but Ibrahim never experienced it.

"I had high self-esteem, so I didn't care if people were rude.
Maybe they were reacting to my being Arabic, but I just thought
they were being unpleasant. It didn't occur to me that people were
discriminating against me because of my race. I thought it was their
problem. I never thought it was because of the colour of my skin,"
he said, shrugging.

Ibrahim and his friends hung out at the international club at college
where they met a group of European au pairs studying English.

"People smoked Woodies in those days, Woodbines," he continued.
"You could buy them in tens. They were small, narrow and thin. In
Iraq, if a teenage boy had a pack of cigarettes, he would just have a

puff and then throw it away to show that he was wealthy. He didn't actually want to smoke it. But here, on my first day of school, I remember seeing a guy on the tea break, smoking half a cigarette intensely, putting it out and then returning it to his top pocket. I thought, What is he doing? Then, at the next break, he took it out and continued smoking it. That was culture shock!"

My mother's older sister, Jane, attended the same college as Ibrahim's friends. Through a group of international students, she had made pen pals all over the world and became friendly with the Iraqis. In the summer of 1961, she was expecting a visit from a Dutch boyfriend, but one of the Iraqis had fallen in love with her. She banned him from the house while the Dutch boy was there, but he was forever dreaming up excuses to visit her anyway.

One day, the Iraqi boy said to Ibrahim, "Come on, you will come with me and I will introduce you to Jane's family, her nice sisters."

In their mackintoshes, they motored on his Vespa to my mother's house.

That first day, my mother, Mary, wasn't home, but Ibrahim met my maternal grandmother. Nasser introduced him as an Iraqi friend from school. My grandmother was a funny, generous woman who loved the vitality of young people, their exuberance and sense of fun. She was warm-hearted and felt for these young men who were so far away from their families and on their own in the world. She wanted to nurture them. They were well mannered and well groomed, compared to some of the local boys who she thought weren't properly polite or respectful towards their elders. She liked Muslims and Christians equally, and it never occurred to her to try to convert anyone, even though she was a fervent Catholic. She was colour-blind and unusual in her openness to foreigners, and the more conservative mothers in the neighbourhood whispered about her; they thought it was a little foolish for her daughters to invite strange boys into the house. Mary's father used to say, chuckling to himself, "It's like the League of Nations in our front room."

On Ibrahim's second visit to the family for tea, he first set eyes on the young girl who was to become my mother. She'd come home from a day out at the seaside to find the house full of her sister's friends. Ibrahim was wearing a fine black wool sweater, and she noticed his long black eyelashes; to her, he looked very fashionable and smart. She was just fifteen and her pale blue summer dress complemented her eyes. They didn't speak, but my mother reports that he gave her a wink as he left the house.

Ibrahim prevailed upon his Iraqi friend to ask Jane to see if Mary would like to go out with him. At first my mother wasn't sure which boy was asking her out, and she feared it was another of her sister's friends whom she hadn't been attracted to. But when she found out that it was the quiet boy who looked so mysterious, she was excited. She agreed, and the date was set for after Sunday mass.

Mary and Ibrahim met and took the bus to the next town. To Ibrahim, she seemed very prim and proper, prettily dressed in her best Sunday clothes, black gloves and a green coat with a fake-fur collar. He took her to an Italian restaurant called Paradise Gardens which was a bit exotic and avant garde for Mary. It was the first real date ever for either of them, and so they were shy and found it difficult to make conversation. Their second date was a secret, because she went alone to Ibrahim's apartment where he made her "some sort of Arabic meal, beans and rice. It tasted terrible."

My mother has given us little morsels of this story over the years. She still has a vivacious and youthful spirit even in her fifties, and she is said to have been rebellious and stubbornly single-minded as a girl. I once asked her if my father had a strong foreign accent when they'd met, because he didn't have one anymore.

"Oh yes, he did. A lovely one," she laughed. "And he was very exotic. The film *Lawrence of Arabia* came out around that time, I can't remember when, and we were all very taken with notions of the 'East.' I remember seeing Omar Sharif in the movie and thinking of your father! The East was very remote, very 'other,' and we romanticized and idealized it, the way you do as a teenager. Baghdad was this exotic city. When I thought of Baghdad then, it was a place bathed in a golden light connected to the Ottoman Empire, a city with a skyline of minarets and domes like Istanbul, but with the Tigris and Euphrates Rivers flowing through it and palm trees everywhere. It was something out of a fairy tale."

Since Mary knew Ibrahim's family was Westernized, she never pictured his parents dressed in flowing robes.

"I was totally naive, and open, and young," she recalled. "I knew he had a large family full of love and care and attention. He didn't say much about Iraq that I can remember, but he described Beirut and how beautiful Lebanon was, and told me about his childhood visits there. Early on before I met him, he planned to meet his whole family in Lebanon because he couldn't go back to Iraq, even then. I don't know why. It was the last chance he'd have to see his grandmother Samira, who died a few years later. There was a lot of excitement while he was preparing to go. And when you think of it, he probably hadn't seen his family for a year or so. He probably missed them dreadfully. But at the last minute the trip was cancelled, and he couldn't meet them. He was terribly disappointed."

When I asked my father what had happened, he said, "I was supposed to go by ship to Beirut, from Southampton or somewhere. My father bought and sent me my ticket. It was a special cheap ticket to be used by foreign students returning home. But when I went to pick it up, I had to show my Iraqi passport and they said, 'You aren't going home, you are going to Beirut. But you are Iraqi. Lebanon isn't home for you.' I tried to explain but they wouldn't let me use the ticket. My parents had already left for Beirut and so I couldn't get a message to them. They were waiting for me at the port, but when the ship arrived I wasn't on it. They must have been so disappointed. They hadn't seen me for over a year. I was upset too."

I asked my mother if she had dreamed of going to Iraq and seeing Baghdad for herself, if she'd wanted to familiarize herself with the place her husband came from. She hardly knows the Middle East to this day, has only visited Lebanon once and has never been to Iraq.

"It was never 'on the table,'" she explained. "Because of politics. Around the time of our wedding, the fear was that if Ibrahim went home he'd have to do military service. He didn't want to do that, and as soon as that emerged as a possibility—the idea of being in the military—he just shut the door to us ever going. And so did I. Too risky."

Her elder sister, Jane, was more knowledgeable about Iraq than my mother was. Jane was bewitched by the whole notion of the Middle East; she even wore a small metallic carved brooch of Lawrence of Arabia's face.

"We were all into that at the time," my mother said. "She forgot the brooch when she left home and I took it, and remember I gave it to you when you started getting interested in the Middle East?" At eighteen, I hadn't realized what it had meant when she gave the brooch to me. She went on, "It was Jane who always talked about how amazing it would be to go to Baghdad, about how ancient the country was, about history and about the Bible. Years later, she moved to Kuwait and had a chance to briefly visit Baghdad and Babylon. She is still grateful that she had that opportunity, especially because of what has come to pass there."

Mary was more interested in being an international couple with my father, and travelling the world.

"I was a sixties person. I suppose I thought I would visit Baghdad one day, but I never thought I'd live there," she said. "And do you know something strange? My father's sister, my auntie Jean, came over once before I even met your father. She looked at me and said, 'You look like May Clayton. You have her smile.' May was my dad's cousin. Later I discovered that May Clayton had married an engineer who worked at the Iraq Petroleum Company. The couple lived in Iraq in the 1930s. Now that I think about it, it's eerie."

Her father, my English grandfather, had once quietly warned her about ever thinking of moving to the Middle East. My mother suspected that he thought about the 'bigger picture' often, and although he loved Ibrahim as a person, he warned Mary in a humorous way, "Now you wouldn't want to go all that way to live, would you?" My mother claims that she answered defiantly, "No one will make me go anywhere to live. It will be my decision." But her parents were not against her marrying an Iraqi.

"So you knew that for the rest of your life you might never go to Baghdad, to Iraq, together?" I asked her.

"I suppose we didn't think it through to that final conclusion," she said. "Probably, we always thought, hoped, that things in the country would improve, that things would change there, that it would be possible to visit. And after we had you children, we thought that it would have been so incredible to take you back to meet all the relatives there. But I must say, I never thought any of you would really feel so connected to Iraq, because you didn't know it, you never lived there."

She was articulating the confusion I often felt. How could I feel even a little bit Iraqi when I didn't know the language or the culture and had never lived there, never even been there? Yet I'd always had this mysterious magnetic pull, a curiosity to know more and more, to get closer and closer. I felt frustrated, because while I was aware that many Iraqis had left the country and never returned, I knew there were some who took the risks and went back periodically to visit their families.

My mother understood. "Many of the Iraqi students did go back without fear. Some even took their English wives with them. But every individual is different. Every person makes choices, makes decisions about what risks they do and don't want to take. Ibrahim doesn't take those kinds of risks. But it wasn't such a culture of fear then, as it is now. He could have finished his degree and gone back to Baghdad. The idea wasn't as unfathomable as it became later on."

GATHERING OF KHALIL'S FRIENDS IN THE COURTYARD OF
A HOUSE IN BAGHDAD

Chapter Four

"It Is Written"

They are a happy, laughing people, the Iraqians [sic], *and they seem to live completely in the present moment, forgetting the past and taking small thought for the future. If misfortune overtakes them, with a shrug of their shoulders they accept it, saying, "Mek-toub-est" (It is written).* —Janet Miller, *Camel-bells of Baghdad*, 1935

In February 1963, Abd al-Karim Qasim was ousted and executed after a show trial. In the days surrounding the coup, which was backed by the British and the CIA who had been alarmed by Qasim's flirtation with communism, about five thousand Iraqis died in a purge and there were house-to-house hunts for communists. In those revolutionary years, different groups controlled Iraq, as coup followed coup and each government resorted to repression and dictatorship to impose its agenda upon the country.

Although Ibrahim was far away in England applying to universities, the unrest and instability at home made him afraid to return. My father recalled this story clearly because his father had told him about life in Iraq after he left.

"So there was a year in the early sixties, when teenagers had a lot of power," he explained. He became animated again, his voice rising over the drone of the plane's engine. The second movie was ending, and we hadn't watched either film. "They had guns and were patrolling the streets. One day, Khalil was driving back from school, and he was stopped at a checkpoint by a young man who asked him for his ID. Khalil looked at him, pointed at a house nearby and said, 'Aren't you the son of the man who owns that house there?' 'Yes, Mr. Nadir,' he replied. 'Mr. Nadir? Well, if you know who I am, why are you asking me for ID?' And my father just drove through the checkpoint in anger. Everyone knew and recognized one another in the neighbourhood, and Muslims and Christians lived alongside each other with few problems. This is the kind of daily life hassle that my father was protecting me from, by sending me away."

When he looks back on his life, my father realizes that everything hinged on a mark on a math test that he took when he was sixteen. "If I had got one per cent higher on this test, let's say 98 per cent instead of 97 per cent, I'd have been one person higher up the list of the two hundred students on scholarship from Iraq that year. One higher up on the list and I'd have been sent to a different part of the country, perhaps Cardiff in Wales instead of Yorkshire, and I'd never have met your mother. You'd never have been born," he concludes with a gentle smile. He saw his life always hanging in the balance, based on minuscule differences that had far-reaching and unforeseen consequences. Whether he believed it was fate or not, he never said.

By August 1963, he had received provisional acceptance at Birmingham University, his place dependent on his A-level marks. That same week, Imperial College in London offered my father an interview for a place in their engineering program. With the letter from Birmingham in his pocket, he took the night train to London. At the end of his interview, which went well, the professor said, "Thank you very much. We will call you and let you know if you are given a place."

It was at this moment that my father took the first in a series of minor risks that changed the destiny of his life forever.

"I remember saying to the professor, 'I've already been accepted at another university, and I need to give them an answer immediately. I need to know right now whether I have a place at Imperial or not.'"

The professor hesitated, looked hard at Ibrahim, and replied slowly, "Well then, well then, if you put it like that." Ibrahim nodded in anticipation. "Well, yes, you are in."

Ibrahim went out into the street and called Mary from the first red telephone box he saw.

"I'm in, I got in!" he shouted over the phone.

He was elated. Imperial College was one of the best universities in the country for engineering and the only school that offered petroleum engineering, since there was hardly any oil business then. They only took ten students a year, and most graduates went overseas to work. Ibrahim moved to London and lived in Maida Vale in northwest London. Mary stayed at home for a year to finish school, and they visited each other in London or Yorkshire whenever they could, keeping their love affair alive.

The next year, Mary was accepted as a nursing student at a large London teaching hospital near St. Paul's Cathedral. She'd also been interviewed for a job as a fashion buyer at Harrods but, at the last minute, had decided to pursue nursing. They lived in the same city, but she didn't see Ibrahim often because she did shift work and lived in residence at the hospital. But they continued dating and seeing each other when they could. This romance continued throughout Ibrahim's studies.

While Ibrahim was doing his third-year final exams, his mother and Aunt Madeline came to London. Victoria had been diagnosed with breast cancer and was to have radiation treatment there. They stayed for a month before returning to Baghdad. Ibrahim didn't do well on his exams, especially in geophysics, which was the subject he had chosen for his master's degree. When the results came out, he went to his professor, who told him that even though his marks weren't sufficient he'd passed Ibrahim anyway because he knew his work well enough to know that something was wrong. Ibrahim confided in him about his mother's illness, and the professor understood the pressure he was under. He advised my father to take his master's degree in petroleum engineering since he didn't need as high marks to get into that program as he would for a geophysics degree. Again, fate made a life decision for Ibrahim.

Once back in Baghdad, his mother's cancer went into remission, but she was always fighting the disease from then on. It was 1967, and my father didn't want to go back to Baghdad. Life hadn't improved there since the revolution. Political life in the sixties was turbulent and dominated by the denial of real representation for the Iraqi people and a changing array of privileged military rulers. Iraqis had dreamed of freedom and democracy, but instead they were living under a worse dictatorship than the monarchy. There were coups and counter-revolutions, and each time they got bloodier and bloodier. Meanwhile, Ibrahim was finishing his master's degree, but he had no idea what to do next. He didn't have a job to go to and his scholarship from Iraq was running out, as was his student visa. He was in love with Mary and wanted to propose to her, but he had nothing to offer her in England, and he knew she wouldn't marry him and move to Iraq.

"I knew that there was no freedom of the press, no freedom of expression, even though this was way before Saddam," my father told me. "I knew that you had to join the Baath party to get along in the government and in society. I'd become used to living in the freedom of England. I was stuck. I was scared. I had no reason to go home, other than my family, and every reason to stay abroad."

Ibrahim wrote fifty letters to companies around the globe asking for employment. One letter was to the president of an oil company in Oklahoma. He'd heard they had offices in Libya. This was before the Gaddafi revolution so it seemed like a suitable place for him to find work. He was sitting his final exams when he got a letter from the company (the only letter he'd received back), asking him to come for an interview in their London office. He had written to the president, which meant that his letter was passed to the international vice president and downwards, and because it had come from the top down, it was taken seriously.

The interviewer liked Ibrahim and wanted to help, but told him that they couldn't send him abroad since he had no practical experience. As Ibrahim didn't want to go back to Iraq, the interviewer suggested Canada and a five-year plan of getting work experience and a Canadian passport. It would be much easier to "go international" if he had a Canadian passport rather than an Iraqi passport.

The company offered him a job in Canada for five years. He accepted the offer and started working on the papers to emigrate. Canada was very receptive to his application; they wanted highly qualified immigrants and were accepting many in the late 1960s. But they were very slow to give him an answer. By now, Ibrahim had a temporary job at an oil company in London and was making money, but he still didn't have the right papers.

Because he had found a job, Ibrahim invited Mary to Odin's, a fashionable new restaurant near Marylebone High Street. By now, according to my mother, he "wore black turtleneck sweaters and trendy black-rimmed glasses like Michael Caine in the *Ipcress Files*." The restaurant was hip for its day, upside-down open umbrellas hung from the ceiling, and the menu was scrawled on a chalkboard. White tablecloths and candles and vases of primroses decorated the tables. Here Ibrahim finally asked Mary, "Will you be my wife?" They had been in love for seven years. He couldn't afford an engagement ring, so the fancy meal was the celebration. My mother said that, at the time, they didn't really believe in getting engaged, marriage seemed like an old-fashioned formality, but they needed the banns if they were to move away together.

When Canadian immigration found out Ibrahim was on an Iraqi scholarship, the officials hesitated again. They didn't want to upset the Iraqi government by poaching one of their graduates. Week after week, Ibrahim had meetings at the Canadian embassy in Grosvenor Square. The officials were concerned about the scholarship and wanted to see the contract between him and the Iraqi government. Before he left Iraq, Ibrahim had signed a contract saying that if he didn't return to Iraq, he would pay the scholarship money back. There was no interest and no penalty. The amount was around six thousand dollars, a year's salary at that time. Ibrahim told them that his parents would pay back the money to the Iraqi government. The Canadians wanted permission from the Iraqi government, but Ibrahim told them that it was impossible for him to go back to ask for anything else from the government authorities. He had already been granted a one-year extension to do his master's degree, and he didn't want to run the risk that the Iraqi ministry would be upset that he wasn't planning to return to Iraq and demand all their money back at once. The Canadians, saying they would see what they could do, sent him away. But he heard nothing.

Meanwhile, Ibrahim's permit to stay in the UK was about to expire and he wasn't supposed to be working. Again, he went back to the Canadian embassy to find out what was going on. As he waited for an interview, he decided that he had to give them an ultimatum. He needed to force their hand because he couldn't wait any longer. He was afraid he'd lose the job offer from the company in Canada.

Sweating, he sat down in front of the official and said, "Time is running out. The job in Canada has been waiting for me for a year now. I need to know right now whether I will get the visa. Otherwise, I will have to go back to Iraq. I need to know now. I cannot wait any longer."

The official didn't change his expression and told him to sit down and wait.

Ibrahim sat down in the office, put his head in his hands and wondered what he had done. His whole life hung in the balance; he had forced an ultimatum that might not work in his favour. He might have to go back to Iraq, break up with the woman he loved and wanted to spend his life with, and the job in Canada would go to someone else. It was the longest hour of his life, and he hardly dared breathe or look up when the official came to get him. The man took him into the office, closed the door and said, "Congratulations, we can give you the visa. You can go to Canada."

Before he could process his relief, they were giving him a list of tasks. He and Mary both had to have a medical exam, get immigration papers and an immigration card, and Mary had to come down to London to do the paperwork. She was waiting at home with her parents to hear what was going to happen. Since the company wanted him immediately, Ibrahim had less than a month to get his life organized.

The following days were a flurry of activity and tension. Ibrahim and Mary had to get married, and so they picked a date two weeks later. Then the church refused to marry them because Ibrahim didn't have a baptism certificate. "I don't even think they issued them in Iraq," he told me. They wrote to the Vatican to request one. Time was pressing, and Ibrahim threatened to marry Mary in a registry office instead. Mary thought that they should just elope. Mary's local parish priest decided that he knew Ibrahim was a good Catholic and agreed to marry them without the certificate. His family in Iraq had only a few days to get ready because driving from Iraq to England took two weeks. Weddings in Iraq are usually elaborate affairs involving a few hundred extended family and friends, with a lead-up of engagement parties, all-women henna parties and other festivities. The whole family dashed out from Baghdad to London—Victoria and Madeline by ship, and Khalil driving through Europe with Auntie Lina and two of Ibrahim's sisters.

Victoria and Madeline made it just in time from Iraq via Beirut. They brought the traditional bridal gold for Mary, the treasures my mother still has in her jewellery box: the gold-and-pearl necklace and matching bracelet from Ibrahim's parents and the bracelet made of tiny gold bars from Aunt Madeline. Victoria and Madeline cornered the couple before the wedding, and Madeline said solemnly, "Canada is too far away. Your mother and I both agree. Why don't you just come back to Iraq with us on the cruise ship? Everything will be fine there and you can come and live with us. You will be very happy. Ibrahim will find a good job."

They were serious. To them, the risk of returning to Iraq wasn't as great as others thought at the time. But Ibrahim didn't want to go back, and my mother had made a strong commitment to herself that she would not move to Iraq. She thought her life would be more restricted there, and she wanted the personal freedom feminists were now agitating to obtain in England. She realized later that they felt free to say these things because Khalil wasn't there yet. Khalil got stuck in a transport strike in Europe on the way to England, and he, Auntie Lina and Ibrahim's two sisters missed the wedding. He didn't get to London in time to see his son and his new wife off to Canada either.

The wedding was held in Mary's local church and was followed by a small reception at a hotel in the countryside nearby. The invitations were bright red and the cake was sky blue and silver. In the photographs, Mary smiles in a wide-brimmed floppy pink hat and a ruffly white bridal minidress; Ibrahim wears a dark suit and a blue Swiss-cotton shirt with his thick black hair combed neatly over to one side. Mary's middle sister, Anne, was her only bridesmaid because Jane had married a German and moved to Germany. Her parents and younger brother and a few friends attended.

After the wedding Mary was alone gathering some last-minute things together and packing. She was preparing to leave the house and say goodbye to her family. Victoria and Madeline knocked on the door. They came in and sat down on her bed. My mother remembers Madeline as a very charismatic woman who was used to getting what she wanted. She had a smile that lit up her face. Madeline pleaded persuasively, "Please think again. If you come with us, we can cruise back together to Beirut. We want you to come back to Iraq with us. It still isn't too late to change your mind. Victoria says you can live with her and Khalil in their big house. She will make sure that you are very happy there. You will be like her daughter. Our house is your house." Victoria nodded hard in agreement.

Mary looked at them, wanting to please her new relatives with the answer they longed to hear. She was slightly intimidated, aware of their power as her new husband's family. She hardly knew them, but knew they were sincere and that she would have a good life if she went with them. She was torn. Her happiness was taking Ibrahim further away from his mother. Despite the commitment she'd made not to move to Iraq, she couldn't help but be tempted by the romance of their entreaty, but at the same time she felt she couldn't let them see her waver or know how attractive their concern and sincerity was. Mary stood firm. The die was cast, the decision had been made; she was already on her way to Canada.

"I said, 'We will come to Baghdad. We will see you again, but the job is waiting there. All the plans are made.'"

Only fifteen years later, as a mother with a son of her own, would she understand how wrenching it must have been for Victoria to give up her only son to an alien and, for her, unreachable place like Canada. Only then did she know what Victoria intuited then, that her grandchildren would never know Iraq or Arabic. The connection was being severed.

The next day Mary and Ibrahim travelled to London for two nights before flying to Canada. Mary's father lent Ibrahim twenty-five pounds and Victoria also gave him a few pounds, but that was all the money they had until they got to Canada. They stayed in the brand-new Lancaster Hotel opposite Hyde Park (for ten pounds a night). Their suitcases were all they had with them. They'd packed trunks to follow by ship.

At Heathrow airport, the officials noticed that Ibrahim's permit to stay in the UK had run out a few months earlier, and his Iraqi passport had expired. My father was surprised. He never expected to have trouble leaving the country. After all, he was leaving anyway, what would they threaten to do? Throw him out of the country? After Ibrahim showed them the visa from the Canadian government, the officials let them board but said that they would write on my father's file that he had overstayed his visa.

The newlyweds flew to Calgary, Alberta, for their honeymoon. They stayed at the Canadian Pacific Palliser Hotel which was meaningful to Mary, for she'd heard about Canada's incredible railway. Three days later, they drove to a small town in the foothills of the Rocky Mountains where they were going to live. In the magnificent mountain scenery, unlike anything either of them had ever seen, they felt that their international adventure had begun.

Still, the small town was a shock to the Londoners, and they were a shock to the town. The Canadians had known an "A-rab" had been hired and were expecting a traditionally robed Gulf Arab with a red head scarf and his exotically veiled submissive wife. Instead, a green Chevrolet pulled into town and the townspeople watched the new engineer, Ibrahim, with his shaggy black hair, trendy tight T-shirt, and jeans, helping out his new bride, Mary, with her long brown hair parted in the middle and flowing down her back, wearing a brightly coloured miniskirt, loud prints on her shirt and platform shoes. This was not the belly-dancing wife that some had expected.

Mary couldn't believe that people drove their cars everywhere despite the town being only a few blocks long, and that they left their cars running while they went into shops and diners. But gas was so cheap at the time. She heard later that some townspeople raised their eyebrows when they saw her walking along with an umbrella, in her high heels and short skirts. The town still had wooden platform sidewalks and a bar with a separate entrance for women. It was the Wild West to Mary and Ibrahim.

Meanwhile, in Iraq in July 1968, there was a military coup carried out by Arab nationalist and Baathist army officers. Then, another Baathist coup ousted the non-Baathist allies. The young Saddam Hussein was named vice president.

The Iraqi government took a while to find out that Ibrahim had not gone back to Iraq. When the authorities contacted his parents, they started paying the scholarship back in monthly instalments. Without being asked, Ibrahim started to send money back from Canada to repay his parents. His father wanted him to send the funds to his account in Lebanon because he thought the bank system there was more stable than Iraq's. In 1974, however, the eruption of the civil war in Lebanon made the currency worthless and all the money was lost.

"I was all right with the Iraqi government with my scholarship," my father said when he told me this. "But if I had gone back, I'd have been drafted into the army. All the men went into the army for two years of military service. Now, at some stage there was a law passed saying that you could buy yourself out of the service. My father paid that money and got a piece of paper exempting me. I wasn't considered a deserter. Maybe I could have gone back and then come out of the country again, but I never wanted to take the risk. They might look at my resumé and decide I should not leave, but instead be the head engineer at IPC. They might offer me everything because there was a drive to lure graduates back with incentives. It would have been nice to visit. I wanted to see Iraq again, my family, show off you, my children, and I would have gone back with different eyes. But even by the early seventies Saddam was already very powerful and things in Iraq were bad."

From then on, my father always had to choose between his present life in Canada and going back to Iraq. To him, it was an either/or choice; he couldn't have both.

I was born in March 1971, and exactly two years later my sister Brigette was born. That Christmas of 1973 we made our only trip to the Middle East as a family. We went to Beirut to stay with my grandfather's sister, Selma, and the Iraqi family came to meet us: my grandparents, my aunts and my great-aunt Lina. We flew from Calgary to Heathrow airport on December 17, but the flight was delayed and we missed our connection to Beirut. While in the air, my parents didn't hear any international news. We got to Heathrow at the height of the miners' strike and the oil embargo, and England was on a three-day week. There was no energy, oil or electricity. The airport was freezing cold without much heat. When we finally got on the plane, we had to go up the stairs from the tarmac the old-fashioned way. The British Airways pilot said to my father as he passed, "Well, I guess we're lucky it's not our turn today."

Ibrahim didn't know what he was talking about. But when he got to Lebanon he heard that a plane had been hijacked in Rome that day by a Palestinian group. They wanted the plane to fly to Beirut, but the government had filled the runway with army trucks, making it impossible for the hijacked plane to land. It went to Libya instead. When we finally got to Beirut, my parents were shocked to see all the military there, and people were only allowed to disembark. British Airways was supposed to notify Ibrahim's parents about the changes, but they hadn't received any information and so they'd waited for the original flight. Of course, no one had arrived. The airport was closed, and they couldn't get in to meet us. Finally, they convinced a BA official to tell them which plane we were on, but they still waited all day for us to arrive.

This was my father's first, last and only trip to the Middle East since leaving at sixteen. Despite the difficulty getting there, my parents had a magical time with his parents Victoria and Khalil. They ate Ibrahim's favourite Lebanese food and toured the country, and he showed his English wife the Roman ruins of Baalbek and the mountains and cedars of Lebanon. On New Year's Eve there was huge party in the streets of Beirut, and they all had champagne in our flat and vowed to return to Lebanon every year. The next year the Lebanese civil war started. They never went back.

MY SYRIAN GREAT-GREAT GRANDFATHER, YOUSIF

CHAPTER FIVE

The Three Graces

*I felt pangs of pain . . . as I watched an American tank crawling across Al-Jumhuriyaa Bridge in the heart of Baghdad. I have crossed that bridge hundreds of times, and I used to linger a bit halfway along, especially when walking alone, and look down at the river. . . . I used to recite Ali Ibn Al-Jahm's famous line about the enchanting, almond-shaped eyes of the Baghdadi women who used to cross from one bank to the other in the ninth century. On a lucky day, I would encounter a descendent of one or two of those women. Now the moon-like faces celebrated in thousands of verses are hiding in houses on both banks, while voyeuristic satellites are hovering above and scrutinizing every inch of the city's body. —*Sinan Antoon, "Of Bridges and Birds," Al-Ahram Weekly, April 17–23, 2003

London is my father's city. As soon as we touch down at Heathrow Airport, he becomes a different man. The sprightly energy of his youth resurges as he walks briskly through the airport he is so familiar with. He has spent fifteen years commuting between Canada and England, a week away every month. Dismal Heathrow airport is as familiar to him as the Calgary neighbourhood he lives in, and he flits through the routine of passport control, baggage pickup and Customs with the air of someone who belongs, who possesses the airport more deeply than the other travellers by dint of the time he has spent here. He has the instinct for the quickest queues, he knows the gates where the Air Canada flights land, which carousels the bags tend to come out on, and how long each part of the routine should take.

London itself is the place of the prime of his youth, for he lived here from ages nineteen to thirty-seven, apart from the five years he spent in Canada between 1968 and 1973. Although my parents moved back to Canada for good twenty-five years ago, I always see them as Londoners.

Imperial College, where Ibrahim went to university, is in Kensington in the heart of London. The Royal Albert Hall, Hyde Park, Brompton Oratory, the Victoria and Albert Museum, the Natural History Museum, Knightsbridge, Harrods, Chelsea and the King's Road were all his domain. He stays in Knightsbridge when he works in London for that one week out of every month, and where we are headed now is an apartment in a mews off the Brompton Road. While I didn't inherit the chance to see Baghdad with my father, I have been given a consolation prize—to know London through him. He loves the bustle, the theatre, museums, restaurants, shopping and food; he loves England and the English. But this time we aren't on holiday. My father is working, and we are both going to visit his sisters who live in Greater London, near where I grew up in Surrey.

The war is everywhere as we enter central London, the headlines blaring from all the papers, the papers stacked at newsstands on every corner and outside every tube station. English soldiers are fighting, and England is rallying around them. The propaganda of war is on full display. I feel like a foreigner, and want to be one. I think about how English I am, and now I want to deny that Englishness and assert my Canadianness. Canada is not at war. I don't believe in war, and now I really feel proud to be Canadian. But I know I am picking and choosing my identity as if from a menu.

Every day B-52 bombers leave England and eight hours later pass over Baghdad, dropping bombs on the city under cover of darkness. Here, in London, the rhythm of life continues unabated: the Underground runs, newspapers are printed, politicians debate, people shop and eat in restaurants, and apart from the news, life has not altered one bit. I sit on a Piccadilly Line train and open a newspaper.

The images from Iraq are more intimate than the pictures I remember from the first Gulf War: thin Iraqi men (who look exactly like my father) with their arms in the air; Iraqi civilians hooded and bound with plastic cuffs sitting by the road, one with a young boy sitting beside him; and then an unforgettable photograph of a boy with bloodied bandages instead of arms, his brown frightened eyes staring into the camera. He lost his parents too.

The feelings are new and awful, and the photographs tear at my heart. The tears are falling, and I cannot control them. People glance up at me, and I catch their eye for a moment before looking away. For the first time I know what the desire for revenge feels like.

This is why my grandfather sacrificed his son to another life. It was as if he was clairvoyant and knew that he had to save him from the horrible destiny of war, and so gave up his only son. I remembered my mother telling me that when the family came from Baghdad to London to visit them in the early years of their marriage, she hadn't truly understood how important those visits were. To a young woman in her twenties with a new family, it was hard to have her in-laws arrive and take over her home, bringing a whole other culture into her domain. She realized then how "Anglo" she was, and how, despite all the strange similarities of their Catholic upbringings, the cooking smells were so unfamiliar, how different the language was, and the customs.

"It was all too strong for me," she once admitted.

She was overwhelmed by their differences; his family was out of context for her so she couldn't understand them. But she saw how much they loved Ibrahim.

"They cared so much about him, so wanted his attention, and he, always being the finest human being, was patient with their need to be near him, understood how limited the time was, how fleeting the possibilities of those meetings were. I wish I'd had more generosity of spirit to understand those things then," my mother says wistfully. "Only now that I am older do I realize how utterly remarkable it was.

They lost their first-born and only son so young. He left home at sixteen and never went back. They'd made the ultimate sacrifice. Not only that, but Khalil made sure that all his daughters had good educations too, so that they had freedom to move away as well. How did he know then that this was so important?"

The last time his parents came to England was the summer before we moved back to Canada, in 1982. My mother told me that when Victoria said goodbye to her, she held my mother's gaze in a deep meaningful look, which seemed to say that she knew she would never see my mother and father again. She never did. She died one year later in Baghdad, while Iraq was at war with Iran, so there was no possibility of my father attending her funeral.

My aunt Amal once let it slip that, every now and then, my grandmother Victoria would get angry at her husband.

"It's because of you that Ibrahim isn't here!" she would shout. "That we never see him, that we never see our grandchildren! Why did you have to send him away to England?"

Khalil never argued because he knew that they both recognized that Ibrahim's exile was for the best, for the greater good, but she had the right to be upset. After the revolution of 1958 and all the bloodshed, Khalil had worried that his teenage son could get caught up in the violence to come.

I told my mother this story later, and she looked at me and said, "You could say that your frustration at not knowing them or Iraq properly was the twin of Victoria's pain." We are at least joined in that; both angry at our helplessness in the face of circumstances beyond our control.

Looking at the images in the newspaper made the possibility of entering Iraq even more remote than ever. Yet I had to admit to myself that even though I was completely against the invasion of Iraq, I couldn't help but wonder, if everything calmed down quickly, would it finally be my chance to go with my father and see his house, his city, his country? Despite all the empty rhetoric of freeing Iraq, every cynical Iraqi secretly wanted to believe, against their better judgment, that this invasion was partly about their future freedom.

As we have done so often before, my father and I take the train to the London suburb, still known locally as a village, to visit his sisters for dinner. When we lived there in the seventies, my Iraqi relatives had come to this very same patch of England to visit us. This is the first part of England that my aunts Amal and Siham had ever seen, and then where they first stayed when they moved here as young women, Amal for her postgraduate studies and Siham to work. And this is where Ibtisam visited Siham, who came here first and where she eventually ended up living after the Gulf War. Not only is London my father's city, it has become my aunts' city as well; despite being immigrants they are synonymous with the place for me. They love Wimbledon, the royal family, the Last Night of the Proms, "Top of the Pops," Hugh Grant (especially in *Four Weddings and a Funeral*) and the BBC.

As the train jogs through the outskirts of London, still grey with wintry light but spring just starting to break through in patches of crocuses and daffodils, I think about how my aunts have finally settled in the same village they'd first visited, all three living together and forced into the same apartment by the Gulf War. Siham lived there on her own all through the 1980s, while the Iran–Iraq War raged and Amal and Ibtisam were still in Baghdad. Then in the spring of 1990, Aunt Lina and Ibtisam were granted travel visas to England for a holiday. Amal was due to join them, but she didn't receive permission to travel until later in the summer. By then, Aunt Lina had been in London for two months and missed Baghdad and decided to go home. Siham and Ibtisam tried to convince her to stay until Amal arrived, but she was homesick and left just before Amal arrived. A few weeks later, Saddam Hussein invaded Kuwait. Ibtisam and Amal have been living in London ever since, and Auntie Lina has been in Baghdad.

At my father's sisters' home, we are greeted by the spicy smells of curry simmering on the stove, and at the door Amal, Siham and

Ibtisam all crowd around to kiss us and welcome us. Despite everything, they are smiling, happy to see us, but very emotional. Immediately, we start talking about the invasion, about the rumours that the Americans will soon seize Baghdad.

"How are you?" we ask them.

I take Amal's hands in mine. Amal is the youngest, warm and expressive.

"It's so terrible," Amal says. "I feel like someone has come into my house, raped me, and stolen everything and burned down my house." Then she says something to Siham in Arabic. They have developed a way of talking to me; they speak in Arabic to each other, translate a bit, speak to me in English for a while, because they can all understand, and in mid-sentence, one of them switches back to Arabic and they consult about whatever they are saying. I wait patiently, and they get back to me in English with the rest of the story.

Siham adds, "Lina is all alone in the house. We spoke to her before it started. We told her to forget the house and go and stay with Karim and the family. But she wouldn't go. She said she wasn't afraid. She wants to protect our house from looters."

It seems incredible to me that the house they are talking about is the house my father, standing beside me, grew up in with his sisters.

"It was all right at the beginning," Ibtisam adds. "We could speak to her every night and make sure she was okay, but now the telephones aren't working. Electricity was cut off a few days after the war started. We're so worried. She must be terrified. Last time we spoke, she said she was sick with fear."

Usually, my aunts fuss over me when they first see me. I am like a daughter to them since none of them have children. They joke as they touch my hair and tell me it's too long or too short or not stylish enough, that I've lost or gained weight, that I am wearing too little or too much make-up. They aren't afraid to hug me or stroke my head or sit close to me. This time they are distracted, and they flit around, not focusing on me long enough to comment upon my appearance.

Dinners with my father and his sisters are a revelation to me. I am in the minority, so my aunts speak in Arabic to my father. The conversations at the table are unlike the ones we have at home in Canada. Suddenly, my father is talking Middle Eastern politics in earnest and discussing relatives in Iraq and people they both know. I see another side of my father, the elder brother who feels responsible for his sisters.

Over the years I had heard conversations about visas, endless paperwork and bureaucracy, lawyers, bank accounts being frozen, the sanctions in Iraq and how they were affecting Iraqis, and all the anxieties of normal people whose lives are suddenly turned upside down by war. It had taken ten years for Amal and Ibtisam to get British citizenship, and with it passports and the right to travel without fear that they may somehow lose their residency claim. They could have obtained temporary visas to travel, but they never wanted to; they didn't feel secure until they had their citizenship.

The television is on in the background and the six o'clock BBC news comes on. We all stand close to the set as if we'll learn more by our proximity to the screen. My aunts have satellite television, so we watch Arabic news as well, flicking back and forth between the different channels trying to piece together the truth through the fog of political biases. Iraq plays across the screen, the bombing lighting up the sky, the tanks rolling along dusty rubbled roads, "embedded" journalists chatting up soldiers, hooded men sitting handcuffed on roadsides. It feels like 1991 all over again. None of us can believe that our embattled homeland is suffering war for the third time in two decades.

Amal and Ibtisam lived through the Iran–Iraq War, and I ask what that was like.

"These two wars, the Gulf War and this one, are—were—much much worse for Baghdad than the Iran–Iraq War," Amal says, bitterly. "They never bombarded Baghdad every single day in the Iran–Iraq War. Only once every one or two weeks."

Amal came to England to study for her Ph.D. in 1975, and then returned to Iraq to work in the early 1980s. Despite the war with Iran, she'd decided to go home. She didn't realize then that she could have applied to stay in England because of the war. Saddam Hussein was in power, and I ask her if she knew about the political repression in Iraq before she went back. She hesitates, not wanting to talk about Saddam even now, when she lives in another country, when Iraq has been invaded and his regime is toppling.

"You see, when I went back, there was always fear that someone would write a report about you to the party. So you don't talk about politics when you are working at your job. You never talk about politics ever. I still don't like talking about it," she admits.

"Was that frightening?" I ask.

She raises her eyebrows. "Yes, but you get used to it. We couldn't complain with our colleagues about not being able to travel, for example. You couldn't complain about the war, or government policies, you just had to ignore it all."

"It must have been hard to go back to Iraq, after living in freedom in England," I say.

"Yes, it was hard, but I adapted." She shrugs. "I was back at home where I belonged. Remember, it was nice for me to be with my parents and sister. Iraq was modernized by then, and Saddam liked to build new roads and make the country clean and tidy, and he built many new buildings. At the time, Baghdad was a relatively nice city to live in, especially compared to now. I mean, you had shortages of things, the government imported everything, so there wasn't selection on the shelves, but there was health care, education, and the country was prospering because of oil. Daily life was stable. And if you wanted a car, you put your name on a list and waited. When I came back I was allowed to buy a car without waiting, which was a privilege of having a foreign degree. It was encouragement for people to return. So I went back and lived in the house that I was born in with Ibtisam and my parents."

Amal is the social one of the three. She has never learned to cook and doesn't like cleaning, but she loves chatting to dinner guests. She toasts the pita bread and brings it to the table; that is her job. But the cooking is left to Siham and Ibtisam. Siham is lively and likes telling stories as well, and she is an excellent cook. Ibtisam is the quiet homemaker and loves looking after the house; she is happiest when she is active, and hates sitting around.

As I set the table, Siham and Ibtisam come in and out of the room, bringing in different dishes heaped with food. When their brother comes to dinner, his sisters always make his favourite meals, providing him with the home cooking that his mother gave him only sporadically on her trips to London. Amal sits with Ibrahim, and I continue the conversation with Amal and Ibtisam about the Iran–Iraq War. They have never spoken about it, but now, in the context of an even more ferocious bombardment of their country, I want to know more about their pasts.

"First of all," Amal says, wringing her hands, "we never thought the war with Iran would end. It went on and on and on. At the beginning, we thought it might take two weeks. But by the end, after years and years of war, people were in despair. They thought they'd never see the end of the war in their lifetimes. When it ended, when it was announced on the radio that there was a ceasefire, we were so happy! We thought we'd won! The people went out spontaneously in the street to celebrate."

"I thought Iraqis didn't believe the news?" I had been given to understand that they were attuned to government propaganda and quick to interpret it cynically.

"I think we thought we had won because Khomeini said that he had to 'drink from the poisoned cup.' It means admitting defeat. We hadn't known all along if we were winning or losing during the war. So everyone went into the streets, some with their cars, honking, dancing, shooting guns in the air and celebrating. It was like when your team wins the World Cup!" Amal says.

"Did you go out as well?" I ask her.

"Yes, Ibtisam and I went out into the street. Our father was still alive, but he was old so he didn't go. We thought there would be no more war, ever." She sighs. "It reminds me of the revolution in 1958. Yes, we were very little, but I remember the same thing the following year, going out into the streets and celebrating. Qasim organized it for the first anniversary of the 1958 revolution, when they erected the Unknown Soldier monument."

"Don't they usually do that when there is a war?" I say.

"Well, it was for the people that died in the revolution."

"What did Iraqis think the Iran–Iraq War was all about?" I ask.

"Well, we thought it was about the Shatt al-Arab waterway [the confluence of the Tigris and Euphrates Rivers and a fluid border between Iraq and Iran]. We thought it was about access to those waters. We've always had problems with Iran about this. There was a treaty, and either we broke the treaty or they did. The war started officially on September 25, 1980, but even before that Iran was attacking our border," Amal states.

"So Iraqis thought you were defending Iraq not invading Iran?"

"We thought we were fighting over this waterway," she repeats.

"How did the people feel about going to war then?"

"No one wanted to go to war."

I tell Amal that I'd read that Saddam had invaded first, but that Iraqis had been told that the Iranians started the conflict, and that America supported Iraq because the US was against the Islamic revolution.

Amal says, "Yes, maybe that is what happened. But not what we knew at the time."

"Did you know anyone who went to war?"

My father says, "Our family is so full of women that we didn't have many male relatives of the right age at the time."

"But our first cousin, Nusrat, was a soldier who was taken prisoner in the first year of the war," Amal adds. "And we have a friend whose husband went to war when she was just newly married and pregnant, and he was, how do you say, MIA, missing in action. She didn't hear anything from him until one year after the war ended, it was almost ten years later. He had been in prison in Iran and finally was released. I never saw him, though, as we were in England by the time he got home, just before the Gulf War."

"What about Nusrat?" I ask.

"He was away for eight years. He left when he was twenty-five but he wasn't married, luckily. He was very very thin when he came back, and he had rheumatism. He is disabled now and in a wheel-chair. He had been with many others in an Iranian cell, and they were hardly given any food and were forced to do hard labour. The war ruined his life," Amal says matter-of-factly.

"We couldn't travel," she continues, "which was hard on my father because he loved travelling. But we couldn't do anything about it; you have to just get on with your life. Without a passport, you can't travel . . . that's it. Unless you want to do it illegally . . . if you are smuggled out."

"Did it feel like you were being held captive?" I ask.

She shrugs. "Yes, you try and put it in the back of your mind, but it is always there. You are in a situation where you can't do anything. So you complain about it, you talk about it secretly at home, but so, what else can you do?"

"And it was always hard to talk to you from Canada," my father says. "We didn't really know what was happening in Iraq then."

"In Iraq we had to go through the operator to call you, but then we'd be in a queue for an international line, sometimes for hours. You couldn't dial direct. The technology wasn't very advanced. Anyway, the phones were tapped. You never knew if you were being listened to or not, so you had to be careful. For very important things, you would send a telegram. Or letters . . . the post was working. Canada seemed so remote to us. Another world that we never thought it would be possible to see. The isolation was suffocating," Amal says.

I remembered being a student at McGill University in Montreal in 1988, and being a member of Amnesty International and sending my grandfather one of their Christmas cards. For a while, my father was worried that if the authorities opened it, the card's contents might be construed as political. Yet I had written nothing more than Christmas wishes.

Amal continues, "Iraq was like a prison and then I was suddenly sent to work in Cairo in 1987. I just couldn't believe I was on a plane, leaving the city and going to another country. Siham came to visit me there; it was so good to see her, I so wished I didn't have to go back to Baghdad. But, of course, my father was still alive and Ibtisam was still there."

Siham and Ibtisam finally stop bustling around us and sit down at the feast they've prepared. They say grace in Arabic, and then Ibtisam insists that my father and I start serving ourselves from the mountainous dishes: chicken and potato curry, rice with almonds and pine nuts, kibbeh cut into triangles, and salad. I look at them all sitting around the table, four Iraqis who have the good fortune not to live in Iraq anymore, and wonder how much of it was luck and how much design, their father's foresight. They escaped their fate. The Arabic dictum "It is written" means that your fate is already decided; you cannot alter it. But it was hard to know what was written: that they should escape this war or that they should never return home.

"Did our family suffer in the Iran–Iraq War then?" Every question I ask seems to lead to another and then another, and it feels that no matter how many things I ask I will never really know or understand what happened.

"We didn't suffer like they are now," Amal says, clucking her tongue, shaking her head.

Ibtisam interrupts. "We always had food shortages, even before the war. Because it was the government that imported everything, we didn't have choices. One day there would be no chicken or no meat. We had vegetables because they weren't imported. And rice and sugar and bread. But nothing extra."

"The air raids were hard," Amal says.

"A siren would go off?"

"Yes," Amal replies. "At the beginning my parents and Ibtisam and Lina used to go down to the shelter, but then they decided not to bother. I never went; we couldn't be bothered by then. Then at the end, we didn't hear air raid sirens anymore, the government stopped sounding them."

"Did the Iranians target government buildings?" I ask.

"No, I think their approach was random," Amal says. "They just fired. Many many many people died. It was sad to see so many people wearing black in the streets; other families had husbands, sons, fathers in the war. We were so lucky."

"Yes, remember that story you told me?" Siham says. I'd forgotten she hadn't lived through the war herself either, as she'd moved to England in 1980. "The one about—"

"Yes, our neighbour's son was in the war," Amal says. "Usually when soldiers were killed, the army brought back the body to the house in a coffin. One day this woman saw a coffin coming down her street and she thought that it contained her son. She had a heart attack instantly and died. But the coffin didn't contain her son." My aunt pauses. "It was someone else."

We are all silent.

Then the evening news comes on again, and we get up from the table to stand in front of the television and hear the latest dispatch. It seems that the Americans are confident that they will take Baghdad in a few days. We all stand motionless, staring at the screen. We aren't surprised because we knew that the US army could easily beat the Iraqi army. I try to imagine what it will mean for Baghdad to be taken over by the Americans. I draw a blank; none of us can imagine what will come next. The idea of Saddam's regime being precarious and possibly destroyed is unfathomable. The prospect doesn't feel real. Saddam Hussein has dominated the waking lives of Iraqis for more than three decades. He was powerful, too, as vice-president for years before he took over in 1979. It is impossible to overstate the impact of his personality on every Iraqi. Even I, who have never lived there, feel his shadow upon the family.

"I wonder what Lina is doing now?" Amal asks.

But we know. The bombs are falling. Baghdad is three hours later and so it is midnight there, and we know that the bombing goes on all night. We clear the table in silence, and Ibtisam goes to make the tea and get the fruit bowl. We sit on the couches with the television on mute, Siham's hand hovering on the remote in case we see anything new about the war.

"So then one day the Iran–Iraq War ended," Amal says. "I couldn't believe it."

"Me neither," says Ibtisam.

"It took a year before we were even allowed to travel," Amal explains. "And, of course, many Iraqis have family abroad, so everyone wanted to travel at the same time. But before we could even book our tickets to London we had to do so many things. I had to get written permission from my employer to say that I was allowed to take a holiday. I had to show the letter at the airport. Then we had to apply and get passports, and then an exit visa from the Iraqi government and then a British visa to travel to England. The British embassy was only open from 8:00 a.m. to 12:00 p.m. every day, and if you didn't get in the door, you had to wait until the next day. Auntie Lina stayed overnight, even sleeping in the street for two nights to get access to the embassy. Ibtisam and I couldn't wait overnight because we were working all day. Lina still didn't gain admittance and so one of my colleagues managed to enter the embassy and put in our application for us. I needed an invitation from someone in Britain, I think, so we must have got that from Siham. This all took a few months. Then I had to book a flight, but the flights were packed because everyone wanted to leave. Even though I had a seat booked, I had to get to the airport really early because they'd overbook every flight and I had to be ready to fight for my seat. By the time I was on the Iraqi Airlines flight, I tell you, I couldn't believe it. And only four or five hours later I was in England, with Siham waiting at the airport. After almost ten years. Ibtisam was already here, Lina had gone back. When you think of it, if I had come with them in March, I would have been home by the time Saddam invaded Kuwait in August. I would have been stuck in Iraq until now. Like Lina. Siham and Ibtisam begged her to stay until I arrived, but she wanted to go home and then, a few weeks later, it all happened. Another war."

Siham gets out the photo albums, as she often does when I visit. Ibtisam replenishes the plate of baklava.

"Amal brought Baba's albums when she came before the Gulf War. Thank God she thought of that," Siham says. "In 1989, when he knew he was terminally ill, he spent the last months of his life creating these albums."

The album is covered in black cloth, and Siham opens it gently, patting the seat beside her, which means that I am to sit close to her. The album is falling apart; there are some blank spots where the glue isn't sticky anymore, and photographs are just loose or lost. Faded black-and-white photographs are attached with corners to the delicate black pages, with thin tracing paper protecting each page. The first page is a collage of portraits of Khalil and his family. The top image is a snapshot of his white-haired Syrian grandfather (my great-great-grandfather), Yousif, wearing a fez and a suit and tie along with a thick white moustache; next comes Khalil's father, looking very stern and high-cheeked.

Surrounding the portrait of Khalil are his three sisters in their thirties, all with 1940s hairstyles, smoothed but kinked black hair. The eldest sister, Safiya, had married and been whisked off to Peru by her husband; Khalil never saw her again. The middle sister, Selma, is the one who stayed in Beirut throughout all the recent turmoil and is still alive, the last survivor of her generation. And the youngest sister, Miriam, lost her husband and daughter, and so lived with Ibrahim's family in Baghdad until she remarried there. Khalil's mother wasn't represented, but his father had had three wives, and his real mother, Agia, had died in childbirth. My aunts didn't mention her often; they said there were no photographs of her that they knew of.

The next page held photos of Khalil's youth in Syria and Lebanon in the 1920s and 1930s. The photos were sepia-toned and small, with writing in blue ink all around them, naming the people and the occasions: school photographs, the basketball team in striped shirts, and a few labelled "Jibran journey," which was a several-day hike Khalil had taken with his best friend, Ibrahim, in the north of Lebanon to the home village of the poet, Kahlil Gibran.

As I look at these pictures, I realize most of the painstakingly written captions are written in English and there are only a few names in Arabic script. Khalil had even marked small X's directly on the photographs with the names printed out in the margin so that people could be identified. It's as if he had purposely written this for us, his grandchildren, knowing that we didn't know Arabic. He didn't make the albums so much for his own children, who knew most of the people and events they contained, but for us, the grandchildren he couldn't know. He knew that all the family history would be lost in a generation if he didn't make the albums. I believe this wasn't an accident—it was his direct intention.

The album continues chronicling Khalil's life, moving to Iraq to teach, his wedding to Victoria (with portraits of each of them on either side of the wedding photo), starting a family, building the house in the suburbs of Baghdad in 1950, trips back to Syria to visit his father, trips to Beirut to see his sister. There is a photograph of a crashed car with the caption "1939. King Ghazi I of Iraq died in a car accident. The car was left at the place of the accident for the public to have a look at. Khalil, with his fifth class from Kirkuk, were on an academic trip to Baghdad."

In the pictures, the women are dressed in Western-tailored form-fitting clothes, and have modern fifties hairstyles and a good deal of makeup on. The photographs are rarely of one person, except in professional portraits, but instead are full of family groups, friends, engagement parties, weddings, graduation ceremonies. Many of the photographs seem to gleam with happiness. There are shots from Iraq, Syria and Lebanon, and many are outdoors on the Tigris River and its sandy islands, in nearby fields and parks, and in the garden at the house my grandparents built almost sixty years ago.

Then there is a photograph of Ibrahim in his first year in England. Beside it is another photograph of the family sitting around the same photograph framed on their mantelpiece in Baghdad. Khalil was making a family portrait despite my father's absence. Finally, there is a photograph of my grandparents sitting by the fireplace: Victoria looks up from a book she's reading, and Khalil browses through the same album that we are looking at now.

I picture him assembling the album, carefully arranging the photos, writing the captions, thinking of who would look at it one day. The future was as exotic to him as the past is to us. But he didn't want us to forget Iraq, our roots. Did he suspect that one day it would be impossible to go back and see the house he built for the family, to collect our possessions, the family heirlooms? Did he know he was recording it all for us to remember? At the time of his death, Iraq had been cut off from the world for almost a decade. Maybe he knew what that meant, and how easy it would be for that to happen again.

We pass the album to my father, and Amal and I clear the teacups away. In the kitchen I ask Amal a question I'd wanted to ask earlier: "Were you ever really frightened during the Iran–Iraq War?"

"No, I wasn't afraid," she states simply.

"You weren't? You didn't think about dying?"

"No, I never thought about it. Ibtisam was scared, but what could I do? I couldn't do anything so why think about it?"

"But I—"

Amal interrupts me. "I told you that at the end of the war, when Iran was bombing Baghdad, they didn't put the air raid siren on every time. The government stopped using it, I don't know why. So you didn't know if an attack was coming. My logic was this, if you hear the bomb then you are alive. If you don't hear it, then you are dead anyway. So you won't know. So if you hear the bomb, it's good, in a way, you are still alive. Once, there was a bomb about ten streets away from us, it made a massive noise. Huge bang, it's impossible to describe how loud a bomb sounds when it explodes. Two houses were destroyed and the people who lived there killed. But when I heard it I knew I was still alive. . . . Do you understand my logic?"

"No. You never thought about dying? I think about it all the time and I'm not even in a war."

"No," she repeats. "I never thought about it. You don't know when it will happen so you don't think about it."

"Precisely, you never know when it will happen, so you think about it all the time," I answer.

She laughs. "I don't know, you have to go to work, you have to get on with your life, and the war was mostly on the front lines, not so much in the city. You just get used to it after eight years," she says.

"So Grandpa was still alive then?" I knew he had been ill and died quickly, and that Amal and Ibtisam were there with him until the end.

"Yes, he died in 1989. In March, six months after the war ended. He had cancer. We went to the hospital every day for two months and looked after him. Actually we lived at the hospital for two months. We slept there overnight, ate our meals there. Lina brought us food and we'd go home only to wash ourselves. I closed my shop for two months and the government paid me my full salary for the whole time. That's what happens in Iraq, the family brings food and washes the patient and does all the things that nurses do here."

"So were people not allowed to travel to Iraq then, is that why my dad and Siham didn't come to see him?"

"We didn't want them to worry, or know how sick he was." I can see she is uncomfortable talking about this. "They didn't realize how sick he was, the communication was so difficult. They wouldn't have come anyway, maybe Siham would, but not Ibrahim, not your father. I don't think it would have made a difference. What could they do anyway? It might have been difficult for them to leave the country again; Siham might have been stopped from going back. You just never knew what would happen with Saddam. The saddest point for me, of course, was losing my father. But the fact that his children were not at his funeral was very sad. He didn't see his children."

"You mean when he was sick?"

"No, I mean, he didn't see them at the funeral. I was so sad for him that they couldn't be there. I think children should be at their parents' funerals, don't you? He is buried in the cemetery in central Baghdad. Because he was a Protestant."

"What about Grandma? Where is she buried?"

"She was buried in a very beautiful old Syrian Catholic church, about three hundred years old," she says. "It's in the old city, Old Baghdad, on a street known as Christian Street because of all the churches. It's where we all celebrated our first communion, even your father. Remember those funny photos of Ibtisam and me in white veils? My father created a beautiful stone for Mama that was engraved with calligraphic writing to mark her burial place. During the Gulf War the church was destroyed. Not by a direct attack, but by the reverberations of the incessant bombing nearby. The walls of the church began to crumble, and the priest summoned Auntie Lina and asked her to move my mother's remains. Now Mama is buried in the same church as my grandmother, in Our Lady of Salvation Catholic Church. Lina always looks like she is about to cry when she tells anyone this story." Amal's eyes moisten as well, but she composes herself.

"If I ever get to Baghdad, could I visit their graves?"

"Yes, underneath the church there is a crypt, with different graves. Like drawers in a wall. Different from here," she says.

"So not everyone is buried in a burial ground?"

"Well, it's better in the church crypt, but there aren't many graves there. The crypt can only hold a few people. Auntie Madeline is buried in the crypt too. My father used to go and visit my mother's grave every single Friday. He took roses from our garden, her garden, with him and never missed one week." Amal is quiet for a moment. "He was so good. Everyone came to him for help if they needed something, and he never denied anyone his assistance. He was unusual for his time; he'd go to the market to buy the groceries. Sometimes he'd be the only man in the market, apart from the stall owners, among all the women.

"I remember at Easter, he used to put parsley leaves on the shells of boiled eggs, and then wrap them in an onion. He'd leave them for a while and then when he took off the onion, it left a beautiful green pattern on the egg. It must have been a Syrian tradition. I don't remember anyone else doing it. We were supposed to go to church on Thursday, Friday, Saturday and Sunday for Easter. We'd try to sneak out and not go. But we always had to. It was warm weather at that time of year, so everyone was outside; a different feeling to the way it is here.

"Baba used to walk two kilometres each morning to get fresh bread for our breakfast. This was when he was retired in the eighties, and Mama was gone. I used to say to him, 'Why are you doing this? Why don't you just put bread in the freezer?' And he would say, 'When I die, there will be no one to do this for you. So while I am here, I want to get bread for you.' And of course, after he passed away in 1989, we didn't have fresh bread in the mornings." She looks down, silent for a few minutes.

Finally, she says, "You know, he used to call us the three graces?"
I shake my head.

She laughs, saying, "You know, from Greek mythology, the daughters of Zeus. Charm, Beauty and Happiness." Then she holds up her index finger, remembering. "Have I shown you the quilt that was made for my parents' wedding bed?"

"No, is it here?"

"Yes, we brought it to give to Siham when we came in 1991. Come up to the loft with me."

We go upstairs and open the square hole in the ceiling that leads to the attic.

Amal gets out a ladder, laughing, saying, "This is always my job, to go up to the loft."

Ibtisam and Siham didn't like going up into the dusty darkness, rummaging around disturbing old boxes. She climbs the ladder slowly while I hold it. Then I clamber up behind her into the dark space where all the extra boxes and suitcases and forgotten items are stored. Amal walks all around, picking up boxes, saying "No, not that one. I think it's this one. No, that's not it."

Finally, she locates what she's looking for, and we climb down again and go into her room. She spreads out a quilt made of peach-coloured shiny silk.

"I'm not sure, but I think my mother made it when she was engaged. There's also another blanket, a matching baby one, for Ibrahim when he was born." She mutters, "I thought it was here," as she rummages through the box. "It must still be in the attic. I'll look for it later, but it looks the same as this one. Just much smaller."

"I don't know why you've never shown me this before or told me the stories you told me tonight," I say.

"I didn't think you were interested."

"Interested? But we are family, you should be talking about it, handing it on."

"Well, we don't know much about our family background. It is over, it is past," she says.

NATIONAL MUSEUM OF IRAQ IN BAGHDAD DISPLAYS THE TREASURES
OF NIMRUD FOR A FEW HOURS, JULY 3, 2003
PHOTO CREDIT: FARAH NOSH

CHAPTER SIX
Pieces of Civilization

They lie across the floor in tens of thousands of pieces, the priceless antiqui-
ties of Iraq's history . . . the statues and pots and amphorae of the Assyrians
and the Babylonians, the Sumerians, the Medes, the Persians and the
Greeks. . . . No one knows what happened to the Assyrian reliefs from the
royal palace of Khorsabad, nor the 5,000-year-old seals nor the 4,500-year-
old gold leaf earrings once buried with Sumerian princesses. It will take
decades to sort through what they have left, the broken stone torsos, the
tomb treasures, the bits of jewellery glinting amid the piles of smashed pots.
—Robert Fisk, "A Civilization Torn to Pieces," *The Independent,*
April 13, 2003

My father and I are still in London for the "liberation" of Iraq. Horror
follows horror; stories of destruction, killings and random violence
seem to overflow the newspapers and television. In the anarchy
that reigns after the invasion of Baghdad, the National Museum
and the National Library and Archives are looted and burned.
Centuries of precious literature, poetry, art and artefacts are wan-
tonly destroyed within a matter of hours. We hear in bewildered
disbelief the reports that the only government building the American
soldiers protected from looting was the Oil Ministry. This is the
beginning of the occupation.

"Why didn't they impose a curfew?" my father mutters.

Iraqis were used to being put under curfew during a revolution,
coup or war. My father couldn't understand why the Americans hadn't
put a curfew in place to control the looting and protect the citizens.

The message we took from this and from all the other acts of reckless violence was that if the invading soldiers were indifferent to priceless artefacts of human history, what value would they place on the lives of the Iraqis they were supposed to be liberating? Any twinges of joy we felt at the end of Saddam Hussein's appalling reign were stifled by the terrible fear that those who would replace him would not end the terror as they had claimed. The one impossible dream Iraqis had nurtured for decades, the end of Saddam's tyranny, was finally coming true. But instead of relief, it was bringing more and more pain in its wake.

Finally, my aunts receive a call from Iraq. It is Karim, the husband of their cousin, Maha. He says that he, his wife, their son and daughter, both his wife's parents and his parents, and Aunt Lina have all survived the war.

"We have no phone, no electricity or water. The call is costing ten dollars a minute," he says.

They had bought two minutes on a mobile phone. He puts Aunt Lina on the line, and when she hears Amal's voice she starts crying. She had not even cried after the Gulf War. She says the war has been catastrophic and admits to being terrified, and that when she had finally left the house at the end of the war, she had literally not recognized the city. She didn't know where she was.

"It's not my city anymore," is the last thing she says. And then the line is dead, and they are both gone.

Amal says to me, "We only heard Lina cry once in the past, when her mother died. She is a very strong woman."

Amal didn't know when we'd hear from them again.

⌘

I first encountered ancient Iraq as a small girl in the Great Hall of the British Museum, which houses Assyrian artefacts alongside Egyptian treasures. My father pointed out two huge black Assyrian *lamasus,*

stone beasts with the body of a bull or a lion, a man's bearded head
and an eagle's wings. They were massive to me. He explained that
they were guardians at the temple gates. As we wandered through
the exhibition halls, he never emphasized that ancient Mesopotamia
was my particular heritage, but explained Iraq's history as a part of
world history, of the beginnings of man. Only later did it occur to
me that the Assyrian sculptures and reliefs, the treasures of Ur and
the Sumerian cylinder seals, were out of place, like my father, in a
museum in London. As he'd shown me the wonders of the ancient
world, he betrayed no bitterness and didn't mention that these treasures rightly belonged to Iraq. He expressed pride in Mesopotamia's
ancient civilization but never referred to Iraq as a British colony.
Iraq's treasures are scattered around the museums of the world:
Philadelphia, New York, London, Paris and Berlin house Assyrian
sculptures, Babylonian gold and Sumerian cylinder seals.

I decide to go to the British Museum to see the Mesopotamian
collection to remind myself of the historical artefacts that are
being plundered in Baghdad. Through a series of serendipities I
manage to secure a meeting with Irving Finkel, a curator at the
British Museum who agrees to show me around the Near Eastern
Hall. When I meet Irving under the great dome, I realize I have
seen him before. He is unmistakable with his wire-rimmed glasses,
shock of white hair and long white beard, and brown corduroy
jacket over a blue shirt. I attended a lecture he gave on cuneiform two years before, and I remembered it was passionate, full
of humour and brought the richness of the ancient society to the
modern world in the arid lecture hall. Cuneiform is the script used
by ancient Mesopotamians. It was written with the wedged end of a
reed impressed in clay tablets. It looks like the imprint of tiny birds'
feet running over clay. It is a syllabary (a set of written symbols that
represent syllables that make up words) rather than an alphabet
and was the written script of several ancient civilizations, including
Sumer and Assyria.

Despite his decades at the museum, Irving's enthusiasm for his subject has not waned. He immediately puts the alien ancient Mesopotamian artefacts into human context, making me feel intimate with the people. As we walk upstairs to the ancient Near East collection, he tells me that in our modern arrogance we don't realize, or can't believe, that the people of ancient Mesopotamia were just like us. True, they believed in many gods rather than one, but they were people who played board games and musical instruments like the harp and the lyre, and wore gold jewellery. The women cried out in childbirth, the men went to war, they wrote and read, had two-storey houses, running water, fortune tellers. There were professional storytellers in Mesopotamian towns and cities as there were throughout the Middle East until this century.

Once upstairs he starts to show me the precious objects in the Victorian wood and glass cabinets. The first is an inlaid board for the Royal Game of Ur, from more than four thousand years ago; ancient games are one of Irving's areas of expertise. He points out an inlaid jewelled ram made of gold and lapis lazuli and the exquisite Queen Pu'abi's headdress decorated with delicate gold leaves and stars dating from 2400 BC. He explains that when the first archaeologists began studying the ancient Near East in the nineteenth century, they went looking primarily for connections with sites that could verify biblical texts. When they found the cultural relics of ancient Mesopotamia with its human-headed winged bulls and pantheon of city gods, they saw them as the creations of a barbarian people who were not civilized compared to the Greco-Roman or Judeo-Christian cultures that followed. Ancient Mesopotamian culture has not inspired the world as ancient Egyptian culture has, despite being older and more intimately connected with Western history. Iraq doesn't have great monuments like the pyramids or tombs of Egypt. Most of the remnants of the culture are buried under the desert sand.

Iraq is mysterious in the abstract: Mesopotamia, Sumeria, Assyria, Nineveh, Gilgamesh, Babylon, Baghdad. The land of the

two rivers, the Tigris and the Euphrates, the birthplace of civilization. Iraq's roots are humanity's roots. As I am guided through
the museum by Irving he reminds me that these cultures, the first
civilizations in the world, not only invented writing, agriculture and
architecture, but also celebrated art and music through religion. Iraqi
art dates back over five thousand years, to the exquisite Sumerian
glazed-brick architecture in colourful designs. The Sumerians also
wrote literature on clay tablets. I ask Irving to read out some of the
ancient language so I can hear it being spoken. The soft melody of
this long-dead tongue comes to life through Irving's voice, sounding
strange in the way foreign languages do, but with the added dimension that the language no longer exists.

"What kind of language is it?" I ask.

He says, "The language is as sophisticated as English, full of puns,
jokes and irony."

I tell him that I revisited the rooms downstairs housing the
superb Assyrian bas-relief carvings of kings hunting lions, and going
to war and bringing back booty from their conquests. Irving doesn't
see these sculptures primarily as works of art, but as an early form of
propaganda, not only created for beauty, but for the narrative they
told about the king and his power.

"Like a newspaper," I laugh.

Finally, he shows me the British Museum's latest acquisition, a
carving of a winged goddess, perhaps Inanna, flanked by lions and
owls, known as the Queen of the Night. Below the sculpture, a photograph shows it as it would have looked in Mesopotamian times, not
pale stone but painted bright red and blue.

The first temples built for the gods were erected in Sumeria,
and were the precursors of synagogues, churches and mosques.
Their religious mythologies form the basis for later myths that
became part of the Old Testament, Greek mythology and the Koran.
Abraham, the founding father of the three great monotheistic reli-
gions, lived in Iraq, which was also the site of the Hanging Gardens

of Babylon, which means Gate of the Gods, and of the Ziggurat of Ur, said to be the inspiration for the Tower of Babel. The Epic of Gilgamesh, rediscovered on a clay tablet in the nineteenth century at the British Museum, gives us the original flood story. The story of Adam and Eve has echoes of Sumerian myth; Al-Qurnah in southern Iraq is reputed to be the site of the biblical Garden of Eden.

When Irving points out burnt-clay tablets from the libraries of Nineveh, I say, "I heard that these tablets can survive any natural disaster."

I was also thinking of the recent burning of the National Library and Archive in Baghdad a few days after the destruction of the Baghdad Museum.

"Well yes, many of the clay tablets survived fire because the clay was dried in the sun and had not been fired," he explains. "When the library was burnt, the tablets were fired thus preserving them. And if there was a flood, because clay is porous, it can withstand water as well." Irving tells me that the Mesopotamians wrote down the first laws on these clay tablets.

"If you are ever in Paris you should see the Code of Hammurabi in the Louvre. The cuneiform script on it includes the formula 'An eye for an eye, a tooth for a tooth.'"

At the end of our meeting I ask, "Have you ever had the chance to visit Iraq?"

Irving replies, "No, I have only seen it over the border from Syria."

"That is the closest I have been as well," I reply. I explain that in 1992 I visited Deir Ezzor, Syria, a nondescript town near the border of Iraq. It is a drab collection of concrete houses, shops, cafés and offices, all covered in a thin layer of desert sand. Most people labour in the nearby oilfields or are peasants who work the land. Bedouin women with tattooed faces wear colourful sequined scarves and dresses, bells on their shoes and gold amulets around their necks. Since oil wealth hasn't accumulated there, few outsiders visit.

I was on my way to the archaeological sites of Dura Europolis and Mari in 1992 when I passed through Deir Ezzor. There, in the middle of a gritty desert, I found out that the townspeople spoke Arabic with an Iraqi accent and listened to Iraqi music. I realized I was so close, and I suddenly wished that I was crossing the border into Iraq.

It was only a year since the Gulf War had ended; I was too afraid to go to Baghdad and visit my relatives. The Baathist regime was known for killing or imprisoning people they thought might be their enemies, and having a foreigner in your house could put you under suspicion, even if he or she was a member of your own family. Saddam Hussein could arbitrarily decide to shut the borders at any time, leaving anyone stranded there. The situation was too volatile, and I was young and scared. My father had not wanted me to go to Iraq, but he never really explained why. Now I know he didn't want to risk another family member being caught in the mire of Iraq's unpredictable politics.

"How do you feel about the fact that you have studied Iraq for your whole life without ever having set foot there?" I ask Irving.

"It drives me crazy," he admits.

In the year Irving started his career—1971, the year of my birth—he wanted to visit, but back then you couldn't get a visa if you were Jewish, even if you were non-practising, as he was. His name would probably have been considered Zionist, and so if he wanted to go, he would have needed written proof that he was not Jewish. Even though he desperately wanted to go to Iraq, he would not deny his identity.

I ask him if he thinks he will ever get to Iraq. He admits that he doesn't hold out much hope. At the moment, anyone employed by the British government—including British Museum staff—has to get a special permit to go, and because of the violence and insecurity in the country no one is being given permission.

"How much have we discovered of ancient Iraq?" I ask.

"We have only found about one percent of what is there," Irving
tells me. "Every tablet that was ever written is still there, unless it
was chucked in the river or deliberately smashed. There must be millions of them still left in the ground; altogether we know of maybe
three hundred thousand tablets in the collections of the world; most
are still awaiting discovery. But at the moment, few sites are being
guarded and things are being stolen and the sites are being destroyed
by war, making it very hard to do archaeology there in the future.
There is so much we still don't know. We have only scratched the
surface."

After our meeting, I wander around the British Museum, in awe
of all the treasures collected under one roof. What would it feel like
if one day it was bombed, or looted or destroyed? How would it feel
to walk through this building and see everything thrown out of the
cases, the captions ripped from the artefacts, the highest, irreplace-
able achievements of man crushed?

Outsiders often talk of modern Iraq as an artificial nation because
it was created out of three provinces of the defeated Ottoman
Empire by the victors of World War I. In the minds of Iraqis, though,
"the land between the two rivers" has existed as an historic, geo-
graphic and cultural region for five thousand years and beyond. It is
hard for Westerners to comprehend how long the historic memory
is in Iraq, where people refer to events hundreds of years ago as easily as they refer to current political machinations. The destruction
of the National Museum was an affront to all Iraqis, who saw it as
a wanton attack on their shared history, almost foreshadowing the
political disintegration of their country. Deprived of the symbols of
their cultural unity, Iraqis could be more easily coerced into other
alliances, whether religious, ethnic or political.

But Iraq is universally regarded as the cradle of civilization, and
the outrage at the destruction of its cultural institutions reverberated
around the world as profoundly as the loss of the British Museum
would. Only Iraqis felt the loss of their country to foreign occupation,

but millions of non-Iraqis mourned the looting of priceless artefacts and archaeological sites and treasures. The grief gave them a taste of the horror Iraqis felt at the pillaging of their homeland.

AMERICAN FORCES IN IRAQ

PHOTO CREDIT: FARAH NOSH

CHAPTER SEVEN

Porthole into Occupied Baghdad

This war started out as a war on WMD [weapons of mass destruction]. When those were not found, and proof was flimsy at best, it turned suddenly into a "War against Terrorism." When links couldn't be made to Al-Qaeda or Osama Bin Laden ... it turned into a "Liberation." Call it whatever you want—to me it's an occupation. —Riverbend, *Baghdad Burning: Girl Blog From Iraq,* 2005

It isn't until June 2003, a month after George W. Bush announced that the war was over and the "mission accomplished" and two months since my cousin's first call after the war, that we hear from Karim again. I am back in Vancouver, and he has an e-mail address, and miraculously, the computer at his office still works. The phone lines in his office's district are working too because his office is in central Baghdad. His home phone is still not connected. A week later, the UN Security Council recognize the US-led administration and officially lift the sanctions after thirteen years. Iraq is open to the world again; Iraqis in exile talk about going home to visit their long-lost relatives, but our family is still waiting, because everything still feels unstable and unsafe. No one can guess what the future will hold.

I decide to send Karim an e-mail. I can tell you that he is a Christian professional in his mid-forties and that I have never met or spoken to him before. The next day I have his reply. He is so happy for us to be in touch.

"This is one of the benefits of war. They say that calamity will combine a nation!" he says. Over the next few days we started a correspondence.

He asks me if I know Arabic, and I have to admit that I don't and blame it quickly on my father for not teaching me.

"You should speak Arabic, you are Iraqi. You must learn!"

I promise him I will.

His English is excellent, considering he spent his whole life in Iraq. I ask him what he thought of the war, and he says that of course he felt very differently from me. He told me that he had survived three wars now spanning twenty years, and that "there is no one that we did not fight." He said Iraqis had become acclimatized to war, and Iraq had lost millions of people. Death has become "an ordinary thing for us."

"We spent most of our life in conscription in the army," he writes.

He was supposed to do twenty months of mandatory service, the same amount my father would have been obliged to serve had he gone back to live in Iraq. As a result of "the continuous wars," he spent over seventy months in the army, which was still less time than many of his friends. To object to army service would have meant prison or death. War was daily life. Many of his best friends were killed.

"All the Iraqi people were looking to this war to bring the end of a tyrannical regime," he says.

Most people didn't make preparations, just stockpiled food and water. He didn't even do that because he thought the war would be quick, knowing first-hand that the Iraqi army was no match for the Americans.

"What was the war like?" I ask.

"It was different from all the last wars," he replies. "Iraq became a laboratory for testing all the Americans' new weapons and disposing of the old ones so that the Americans could keep their factories working."

I was shocked he'd phrased it this way, not citing oil or freedom.

The war took twenty days, and they were the most miserable days of his life. From his own front door, he could see the airplanes and cruise missiles flying overhead, and everyone expected the bombs would fall on their houses.

"The explosions made a terrifying noise, and each time we thought that the house would fall down, and the doors and windows shook as if they would burst out," he tells me.

One night, the British and American forces attacked at ten in the evening and didn't stop until ten the next morning.

"Twelve hours, and you might not believe it, but they did not stop for a moment." His wife and twelve-year-old daughter could not stop shaking, "even though I gave my wife tablets." At first, they thought an earthquake had hit the city because the house moved. "I felt the tiles on the ground would jump in my face." They were standing beside the walls and could not move, even for a drink of water, for twelve hours. "It is difficult, I know, for you to believe, but it is the truth. The Americans said that it was a clean war, but it was the dirtiest war for civilians."

At the beginning of the war, they had water, electricity and telephones. After a week, they heard on the news that American communications companies were complaining because these centres had not been attacked, and this was part of "the deal." Then the forces destroyed all the power plants and communications centres.

"So we lost electricity and lived in darkness. And we lost each other without the telephone, and then the explosions at night were even more terrifying," Karim says.

I keep thinking of my great-aunt Lina, living alone in the dark to protect our house as the bombs fall night after night, without even the phone to comfort her.

Then Karim stops writing, saying that maybe I don't want to hear any more about their miserable lives.

Karim doesn't e-mail me for a few weeks, and when he finally does, he apologizes for not being in touch, but they have not had any electricity or water for twenty-five days. None. I mentally unplug everything that needs electricity or water in my apartment; it would be like stopping blood flowing in the veins of the house. And yet, in the next sentence, he says that he thinks it is wonderful that I am a writer, but that he would prefer that, as a young woman, I would "choose to write romantic stories, not sad ones."

He describes the trauma of the Americans entering Baghdad. He never says the word "coalition" or mentions the British; it is always the Americans. No one had expected to see tanks in the streets.

"Now I must tell you a terrible story that happened to my friend's daughter who was only in her early twenties and her husband and young family on that same day, the day they entered Baghdad," Karim begins.

The family was at her husband's parents' house to check on them when they decided to return to their own house near the centre of Baghdad. She drove with her husband and their children, two boys and one daughter.

"Suddenly, they saw an American tank up the road," Karim continues, "and without warning, the tank began to shoot at the car with the huge tank machine gun. Instantly, the father and their three children were killed. My friend's daughter survived and leapt out of the car, waving at the soldiers to stop." The soldiers started shooting at her. "She ran through the shooting and found a house. It was a miracle she survived. She was taken back to her father's home. Her clothes were soaked with blood. She was like someone who had lost her mind.

"A few days later, her brothers went to the place where the catastrophe had taken place, but the Americans threw them out. After five days, they were allowed to take the bodies, which the Americans had buried quickly, using only a shovel to dig the shallow graves.

"When her brothers asked the Americans, 'Why did you kill this family?' the answer was simple: 'We are sorry, it was an accident.'"

He says the situation in Iraq is much worse than before the war. Baghdad is "following the law of the jungle." Soldiers are "savage and ready to kill for any easy matter," tanks push past cars in the street and if you do not stop your car, "they will crush it so easily." They are drinking hot water from the local well because there is no running water and it is the height of summer. "And these attacks on the American soldiers, it is because the Iraqi people cannot bear this situation anymore." The last thing he says is, "Don't worry if you don't hear from me for a while, because we are living a different life than yours."

❉

But I can't stop worrying. Now that I've made direct contact with my family, I want to know that they are all right, that they are still safe. I think about them every day. My friend Farah Nosh, an Iraqi-Canadian photojournalist, had stayed with her Iraqi family throughout the war, against her parents' wishes. She was taking photographs of the war and its aftermath for all kinds of international media, but primarily for the *New York Times*. She had remained in Baghdad, so I ask her if she would mind going to see my great-aunt Lina, who is still looking after our house, despite being told that the war is over and she should go and live with Karim and the family. Now she is protecting the house from the looting and anarchy that had accompanied the fall of Baghdad. Farah agrees to go and take photographs of her.

The first time I saw Farah was in Vancouver in the spring of 2001 at a protest against the devastating effect of ten years of sanctions on Iraqi society. Until then I'd only been peripherally aware of what the sanctions meant for average Iraqis. My aunts had told me that cancer medicines were becoming scarce, and that children were dying of malnutrition. Basic chemicals and foods were not allowed to be imported, spare parts needed for machines were banned. Western newspapers hardly covered the story even though these were the most draconian sanctions ever imposed on a country and were responsible for the deaths of a million people and the total disintegration of Iraqi civil society. The sanctions were an attempt to prevent Saddam Hussein from developing his weapons arsenal; instead, the average Iraqi was impoverished while Saddam continued trying to prove his power by building palaces and monuments to himself with funds from illegal oil smuggling.

I invited two new friends, one of whom was Iraqi, to the protest. It was pouring rain and we marched slowly down Robson Street.

"That's my cousin Farah," my friend pointed out. I saw a slight figure rushing by in a rain jacket, her dark hair pulled back into a ponytail. "She's very involved in the anti-sanctions movement in Vancouver, you should meet her."

Next I heard Farah had been invited to go to Iraq with a group of sanction-busters who were defying the import ban on essential products needed for hospitals and schools. She hadn't been there since she was a child. I was shocked that she was going to Iraq, and wanted to know more. I begged my friend to introduce me to her.

We didn't actually meet until Farah returned from her trip. Farah struck me that day as a very modest, unassuming, quiet woman who could be tough and brave if she needed to be. Beautiful, with a gentleness that belies her fierce strength, she has dark eyes and long dark wavy hair pulled back, and her olive skin was slightly tanned from her trip. She was even more petite than I'd thought when I first saw her. She moved slowly and precisely, unhurried, and she looked directly at me when she spoke, listening intently. I found out later that she'd been one of the only photographers to witness a meeting between the Iraqi deputy president Tariq Aziz and British MP George Galloway. I also found out that like me, she'd only recently "woken up" to the tragedy unfolding in Iraq.

On September 11, 2002, Farah flew in defiance of the fear of terrorism from Vancouver to Amman, Jordan, and from there took a bus to Baghdad. By then, the likelihood of war was growing more and more obvious all over the Western world. The Bush administration was relentless in its attacks on Saddam Hussein and his regime, and in connecting the attacks on the World Trade Center and the Pentagon on September 11, 2001, with Iraq, directly and indirectly. As a photojournalist Farah wanted to document the end of Saddam's regime and see how her extended family was coping with the build-up to a new aggression. I was envious. I deeply desired to go as well, but I told myself I had a job and a mortgage in Canada, and besides I was not brave enough to join her. She promised her friends and family that she would come back home if a war began.

On July 18, 2003, I open my e-mail to a photograph of my great-aunt Lina, sitting on a threadbare couch in the house in Baghdad where my father grew up. I've only seen the house in the peaceful photographs in Khalil's album. One look at these photographs confirm that the house is in disrepair and is slowly becoming dilapidated despite all the best efforts of the people left behind. A house cannot survive without a family living in it.

Farah writes: "She was there alone when I arrived by taxi and hadn't been feeling well. There was no electricity, and it was very hot without a fan. She was sitting in the dark. But she felt like getting out of the house."

The photographs show a woman who looks much older than her seventy years, but is unmistakably my great-aunt whom I had teased on holiday in Greece many years ago because she didn't know how to swim. She wasn't smiling.

When he sees the photographs, my father says, "She was a very tough lady. All the women in my family were strong and powerful. You know, she worked in Customs, very high up."

Her eyes are intense and alive, but she looks angry. She looks sad. In her hand is a woven straw fan. The roots of her hair are grey, but she has obviously still been dying her hair red with henna until the invasion. The roots have probably grown in during the months since the war began.

Farah says it is strange to walk into that house in the middle of Baghdad, so far from her own home, after everything she's been through in the war, and see photographs of me and my family framed around the room. Some are photographs that my mother had sent to her in-laws during the 1980s when the post was still working. Farah took a picture of a silver-framed black-and-white photograph of my father at age forty, who looks young and handsome, and behind the frame sits a light bulb, useless and forgotten on the mantelpiece. She captioned the photo Abu Leilah, Leilah's father, which is the way Iraqis refer to one another, as the father of their eldest child, so much are children valued.

Another photograph is of my great-aunt Lina's wrinkled hands holding a photograph of our whole Iraqi family from the late 1970s during one of their London trips. In it, I must be seven or eight, and I sit on my grandfather's knee, looking over at my father who is crouched beside us. Behind us sit my grandmother Victoria, and beside her are my great-aunts Madeline and Lina, who is cradling my younger sister on her knee. Behind them stand my three attractive young aunts, Amal, Siham and Ibtisam, in close-fitting T-shirts typical of London fashion of the day. It was the last time we were all gathered together like that. Farah's photographs were the first that my father and his sisters had seen of their aunt, who had been like a second mother to them, in thirteen years. The house was a place of stopped time; memories more alive than the living present.

The next day Farah sends two more photographs. The first is of Lina driving Farah through the streets of Baghdad. Her arm is raised, hand flexed open, and she is obviously talking while a cross dangles from the rearview mirror in the foreground of the photograph. Farah says Lina was driving her to Karim's house, and while they drove Farah asked her what she thought of the Americans.

She writes, "I knew her answer before she started. 'No security, people afraid to drive their cars'—although she seems to have no problem—'no electricity.... What have they done?'"

The second picture is of Karim and his wife, Maha, who is my father's first cousin; her father, Clement, and Victoria are brother and sister. This is the first picture I have ever seen of Karim. He has short black hair, slightly receding around his youthful face, and soft brown eyes. He wears a short-sleeved white polo shirt. Farah promises she'll send more photographs soon; it isn't easy for her to send e-mails. She tells me Lina asked when I was coming to Iraq and then describes what it's like to cross the border from Jordan.

"No visa, no papers, no bag check, just a few dollars with the Jordanians and a bit of a wait, maybe a bit longer . . . and you're in Iraq." She made it sound so easy.

On July 22, Saddam Hussein's sons, Uday and Qusay, are reported shot and killed. Farah tells me later that she was one of the few Western journalists at their funeral in Tikrit.

❊

In August 2003, American soldiers are being attacked while out on patrol in Iraqi cities and towns, and one or two are killed every day. The media is banned from broadcasting footage of military funerals in the US and so the public doesn't realize yet just how violent Iraq is for their soldiers. The violence is being blamed on ex-Baathists who had lost power with the collapse of Saddam Hussein's regime and on "foreigner fighters" who are sympathetic with Al-Qaeda. These are the first warnings that the war has not been won as easily as first assumed.

I hear from Karim who, despite all this, is feeling slightly more hopeful.

"I think the Americans had the wrong idea about Iraq and the Iraqi people when they first came here," he writes. "They have done nothing for us. But now they are becoming more responsive to the Iraqi people, and we are now beginning to accommodate this new situation, the occupation."

He feels cautiously optimistic. Iraqis should give the Americans a chance to prove themselves. He is quick to point out that he is not a traitor for saying this.

"Now they are starting to move in the right way, and we touch some difference in our lives. In my opinion, it will be better, but it needs patience and time, and people here do not have either because we suffered too much from the last regime. Everyone hoped that America would have a magic way to change everything."

He still doesn't have any work, even though he routinely goes to his office, and he is asking me to find contacts for him in the West. He usually works on contract as a civil engineer, but he has had no contracts since the war began. I do what I can and ask around, but I don't know anyone in his line of work. What could I do from here? The only company that I know that is working in Iraq is the multi-national construction giant Bechtel.

A few weeks later, on September 17, 2003, the news reports that the UN chief weapons inspector Hans Blix said that the Iraqi regime probably did destroy most of its weapons of mass destruction. The fact that this would have been true without the war and subsequent anarchy and death is not made much of in the Western media. All the assertions, speeches and intelligence before the war that claimed these weapons not only existed but were an actual threat to Western society has been to a large extent forgotten. And the occupation has not ended; the war does not stop.

Eventually, after a few weeks, Karim sends me his office phone number in Baghdad. He wants to speak to me. I am nervous about talking to him. We have built up a level of intimacy in the e-mails we'd exchanged, but we do not know each other. I dial the number, and the line takes about a minute to connect. The blank space of the quiet line gives me the feeling that Karim is beyond some barrier I cannot cross. When he answers "Merhaba," his voice is heavy and weak, but my "hello" enlivens him. The line is muffled, and we have to keep repeating ourselves. I find that I am shouting into the phone.

First, he wants to know why I spell my name wrong, "Leilah" instead of "Layla," and he asks if I'd noticed he'd been spelling it "Layla" in his e-mails on purpose to correct me. I tell him that "Leilah" is the way I spell it, but he says, laughing, "No, it's not correct. Because you are Layla, not Leilah." There are two words in Arabic that sound similar, one is Leilah, which means "night," and one is Layla, the proper name.

"No, but my name is the word for night. That's what my parents named me. Not Layla," I insist.

"No, no, no, I looked it up in the dictionary, and it says that the English way to spell Layla is L-A-Y-L-A." I am confused now. I resolve to ask my aunts and my father to explain this to me. But for now, Karim has decided how to spell my name; he continues to spell it like that for the rest of our correspondence.

He tells me that Lina has just had a back operation and that she can barely walk, but her phone still doesn't work so I can't call her. He has a friend who is an excellent doctor, so he got "a very low price." He laughs again. He says that the Iraqi police had finally been given some good weapons and some authority by the Americans, that they were very brave and doing an excellent job. I tell him that we were only hearing bad news about Iraq since the truck bombing of the UN headquarters in Baghdad and the killing of Sergio Vieira de Mello, the UN High Commissioner for Human Rights and the envoy to Iraq on August 19, 2003. To us, this bombing seemed ominous. The UN was a symbol of international co-operation for many, but of course from the Iraqi point of view it was the UN that had gone to war in 1991 and the UN inspectors who had been in and out of Iraq for twelve years. It was the UN that had imposed the twelve years of sanctions that had ripped the fabric of daily life apart.

He says of the recent violence, "This is an old film; we have seen all of this before. The Americans want an excuse to stay here." Then he adds, "We all know that Saddam was an agent of America, and he has finally delivered Iraq to America."

I am stunned by his frankness.

Karim still can't believe that American soldiers are in the streets of Baghdad.

"You see, for fifteen years we can't think about America. It was the enemy. We can't say the word 'America,' we know nothing about America. It was completely banned, it didn't exist. No Iraqis were allowed to travel to other countries. We didn't have satellite television, and even when the Internet came to Iraq most of the sites were 'Access Denied,' and our newspapers were controlled by Saddam. The world didn't know us, and we didn't know the world, especially America," he concludes.

It has been twenty years since regular commercial flights came in and out of Iraq. His children have never seen a passenger airplane.

"I tried to show them one on television, but they don't understand." He sighs. "American aircraft fly over Baghdad and the children hear the noise but don't really know what it is." Iraqis are afraid that when the airport opens, no one will know how to behave on a plane. "I have travelled in the past, though. I once went to Scotland. Beautiful country, beautiful place."

Just before the invasion he finally received a car that he had paid for ten years earlier. The system under Saddam for purchasing cars was convoluted, and you didn't know what you would get or when. You just paid a sum of money and put your name on a list and waited and waited. But under Saddam, Karim's life was at least stable. He had a job, a house, and could bring up a family. But society was also extremely controlled and claustrophobic, and the threat of violence ever present.

On April 9, 2003, the day the American army entered Baghdad, Karim says he was listening to an Iraqi station on a small battery-powered radio, which was reporting that the Americans were not in the city. Suddenly, his neighbour ran up to the house and came in.

"Look down the street, there are the Americans! In Baghdad!"

Karim said, "No, no. That is the Iraqi army."

His neighbour insisted it was the Americans. Many Iraqis didn't know that the Americans had arrived and so they were driving around as usual checking on elderly relatives and friends. Suddenly, a car came down his street.

"The soldiers shot at the car and killed everyone in it. We knew then it was the Americans." There is a pause; the line crackles. "They have done many mistakes to the Iraqi people."

"When the soldiers arrived we were so frightened," he continues angrily. "We thought the American soldiers would be so special, strong and powerful. But they were not more than twenty years old, just boys. They were nothing."

He then tells me about a relative from Fallujah who was in the Iraqi army, and who survived the war.

"He told me that the soldiers didn't know why the Americans wouldn't die when you shot them. You would shoot at their bodies and nothing happened. My relative said, 'They won't die.' I said, 'What are you saying? That the Americans are immortal? Like angels?' Soon after the war he told me that they had shields under their clothes, but if they were shot in the head, then they could die."

"At least now you have freedom of speech, with Saddam gone," I say tentatively. "We couldn't have had this conversation before."

Mostly when people in Canada talk to me about the war, they say something like this to justify the invasion, thinking this freedom is worth a war.

"We are free to speak, but no one is listening anyway." He laughs his belly laugh again. "We used to hear the word 'no' for everything in our lives, and now we feel free. We have to thank the Americans for that. But we all know that the Americans came to Iraq for oil."

He can't believe that still the Americans have not restored anything: no power grids, no sewage or water treatment, no telephones. He says this is why there is resistance to the occupation; after the Gulf War, Iraqis had all of these things operational very quickly.

"How can we enjoy our new freedom without any of these things?" he asks me.

Karim goes on to say how sorry he felt for the American soldiers in Baghdad because the temperature had risen to 40 and 45 degrees Celsius.

"Their faces are so red, like tomatoes, and they have these small tanks on their backs and a little tube coming out and they drink water from it. Just drinking water all the time, but I don't think it helps them. They are still hot," he says.

Then Karim's thoughts swing back to the strangeness of their presence.

"It is still like a weird dream when I see the American soldiers at a checkpoint," he muses. "They don't understand the Muslim culture. Even though our family is Christian, we respect Islam because the Muslims are in the majority here. I mean, even my young daughter respects Ramadan. She won't eat her lunch sandwich while her classmates are not eating anything all day." He points out that the Americans search women at the checkpoints and that no Iraqi man would let another man near his wife. "Now they are starting to have women soldiers checking our wives at the checkpoints, which is much better."

Some American soldiers even go to Karim's church. They talk to him afterwards, saying they like the Iraqi women coming out after church.

"The young Iraqi women are dressing in jeans and T-shirts, and the soldiers asked me if they can ask out an Iraqi girl. I said, 'If you do, probably her father or brother will kill you.'" He laughs very hard. "They said, 'Oh, in Iraq there is a lot of killing, isn't there?'"

When I next speak to him a few weeks later, Karim has stopped laughing. He is worried now. He still hasn't gotten any contracts and is living on money he had saved.

"The Americans have so much money; they have all of Saddam's two hundred palaces that were filled with money and gold. Where is that money? Where is the money from the oil we have sold? Why doesn't the Iraqi Governing Council use that to rebuild the country? Give people jobs? Iraqis want to work," he says.

I cannot answer him. Paul Bremer (head of the Coalition Provisional Authority, the transitional government set up by the US and UK following the "liberation" of Iraq) is living in Saddam's lavish palace in Karradah-Miriam (a symbol not lost on Iraqis), near where my family lives, which eventually becomes known in Western newspapers as the Green Zone.

"The palaces were all filled with gold and marble, ten times better than the palaces of Haroun al-Rasheed." Karim was referring to the glory days of Baghdad over a thousand years ago.

"When we couldn't even get textbooks for our universities, how did they import all these luxurious things?" He pauses, then says angrily, "We are thirty years behind the world."

AN AMERICAN HELICOPTER FLYING OVER BAGHDAD

PHOTO CREDIT: FARAH NOSH

CHAPTER EIGHT
Occupation Limbo

When last we saw him, he was on a presidential platform, waving to the masses below, unsheathing a sword or firing a ceremonial rifle. Now we see him as a wild man, dirty and mangy as a stray dog. And we have to keep reminding ourselves, it is the same person.... Taken together—the bearded Saddam and his underground living grave—they are almost mythic, redolent of legends and fables that are hard-wired into the human mind. With this twist, the Saddam story has become a blend of Bible parable, folk tale, Greek and Shakespearean tragedy—and it is unexpectedly powerful.
—Jonathan Freedland, "Blood Feud Ends in the Spider Hole," *Guardian*, December 17, 2003

When Saddam Hussein, hated by most Iraqis, is captured by US forces on December 13, 2003, many Iraqis do not react with the expected howl of sweet revenge. To see a figure so powerful who had tyrannized his people for so long, suddenly reduced to a bearded old man hiding in desperation in a hole the size and shape of his future grave, and then paraded on international television having his teeth examined like an animal, is distressing. They feel strangely depressed; not necessarily out of concern for him as a person, as he was feared and hated, but for what his capture represents. Even if it had been a dictatorship, corrupt and poor, the government was still Iraqi. Saddam's humiliation symbolizes the humiliation of Iraq. Iraqis are no longer in control; the Americans are. It is a return to seventy years earlier when they were occupied by the British, before Iraqis had gained their true independence in 1958. Now they have lost it again. If someone as seemingly powerful and secure as Saddam could fall so far, no one was safe.

In Dante's *Inferno*, Limbo is the first circle of hell, a place where souls persist in desire without hope, living upon the brink of grief's abysmal valley. In March 2004, a year after the invasion, Iraq is in a terrible limbo and is fast becoming a hellish place to live. But the American administration claims that now that Saddam has been captured, the violence would die down, not immediately maybe, but that all the "remnants" of Saddam's regime would stop fighting now that their leader was in prison.

When Karim finally searches for work behind the concrete ramparts of the Green Zone, he is shocked to see Americans driving around, eating happily in cafés, while his own family still struggles with lack of electricity, water and security. Huge American and British flags flank a tiny Iraqi one in the courtyard. Since then, he has tried desperately to get work, but without the right contacts in the Coalition Provisional Authority (CPA), he has little chance. It is rumoured that many Western companies have signed contracts with the US military, promising not to hire Iraqis for "security reasons."

He can't understand how the most powerful country in the world still cannot provide electricity, phone service, oil and most of all, security. "Freedom" has meant that he can express his opinion and contact us in exile freely. But he and his family haven't tasted daily freedom, because without security, freedom is still meaningless. Karim's dark sense of humour masks his deep disappointment. After hearing Paul Bremer's optimistic weekly radio address that schools and hospitals were open and that life was improving, he laughed.

"Mr. Bremer thinks that we are living in the best country in the entire world."

After twenty-five years of war and sanctions, Karim, like his fellow Iraqis, is exhausted. Unemployment is at 60 percent, especially if you are not "lucky" enough to be working with the occupation power. If you do risk looking for work, you could be blown up by those who are trying to disrupt the occupation. The world is still concerned with whether or not George W. Bush will be re-elected, but Iraqis are consumed by the anxiety of their daily lives. Before the war, under sanctions, women hardly went out because they were too busy surviving in harsh conditions. But they could dress as they pleased, and Karim's wife and daughter were not afraid to go to school or the market. Now, women often won't leave the house for days, preferring their men to bring home the groceries, for fear of kidnapping, bombings, criminals in the streets or random murder.

As the car bombs and suicide attacks escalate, our family in Canada and England turn to my conversations with Karim for an understanding of what is going on inside Iraq. The Western media and the CPA don't appear to know who is responsible, and there seem to be as many theories about who is carrying out attacks as there are attackers. The Americans are claiming that the culprits are ex-Baathists or "foreign fighters" (not acknowledging the irony that their own soldiers were foreign fighters too) or the helpfully vague term "insurgents." At first Karim thought the attackers must be outsiders, but sometimes he believes that the Americans are provoking the instability, since it is mostly Iraqis who are dying in the attacks. He insists that Iraqis would not submit their own countrymen to such random violence. I ask him if he thinks there will be a civil war.

"Who would benefit from such chaos?" he says.

Certainly not Iraqis, most of whom are baffled by constant Western references to the Sunni, Shia, Christian and Kurdish divides as most families are a mixture, and there has never been a civil war in Iraq.

Karim is scathing when the Iraqi Governing Council, which had been appointed by the CPA, unveils a new flag for Iraq. Karim thinks the CPA is very efficient at minting new money, creating new embassies, designating new holidays and now designing this new flag for a new country, but there is no security outside the Green Zone. The day before, he heard thirteen explosions in Baghdad, and saw the aftermath of one near his house, church and son's school. These explosions went unreported in the international news, like so many of these incidents, because they were so frequent.

Karim also tells me that more and more suicide bombers have been blowing themselves up in Iraq. The frequency is overwhelming. The first suicide bomb occurred two days after Baghdad fell: a soldier was killed near Firdous Square where the statue of Saddam had been pulled down. Karim was shocked.

"There were no suicide bombers in Iraq under Saddam," he says.

He sounds very tired and depressed. I feel hopeless. I keep saying I wish I could do something and that no one should have to live like he was, but I knew that when we hung up, he had to risk his life walking out into the streets of Baghdad, while I was safe in Vancouver.

"Please find us a way out of here, we'll go anywhere, an island in the middle of nowhere, the situation is absolute anarchy," he says.

One of their neighbours said to him, "I wish the Americans would hurry up and put Saddam Hussein on trial, find him innocent and bring him back to sort out this chaos."

It is Iraqi humour, but it barely masks the despair and disillusionment the people feel. To even joke about wanting Saddam back is like wanting to go back to prison, because despite the loss of liberty, at least prison life is predictable. But my relatives can't just leave Iraq because no other country is accepting Iraqis as immigrants. Wherever they go, they'll be refugees. In fact, there is no functioning passport office in Iraq, so the most that an Iraqi can get is a one-page travel document, and it is unclear how many countries would accept it. At least in Baghdad, Karim has a house, car, relatives and friends and his office, even if he has no work. I look into the rules for immigrating to Canada, and discover that if you apply from outside the country it takes three to five years to be accepted.

On March 8, 2004, a year after the invasion, Iraq's Governing Council (or, as Iraqis joke, the "Puppet Council") signs the Transitional Administrative Law that will govern Iraq when the occupation ends until the national elections in 2005. The US–appointed signatories are mostly exiles and so Iraqis distrust them, fearing their actions are not in the country's best interests. Many Iraqis see the upcoming hando-ver of "sovereignty" as the US changing only the face of occupation while underneath everything remains the same. The US wants to be seen by the world as invited guests of the Iraqis rather than occupi-ers. But they are barely bothering to cosmetically change the face of who is ruling Iraq. When the government is "handed over," the palace housing the Coalition Provisional Authority will become the US embassy in Iraq staffed by three thousand people, most of them Americans. It is obvious to Iraqis who will still be pulling the strings.

In this climate of growing distrust of the political environment, Karim has a new fear—kidnappings. Not of foreigners, the ones we read about in our press, but of Iraqi doctors, professors, intellectuals or anyone in the middle classes who might have money. He says no one knows who is really responsible, but various mafia-like groups kidnap civilians and then demand huge amounts of money for ransom. This has been going on since the beginning of the occupation, but is now becoming extremely common. The police are either powerless or are partners of the kidnappers. Many records were destroyed during the war, so it is hard to do background checks on the new Iraqi-police recruits. Frighteningly, there seems to be a systematic attempt to rob the country of its educated class, because prominent intellec-tuals are being assassinated. Iraqis also fear that the Americans don't want the Iraqis to really take control of the country. Karim seems as confused as we are about what is going on.

When I talk to my father about what Karim has been telling me, he is cynical. I feel like I need an interpreter to understand what is happening in Iraq, and to filter the news I'm hearing through the media and that I am hearing from Karim. "You see, the Coalition Provisional Authority is using all the same tactics that Saddam used to control the country. They rule from the same palaces, they torture in the same jails, like Abu Ghraib [Saddam's notorious prison that was taken over by the US occupiers], they take people from their homes in the night and detain them without trial because they suspect them of being against them politically. They close newspapers that they don't like. They use collective punishment, crushing whole towns that they suspect of harbouring people fighting them. People used to know that they couldn't say anything against Saddam Hussein and his regime. Now they don't know who they should keep quiet about, as they don't know what all the forces fighting for power are."

※

Karim e-mails me from an internet café in June 2004 because his phone isn't working again. Since I last heard from him, we have watched helplessly as the US carried out a siege of Fallujah, demolishing the city and killing at least eight hundred civilians, of which three hundred were women and children. This was retaliation for the murder of four contractors (the media's new euphemism for mercenaries) after a bloody demonstration in which US forces shot into the crowd and killed innocent people. The images of the prisoners abused at Abu Ghraib have been splashed all over the world. After seeing one of a hooded man with wires coming out of his sleeves, which an Iraqi friend says has been nicknamed "The Statue of Liberty," I can't bear to look at the rest of them.

I ask Karim how he is, and he writes back, "Still alive."

A few days earlier he went to the central bank on Rasheed Street in central Baghdad, and the next day a huge bomb exploded in the exact place where he had been standing. This was the second time he had cheated death in a week.

"They're trying to get me," he jokes.

Our media is talking about elections as an answer to Iraq's problems. I ask him if he believes in the elections and if they will work.

"First, we have to see whose names are on the ballot," he says.

This isn't as easy as it sounds, since many campaigning for office are so terrified of being assassinated that they aren't releasing their names or pictures. And then once again, the line is cut and the Internet isn't working anymore.

In his next message, Karim says that my great-aunt Lina's phone is finally working and tells me I should call her. My heart beats wildly as the phone rings and rings. Finally, she answers.

"Ha-llo." It's as if she knows it is going to be me. Immediately, she starts speaking in English, good English. I am shocked.

"I can't walk well because I have had my back operation," she says.

I realize that is why it took her so long to get to the phone. We chat. We don't talk about the war. We don't talk about the occupation. We don't talk about the lack of electricity, money or freedom. We talk about my love life. She wants to know when I am getting married and is worried that my younger sister is getting married before me. I laugh it off, but she is persistent and I forget under the pressure that she herself never married. As I listen to her my skin prickles, and I suddenly know what she smells like. I can feel her enfolding me in her soft fleshy arms as she did when I was a child. I recognize the familiar rasp in her throat as she speaks English with a guttural accent. She is so close, and the memories of the times when I saw her in Europe flood back. I was eight when I tried to teach her to swim in the Mediterranean Sea in Greece and she repaid me with bottles of Pepsi and plates of chips at a taverna. She is real, she has lived through all of this, and she is talking to me. I realize I have missed her. I ask her if I should come and visit.

"In six months . . . come in six months," she says.

Afterwards my father tells me that in Iraq, six months means never. It is a figure of speech, like saying, "Back in a second."

"I love you. I love you, Leilah," she says.

I hang up the phone and cry.

The next day, Farah, who has finally returned back safely from Baghdad, comes over to see me, and when I open the door she says, "I have a gift for you." I open the soft cloth and pull out a silver jug with an elongated, curvaceous spout and Arabic calligraphy etched onto the front. Farah's mother told her that in Ottoman times the object would have been used at wedding ceremonies. It would have been filled with rose-petal water—symbolizing a sweet life—which is sprinkled on the hands of guests before the wedding ceremony.

"I told the man selling antiques in the *souq* that I needed a present for an Iraqi girl who has never been to Baghdad, something to encourage her to come and visit."

It sits on my mantelpiece beside a silver plate that Jane, my mother's sister, gave to me recently, one she brought back from Baghdad in the late 1960s when she was living in Kuwait. She wanted to hand it on to me, felt it belonged to me now. The silver still life whispers to me. Maybe in six months . . .

A MASS IN BAGHDAD
PHOTO CREDIT: FARAH NOSH

CHAPTER NINE
The Christians

Next morning, at 4:30 a.m. . . . my hostess and I were already on our way to Mass in the Syriac Church. We reached the Christian quarter across the early silence of New Street, and found its dark alleys filled with quiet streams of people on their way to the Chaldean, Armenian, Latin, Syriac, or Jacobite churches, which are all hidden away unobtrusively among the labyrinth of houses. . . . Now, as we came from the half-light outside, we opened the heavy door on what looked like a bed of tulips brilliantly illuminated, so vivid and rustling and shimmering were the many-coloured silk izars of the women who filled the nave in the light of lamps and candles.
—Freya Stark, *Baghdad Sketches*, 1938

A month later, on August 1, 2004, I hear on the news that a series of coordinated car bomb attacks has been unleashed on four churches in Baghdad and one in Mosul at around six o'clock in the evening, when they are packed with worshippers. Sunday is a working day in Iraq, so Christians usually attend mass after work. Fourteen people are killed and at least sixty injured. According to news reports, the Syriac Catholic church, Our Lady of Salvation, was bombed from a Chevrolet driving by, and the blast blew out stained-glass windows, creating a carpet of coloured fragments outside. The insides of the churches were blackened with fire and smoke. Windows and doors were smashed and many of the churches suffered fundamental structural damage.

I am afraid that Karim, Lina and the family are hurt. The next day, I hear from Amal that Karim and the family are safe; his wife is a

Catholic but he is a Protestant and they had gone to his church that
Sunday, a church that had not been targeted. Amal gently reminds
me that Our Lady of Salvation contains the remains of my grandmother Victoria, as well as the remains of my great-grandmother
Samira and my great-great-aunt Madeline. Did their graves survive
intact? Amal doesn't know, and she doesn't show how she feels
about this painful news. I contact Karim to find out what he knows.

"I heard the explosions, as we weren't that far away," he writes
to me. "We all ran out of our church. I saw all the ambulances, fire-
men and policemen swarming around the area. I knew many people
from the Christian community that were in the churches; many had
injuries from the attacks and even just from the shattered stained
glass from the windows." He says that all Iraqis are upset about
these attacks, especially his Muslim friends who called immediately
to express their condolences, saying, "We are all Iraqis, we are brothers. We are ashamed, embarrassed and sad about these atrocities."

These attacks are meant to pit Muslims against Christians, to
divide the communities; instead, they seem to be uniting Iraqis.
Mosques and Muslim holy places have been targeted by bombers
already and various convents and Christian religious schools had
been attacked, but this is the first time in living memory that a
church has been attacked in Iraq. The Christians have never been
persecuted before, despite the periodic resurgence of accusations
that they are sympathetic to the West. The rise of Islamic funda-
mentalism since the invasion has had a major influence in reversing
the previously good relationships between Muslims and Christians.
Also, evangelical missionaries arrived with the occupying US forces
and distributed bibles with food parcels, which made the situation
worse by psychologically connecting Christianity with the invasion.

Iraq has no history of religiously motivated violence between
Muslims and Christians. Initially, after the invasion, a few small
groups threw pamphlets into the churches, threatening priests, and
as the occupation has turned uglier the threat has grown. Iraq's

Christians are among the oldest in the world, and the origins of their community date back to the earliest days of the faith. Westerners forget that Christianity is a Middle Eastern religion, that before the rise of Islam, it was the dominant religion in the region for over three hundred years. Many of the descendants of those first Christians still survive, although many more have emigrated to the West over the last century of upheaval in the Middle East. When my father was growing up, he lived in mixed neighbourhoods and went to mixed schools where religious differences were not an important issue. Muslims attended his school, which was run by American Jesuit priests.

The pope has called on the United Nations to intervene to create peace in the Middle East, but I searched in vain for any comment or expression of sorrow from Tony Blair or George W. Bush, who both claim to be fervent Christians. No one knows who is responsible for the carnage, but Iraqi Christians are afraid that they might be caught in the middle. Islamists can point to the invasions of Iraq and Afghanistan as proof of a new crusade against Islam, and Christians in the Middle East end up being targeted for their supposed Western leanings or their family connections abroad. This religious intolerance is new; it did not exist under the monarchy or the republic, when Iraq was primarily a secular dictatorship.

Since the Gulf War, Christians have been fleeing Iraq to live abroad in Europe, Canada, the United States and Australia; forty thousand have left the country since the war began. The approximately seven hundred thousand that remain have become increasingly terrified for their lives. The American forces cannot guarantee anyone's safety.

Farah phones me a week later from New York; she is distraught. She has just found out that her cousin has been killed in a car accident in Baghdad. He was married and the father of four children, and Farah had become close to him over the year she'd spent in Iraq before and after the war. She had helped him get a job as a driver for a Western newspaper after the invasion. At first she was terrified that he had been targeted for being connected to the occupiers, but her family assured her that it was just a car accident, another tragedy in a country full of grief. Her heart was aching for her cousin's wife; after everything they had been through, to lose her husband now was too devastating to comprehend.

On November 2, 2004, despite all the lies that the Bush administration had told regarding the war, despite the slow realization that there were no weapons of mass destruction, that the evidence to go to war had been fabricated, and that it was not helping to bring democracy to Iraqis, fifty million Americans voted to re-elect George W. Bush.

Later that month, Bush made his first official visit to Canada. My sister Rose attended a demonstration in Ottawa. The protest consisted of about fifteen thousand people, and lasted all day. The march ended at the Museum of Civilisation where Bush was having dinner with seven hundred guests. Ottawa was shut down and security was heavy, with thousands of police helicopters whirring overhead and snipers stationed around the city.

At Bush's press conference on November 30, a *Globe and Mail* reporter reminded the president that after September 11, 2001, Canadians staged demonstrations of solidarity with the American people. But now, there were large protests against Bush's visit in every major Canadian city. The reporter asked Bush if he thought the protests had anything to do with him or his policies. Bush replied that he understood that some Canadians didn't think that Iraqis could be free and live in democracy, but he had faith that they could. Apart from ignoring the question, Bush's answer tried to deflect attention from the illegal invasion and occupation, to an accusation that "some" Canadians were racist and thought Iraqis were not capable of living in democracy.

At the beginning of December, my great-uncle Clement died of leukemia in Baghdad. His disease might have been treatable under normal circumstances before two wars and sanctions, with functioning hospitals, good doctors (many of the best had already fled the country), peace and stability. Clement was the suave, handsome man who my father remembers as having had many girlfriends in his youth. Photographs prove that he was good-looking. When my father was a boy in the late 1950s, he'd watch Clement getting dressed to go out to parties. He viewed him with the natural awe that a young boy has for an uncle. Clement was the least studious of his uncles, the one who liked most in life to have a good time, to go to parties and cafés. He was the one who lived on an island in the Tigris during the summer, once in a while organizing a picnic for the family. He finally settled down and married and had a daughter, Maha, Karim's wife.

Now, if an organization was counting causes of death in Iraq, his death would probably be categorized as a natural one caused by leukemia. But we know that the incidence of leukemia in Iraq is extremely high, thought to be due to depleted uranium left behind from the weapons used against Iraq in the Gulf War and in the recent invasion. Nevertheless, Clement was in his seventies and had lived a decent life. On the other hand, what followed afterwards was caused by the unnatural circumstances created by the invasion.

It was the family's responsibility to take Clement's body from the hospital to the morgue after he died. Uncle Clement had lived with Karim and Maha for many years, and since Maha was an only child, there were no sons to carry out the responsibilities. So Karim, his son-in-law, had to take on this task, which he did willingly. They couldn't go to a funeral parlour and hire a hearse to take my great-uncle's body to the morgue because there were none available to rent. With all the deaths in the country, hearses were much in demand. Instead, they borrowed a station wagon from a friend and bent the seats back to fit the coffin inside the car. They drove to the Baghdad morgue. It was overflowing with bodies; the number of people dying in Iraq every day was catastrophically high. Bombing raids, suicide bombs, car bombs, IEDs (improvised explosive devices) as well as random killings at checkpoints and other murders all contributed to the high death rate. Karim was told he was forbidden to leave the body of his father-in-law at the morgue because there was no room, but that he should take it straight to the cemetery for burial. When Karim got to the cemetery, he was told that the number of dead waiting to be buried exceeded capacity so he couldn't bury Clement there.

Karim was sent to Baqubah, a town sixty kilometres north of Baghdad where the church had recently purchased some land for a new cemetery. He was told he could bury Clement's body there instead. As the journey to Baqubah would be very dangerous (roadside bombings targeting US forces and counterattacks by the US army were frequent on that road), only Karim and his brother could risk going. The rest of the family stayed at home and mourned privately. When the two men finally got to Baqubah, they hired some young men to dig the grave. Then they lowered the coffin into the ground, covered it up and left. There was no ceremony, no prayers, no eulogy, no celebration of Clement's life, no hymns, no blessing by a priest, and none of my other relatives were able to pay their last respects.

When they finally got back to Karim's brother's house in Baghdad, they were surprised to find an American tank parked in the driveway. They drove slowly around the tank to park in the driveway themselves, but were afraid to be so close to the soldiers. As Karim entered the driveway, his side mirror accidentally brushed the side of the tank. A soldier leapt out and started shooting at the car. Karim and his brother jumped out of the car and ran into the house, dodging bullets to the front door. Karim tells me the story so casually, as if getting shot at were a normal occurrence. He doesn't even question why the soldiers were parked there in the first place.

Because of the bombing of the churches in August, there was no chance of even having a commemorative service for my great-uncle in the church that the family usually attended. The church had been ruined and was now closed. So Clement's wife was not able to mourn her husband properly. And Maha cannot mourn her father.

FARAH'S FAMILY ON THE STAIRS OF THEIR HOUSE, APRIL 9, 2003
PHOTO CREDIT: FARAH NOSH

CHAPTER TEN
A Sugar Depression

[Day 17 of 1991 Gulf War] *Rocketing non-stop and the biggest and loudest explosion ever. It was apparently heard all over Baghdad but no one seems to know where it was. Not atomic anyway. We are still alive. I can understand the Kuwaitis hating us but what did we do to you, George Bush, that you should hate us with such venom? ... Tonight we shall have music. Amal has an old crank-up Victrola gramophone and ... a lot of 78 rpm records that we can now play on it. Who could have conceived of such a day when the rest of the world has CDs?* —Nuha al-Radi, *Baghdad Diaries*, 2003

It is the middle of December 2004, and Farah tells me that she is planning to go to Iraq again soon. We still don't know how to get money to our family directly, and so we ask Farah if she would mind taking a Christmas gift for Great-aunt Lina. Even under these extreme circumstances, we know that Lina would not want us to give her money, but we want to help her and she wouldn't refuse a gift. Farah agrees to take whatever we want to send. Once again, she is planning a trip to Baghdad while I stay at home. She wants to visit the wife of her cousin who was killed in the car accident. We send Farah a package of recent family photographs and wire her some money to take for Lina. Farah leaves a few days before Christmas and plans to meet Karim to give him the package.

Christmas isn't being celebrated quite so openly this year in Iraq. Since the church bombings, more people are afraid to attend mass, and big holidays like Christmas are obvious targets. I send Karim and the family an e-mail with Christmas greetings, but I don't hear back. Later, Amal tells me that Karim was surprised to hear from me. In Iraq, when there is a death in the immediate family, the family doesn't celebrate Christmas. They don't send or receive Christmas wishes. I feel terrible about my faux pas.

Great-aunt Lina has been bedridden now for many months; she has moved in with Karim and Maha because she is too ill to live alone. No one knows exactly what is wrong with her; perhaps her back pain that led to her operation was the beginning of the illness. But now her spine seems to be crumbling and disintegrating, and she has neurological problems and is starting to lose her ability to communicate.

Just before Farah leaves for Iraq, she gets more bad news. Sima, wife of Shihab (the cousin who died in the car accident), was caught in the crossfire of a gun battle at the end of her street. Farah thinks that it was a fight between rival militias. Sima had gone out and walked a few blocks from her house to buy tomatoes at a nearby stall. On the way, she was hit by two stray bullets: one went straight through her and the other stayed lodged inside her body. She is in hospital, close to death, almost orphaning her four children, and Farah is distraught again, afraid of what might happen by the time she gets to Iraq.

Before she leaves, she drops by and gives me the journal she kept while she was living with her family during the 2003 invasion. I've wanted to talk to her about that experience and find out what it was really like for her, but there is never enough time for us to catch up. She explains that she was working with all the other international journalists up until the war started, but then she moved in with her family, who are Muslim and lived near the airport. The regime forced many of the hundreds of foreign journalists to leave Iraq. Others left for Amman before the bombs starting falling because they were afraid for their safety, while others moved into the compound of the Palestine and Sheraton Hotels where the government was forcing media to stay. As the war began in the south, the regime organized school buses to ferry journalists to bombed sites, forcing all of them to cover the same events. Farah realized that she had access to a different reality, to be able to show what a normal Iraqi family was experiencing. Most Western journalists would have loved a similar opportunity but couldn't stay with a family without putting those people in danger.

Farah went from being in the heart of the Western media, saturated with news from many different channels and bombarded by conflicting information, to being with her family and starved of any facts other than what she was living directly. Like all Iraqis, she only heard the official news, which couldn't be trusted. Instead, innuendo and rumour passed from one family to another by telephone or by neighbourhood gossip. Her perspective went from being global and complex to craving any morsel of information beyond the immediate happenings in the house she was confined to.

As soon as she leaves for the airport, I make a cup of tea and sit down to read the journal. I am suddenly right with her, in her thoughts, as she "wears this war in one house crammed with fourteen people."

The journal begins on Saturday April 5, 2003. I now know that the invading army had reached the outskirts of Baghdad by then, but Farah knew only what was happening around her. Intense fire behind their house, on the road to the airport, triggers the family to want to leave for a safer spot, northeast of Baghdad. But they don't get beyond a relative's house in the next neighbourhood, where there are thirty people all packed together, sleeping in the same room, terrified of what might happen next. The women stress about what to cook; the men sit in the garden sharing war rumours and yelling at the children to go inside each time a bomb explodes. The men have heard that the district they were planning to flee to has turned into a refugee camp of Baghdadis escaping the city. One of Farah's cousins is a brigadier for Saddam Hussein's military, and everyone is terrified the regime will discover her in the same house as him.

Since it is too cramped in the relative's house they go back home only to find Republican Guards resting on their street. The guards are hungry, and so the family feeds them. The two mothers, Luma and Sima (wives of Ehab and Shihab, Aunt Lamaan and Uncle Ahmed's sons), have six children between them to think of as well. Luma feeds her youngest son with a bottle, not even realizing that he is finished drinking and milk is spilling all over his face. She cries constantly, afraid that she will be killed and her children orphaned. They are most terrified of cluster bombs (air-dropped bombs that eject up to two thousand smaller submunitions or bomblets), having heard stories of the latest neighbourhood casualties.

Sima's husband regrets that he didn't evacuate his wife and four children out of Baghdad earlier. The day before, Sima threatened to walk out of the city with the children, but Shihab said he couldn't leave his parents behind. Everyone is suddenly restless; they just want the fight for Baghdad to come and be over with. They dread the unknown.

"My cousins, Shihab and Ehab, fear it's all a bad joke, that once again the Americans will leave their business unfinished here," Farah writes. "They don't feel they have legitimate business here in the first place but if they come, they must finish. 'Saddam is so bad already,' they say, 'imagine if the Americans don't finish with Baghdad, if they don't take him, he will think he was victorious, then do you know what that will do to him? Make him even worse.'"

The family forbids Farah from using her camera outside of the house. She tries to find BBC or Voice of America on the radio in the yard, but keeps the volume down because her family doesn't want the Republican Guard to hear English blasting from the radio. Before the war, Aunt Lamaan told curious neighbours that Farah had returned to Canada, and her neighbours told Lamaan that they would never leave Baghdad. But then a few days ago they were piling into a pickup truck. The regime has made everyone suspicious of everyone else so everyone tells half-truths. Farah never does find English radio, leaving her famished for news, upset and with no idea what is going on. All she can do is listen to Arabic radio and filter rumours.

The Republican Guard has been using the courtyard to wash themselves, wash their clothes and pray, and they love to come to the back door to politely return the tea trays. They wear red scarves, a reminder of their loyalty to Saddam Hussein. Farah wonders how loyal their hearts are. Are they wondering when it will be time to put their civilian clothes on and walk home? They've slapped a large antenna onto the side of the house; the men of the family think it is some sort of communications station. Farah asks her uncle what he thinks of it, and he replies that it's the reason they are leaving the next morning, but he doesn't know where they'll go. Later that night, a few guards are sleeping in an empty lot beside the house. Everyone is asleep, and Farah enjoys the moment of calm, listening to the guards outside murmur, almost inaudibly, about what to eat.

The next morning, as the family is packing and debating where to go, the son of a family friend, Thikra, arrives and starts yelling at them, telling them that he came back to see if they were still there and that they have to get out immediately. He insists that the whole family go to his house to wait out the war. On the way, Farah sees a few hundred Iraqi soldiers tucked under a bridge, some standing in military trucks and others crouching against the huge concrete pillars that hold up the bridge, just waiting. Her camera remains at her feet. Her uncle Ahmed sees her sit up in awe and stare. She is wearing local clothes and her hair is covered, so that no one will suspect who she really is.

"I hope you don't have your camera with you." Silence.

"It's at my feet, Uncle." He doesn't say anything.

It's April 8, 2003, and now that they've moved into another house off Palestine Street in the Engineers District. No one knows how to reach Farah. Far off in the distance, she can see the Ministry of Oil.

"I have just heard my first helicopter during this war," she writes. "The bombing was quiet last night, kept at a distance. I dreamt early this morning that I was in Vancouver, in a classroom sitting among people discussing the war which was still going on. In the dream, I'd been in Iraq for the start of the war, but unable to handle the isolation of being locked in this house, I left. The feeling of regret at leaving Iraq was so incredibly heavy, and just as the regret was nearly unbearable, I woke from the dream to the sound of an American plane. I am relieved I am still inside. The plane flew low, accompanied by heavy rattling as it dropped clusters of what we thought were bombs. Still confused we are."

She got up that morning to a debate in the apartment as to whether or not Hassan Ali Majid, better known as "Chemical Ali," (he earned this nickname because he ordered the horrific chemical attack on the Kurdish town of Halabja in March 1988), has been caught or killed. It started when Sima suggested he should rightfully be one of the first to be killed.

Her husband argues, saying, "Where have you been? That's old news. He was caught outside of Basra days ago."

After convincing the family that Chemical Ali had been caught his mother Lamaan says, "See, let only those who have killed be killed. Please, Allah, let the rest of us be in peace."

Thikra came into the room, and she's just found out that the American plane they heard hovering overhead earlier today fired at an air defence site in Zayuna district, which is just over the next bridge, not far from their house.

"An entire air defence site was hit, completely wiped out. 'All just kids, of course,' said Thikra. Her eyes were stunned and started to fill with tears," Farah records.

"'*Kelb ibn al-kelb.*'" Lamaan throws her arms up immediately and sits down on the sofa chair in the kitchen. She starts to wail as she rocks back and forth. In the same sentence she starts sobbing to God, and cursing Saddam. "'*Allah*, why?'" Her arms up to the sky, "'No, no, *ya Allah*. Saddam, dog, son of a dog. They are all dying for you,

Saddam. Why don't you leave or take a bullet to your head and spare us? All of this is happening for you. You are one, us millions. Dog, son of a dog.'"

As Lamaan wails, Farah sits on the edge of the wooden sofa chair and rubs her back. Still sobbing, Lamaan she tells Jihan, her eldest granddaughter, to continue sweeping the floor. Lamaan gets up and starts cooking, still crying.

"Lamaan relates everything to her own two sons, but her cries were not just for the lost boys of the defence site," Farah writes. "She's had enough. She's tired of having left her home because of the bombing, and she's tired of worrying that none of it will be there when she returns. She's tired of this fourteen-person apartment suite and these crying kids. She's tired of this tired Iraqi life that has resulted from the brutal regime, brutal sanctions and endless war."

Then Luma starts talking, reminding the family why her sister Suhad locked her twin sons up ten days before the war started, forcing them to desert their military service. They've spent the entire war on the top floor of the house, forbidden from answering the door, or the telephone, or even stepping out on the rooftop.

Suhad says, "Leaving them at their air defence site would be consenting to their deaths. That site will definitely be hit."

Lamaan continues wailing for the mothers; until now she's not shed a tear. As she continues to sob, Sima continues cooking, Jihan continues to wring out the dirty wet cloths that she's used to clean the floor and Luma goes back into the room to the kids. Life goes on.

Lamaan said one day her tears just stopped. She ran out. Weeks ago, she told Farah of the frustration of wanting to cry but not being able to. Between both her sons' visits to Abu Ghraib prison, and the death of her mother and brother, she'd run out of tears.

"A doctor once told her that surgery would bring tears back. 'But none of our doctors are good enough, and who has money for that? Sometimes I need the relief of crying. I just want to cry, and I can't,

how can you cry with no tears. See? Are you starting to see our sadness now?'" Lamaan asks.

Farah is tired, and it's been only a few months for her. She tries to
be patient when she remembers Iraqis have been living in this cage
for decades. Shihab says that because she's just come into the cage,
her memory as a free bird is too long and recent. She is just not used
to the bars constraining her movement, her mind.

On the morning of April 9, 2003, Farah sits in a window of an
apartment off Palestine Street. She watches from behind a palm tree
that camouflages her as a middle-aged man hands out refill cartridges
for Kalashnikovs.

"His hand is in a pink plastic grocery bag the whole time I watch
him make his way towards the house," she describes. "He reaches
the edge of this property. I wonder what his thoughts were as he
walked down the road, his hand clenched the entire time on Russian
Kalashnikov cartridges. I wonder where he got them, how much he
paid and if he's just giving them free to these neighbourhood men. I
haven't seen any exchange of money.

"Yesterday, the men heard rumours of Americans doing house-
to-house searches, so they hid their weapons," she continues.
"Kalashnikovs are illegal under the regime unless government-
supplied, so they fear that Americans will mistake them for Baath
party members (*hisib*) or Iraqi military. They're only to protect their
homes. It's the only fighting these men intend on doing. They think
a dangerous chaos will hit the streets and homes once the Americans
have moved in and the regime has broken. It seems everybody has a
Kalashnikov in Iraq—some I know are official Baath party members,
and many aren't. You can get anything in a black-market system in
Iraq. Somehow, the country just feels out whether or not the government is serious about its regulations. I suppose a few test it; if they're
not executed or disappear, then more brave men do the same, until
it becomes a quiet joke that something everybody has is supposedly
illegal. That happened years ago with American cigarettes and street

vendors. And on two occasions I've heard it happened with sugar at the start of sanctions. A sugar depression. Not even honey. You could be hung if you were caught offering sweets to your guests."

OVERLOOKING DAMASCUS
PHOTO CREDIT: FARAH NOSH

CHAPTER ELEVEN

Snow in the Desert

The past is another country.—L.P. Hartley, *The Go-Between*, 1953

I wake up on January 30, 2005, at 5:00 a.m. to the lamenting sound of the call to prayer, "Allah Akbar." I am in Beirut staying in a hotel on the Rue Hamra, a few blocks from where I had stayed with my parents as a two-year-old in 1973 on their only trip to the Middle East together, just before the Lebanese civil war broke out.

My fiancé, Scott, and I arrived just a few hours earlier in the middle of the night to a renovated and slick Beirut airport. Because of the late hour, we weren't prepared for the crowds when we walked through Arrivals. The barriers were heaving with a press of people beautifully robed in white, women in chadors, waiting for their relatives returning from the *hajj*, the pilgrimage to Mecca. There were hundreds and hundreds of people, and whenever a *hajji*, a pilgrim, appeared framed in the doorway, the crowd clapped and ululated in celebration. They have made their obligatory once-in-a-lifetime trip to the holy city, and they are greeted ecstatically by their families, who embrace and kiss them. We stood out completely, obviously not on our return from Mecca, and were greeted with silence when we walked out, so we tried to slink through the stifling crowds to find a taxi to the hotel. The air was humid even though it was January, and the taxi driver said the weather had been unseasonably mild.

Once at the hotel I was relieved. I had felt deep trepidation about coming to the Middle East again; it brought back memories of an earlier trip to Beirut, twelve years ago, when I had come with Siham to visit my elderly great-aunt Selma. I had memories of the destruction of war, ruined buildings and destroyed lives on a scale I had never seen. But now, I realize, Beirut has changed. Back then the airport had been a concrete bunker full of guards who looked at you with suspicion. There was no electricity, and we drove home through the dark streets, totally disoriented and on edge. Arriving this time at the hotel felt like arriving in a sophisticated city, the staff dressed smartly and ready to offer advice and help with anything we needed.

That morning I was too excited to sleep in, and had jet lag, anyway, so we turn on the television. It is the day of Iraq's first "democratic" elections in fifty years, to elect the Iraqi National Assembly. We watch on CNN as people vote under occupation. A curfew was enforced and no one is allowed to drive in Baghdad. There are images of Iraqis walking through the grim, empty streets to the voting booths. The occupation and curfew mean that many people can't or don't vote, and that most candidates running for office are too afraid to show their faces. Even the legality of elections under occupation is unclear, but the Western media is in full gear, reminding people of the historic occasion and that no election is perfect. The television shows ecstatic Iraqis voting for the first time. So far there has only been one bombing at a polling station. I find out later that two hundred and fifty people died in violence that day. It is as if there has never been an election in Iraq, but then I remember that my father had joked that elections, albeit rigged ones, were held before, under the monarchy and even under Saddam. We won't know the results of this one for weeks.

For many Iraqis, it is the first time that they have ever voted freely. Even I am eligible to vote, despite having never been to the country, because my father is Iraqi. I would just have to show my father's Iraqi passport, and then I'd have the right to cast my ballot. But I have decided not to. I don't believe in these elections, don't see how I have a right to vote when I have never stepped foot in the place and when many Iraqis within the country live in areas that are too violent to allow them to get to polling stations. Besides, to me, voting would mean supporting or giving legitimacy to a government that has been created out of the violence and killing wrought by the invasion.

When I get back to Canada a few weeks later, I hear that Maha's mother, Haifa, despite being in her seventies and barely able to walk, insisted on going to vote. This was the first, and likely the last, "free" election she would ever vote in in her life and she didn't want to miss it. Baghdad was under curfew and driving was forbidden, so Karim, Maha and Haifa had to walk to the voting booth. They left the house at 7:00 a.m., and Haifa insisted on walking over a kilometre to the nearest voting booth. Karim said she usually couldn't walk ten steps on her own. She took many painkillers but managed to get there and mark her ballot. Karim and Maha risked their lives to vote because they want so much to believe that Iraq is going forward. They had no choice but to take part.

After a few minutes of watching TV, we go to breakfast, a Middle Eastern spread of *lebne*, olives, bread, cucumber, tomato, with a nod to the French influence in croissants and freshly made crepes. I can't help feeling strange that the elections are happening, and here I am in Beirut, when I could have been in Baghdad by the end of the day, driving to Damascus and over the desert as travellers have done all through the century. But when I'd told my family (both in and outside of Iraq) that we were planning this trip, they had all unanimously insisted that we not go to Baghdad. Not now, not yet. It wasn't the right time; things would be better after the elections, after a sovereign government took power, after the army was rebuilt, after there was security in the city. We also knew that as Westerners, we would put anyone that we met in danger of being seen as collaborators. So despite being within a day's reach of Baghdad, we are not planning to go. I have to make do with Beirut instead. It strikes me how different it feels to be witnessing events in Iraq from here, the Middle East, than at home in Vancouver. I am relieved to be closer; it feels more real.

Farah and I had talked about my not going to Iraq. She'd always understood that it was a big decision for me and insisted that because it was so dangerous, she could never encourage me to go.

She'd said, "It's only a decision you can make. You only know when not going is more painful than going. I have to go there to do my work. I can't do it from here so I don't have a choice. It's different to have a choice."

Scott and I spend the day wandering through central Beirut, adjusting to the Middle East. The city streets are still broken down; wild skeletal stray cats pick at garbage, rundown Ottoman-era villas stand amidst hastily erected ugly concrete buildings. Straggly palm trees line the potholed sidewalks, but bright lights shine out over Rue Hamra. We lunch in a lively, sleek restaurant where well-dressed families eat lemony tabbouleh (parsley and tomato salad), taratour (sesame sauce) with shish tauok, chicken kebab and fresh orange juice.

We arrive at the Corniche, the promenade by the sea, close to sunset. This is when all Beirut seems to be walking along by the light sage-green water, breathing in the sea air and forgetting their troubles. We buy nuts from a cart flying Lebanese flags, and the vendor scoops them with a tea saucer into a paper bag. Men at kiosks sell corn on the cob, and people are fishing over the side of the Corniche. There are big fancy cafés overlooking La Rocha, the arched rocks that are synonymous with the tourist image of Beirut. Cars blare out Arabic pop music from their windows, some full of young men out cruising the city, while a whole family clambers into a beaten-up Mercedes, squeezing two grandparents, two parents and five children into the ancient car.

After the Corniche, we head towards the American University of Beirut and stumble upon a bookstore on the way. Stacks of books teeter on the shelves, seemingly on the verge of tumbling down on the sombre proprietor, who sits with a cigar hanging out of his mouth at his desk We recognize many English books about the Middle East by the British publisher Saqi Books, and Arabic books translated into several European languages.

We end up at a café near the walls of the university where my grandfather Khalil studied theology in the 1930s. Before going in, we decide to walk around the grounds in the growing darkness. This is as close as I've ever come to my grandfather's life. Despite various renovations, many of the golden sandstone buildings were the same when my grandfather studied there. I try to picture Beirut then, a small town, really, in a beautiful location; this campus overlooking the Mediterranean Sea.

The high-ceilinged café is decorated with Arabic tiles, and students sit in high-backed wicker chairs, playing backgammon or drinking coffee, some smoking the narghile, hugging the pipe to them, cradling it under their chins so the mouthpiece stays in their lips as they puff steadily. The delicious scent of apple-infused tobacco smoke and the burning charcoal of the pipes perfume the air. Arabic pop videos flash on television screens behind Scott, and we sit feeling relaxed and happy.

We talk about our upcoming trips to visit two of my relatives. The next day we are being taken by a friend of Siham's to see Greataunt Selma who lives in a convent that has been transformed into an old-age home run by nuns. She is ninety-seven years old. The following day we plan to travel to northern Lebanon to a tiny village in the mountains where my father's namesake, Ibrahim, my grandfather's best friend, still lives. Khalil was also an only son, like my father, and so was Khalil's friend, Ibrahim.

My aunts always visited Ammu Ibrahim—Uncle Ibrahim as they always called him—with their father when they were young, but since the civil war, our family has lost touch with him. I hadn't even known of his existence until Siham found out I was going to Beirut.

"You have to visit your grandfather's best friend!" Siham said to me. "I looked him up on the Internet a couple of months ago. Just as a joke, I never expected to find him that way. But I looked up his full name and it came up, his phone number in his village in Lebanon. So

I called him. Just like that! His voice was so deep and strong, I thought it was his son. I asked for Ibrahim, saying who I was, thinking that he was likely dead. Immediately, he knew it was me, and said, 'I am Ibrahim.' I couldn't believe it for a few minutes, I kept insisting who I was and who I wanted to speak to until I realized it was really him. 'Ammu Ibrahim?' I said. He is ninety-two years old, and has only just retired from being the mayor of the village. They wouldn't let him retire, he said. I'll phone him again and tell him you are coming and then you can phone him."

So it was arranged; we would visit him. It felt strange that instead of visiting Lina and Karim and Maha in Baghdad, I would be visiting my grandfather's best friend, who had been like a brother to him in Lebanon, but my father and aunts who actually knew him were not. This is the Middle East where simplicity itself is complicated.

I am nervous about the next day; the last time I had been in Beirut in 1993, Siham and I had spent two weeks at Great-aunt Selma's apartment in the hills, hearing her stories and trying to be tourists in a war-ravaged city. At eighty-four Selma had lived through twenty years of war but was still cooking and cleaning for herself. She and her neighbours were full of war stories: running to bomb shelters, seeing family members dying, celebrating Easter underground, militiamen smoking hashish by campfires in the hills. Siham's happy memories of Beirut in the fifties and sixties were superimposed on the tragedy I saw all around me. At the time Selma had been relatively strong; despite her age, she had been living alone, being looked in on by kind neighbours but still independent. Now she was confined to her bed after a hip injury that she'd never recovered from. She didn't have relatives to help her, or access to the kind of care we have in Canada. I had been told she was senile and wouldn't remember me. I do not know what I will find the next day at the convent.

⚜

As Khalil used to say to my father, "There are no bad drivers in Lebanon, only dead bad drivers." Driving in Lebanon is always a spectacular event; whether in the city skidding through unmarked intersections missing crashing by a hair's breadth or careering up and down the mountain roads that lace across the country, your life always feels in danger. Today, we are picked up by Siham's vivacious and still attractive Iraqi friend Nebal who has kindly, and without fail, visited our great-aunt Selma every month for the past decade.

The first thing she says to me is, "I knew you were a Nadir, you look like the sisters."

Siham had said that Nebal was always laughing, despite having had a life full of tragedy, and that she was always telling stories. She drives us to Jouneh and up the mountain road to the convent where Selma lives. She ushers us into the reception area, talking all the while about her two sons who live in Sweden and how she can't move there because her husband and mother-in-law are ill in Beirut and she needs to be with them.

A nun dressed in a white habit escorts us into the ward. Six ancient women sit in pristine white beds in a room that overlooks palm trees and the Mediterranean. I bubble over with tears when I recognize Selma, a shrunken version of herself at ninety-seven years old. Her wrinkled brown hands peek over the top of the white sheets, and the sister goes to find her glasses so she can see us. I remember how, when we'd been there twelve years ago, she had broken her glasses and we had to insist angrily that she let us buy her new frames before she relented and allowed us to. Nebal introduces us to her. Selma looks up at me, blinking slowly, and then smiles.

"Bint Ibrahim," she says.

"She remembers you, 'Ibrahim's daughter,'" translates Nebal. "Of course, she has no idea who I am even though I come and see her every week, but she knows you!" Her laugh tinkles out.

Selma keeps talking in Arabic, and I recognize the tones of her voice.

"She's saying she wants to see your father. She is asking where he is." My heart catches on itself.

"Tell her I am coming as his representative, that he sent me to see her because he could not come."

Nebal translates and says, "Good. She knows you, and today she remembers her father's and grandfather's names too. She says she remembers when you came with Siham and stayed with her."

Nebal is beaming, so happy and proud that Selma remembers me. Then she starts laughing uncontrollably.

"Now she is saying that her brother Khalil, your grandfather, was such a wonderful man. And that he was the president of Syria. The best one they've ever had."

Nebal has tears smarting at the corners of her eyes at the ridiculousness of the thought. The old lady in the bed beside us suddenly turns and glares, then opens her toothless mouth and shouts at us to be quiet. She seems to shout for five minutes, before Nebal can interrupt her and assure her that we won't be long. And then the sister comes in and tells her that Selma never has visitors and that we have come all the way from Canada and that her loud family comes every week and no one complains. The woman continues to glare at us and shout every once in a while. There is nothing to say or do but kiss Selma and hold her hands, and introduce Scott, whom she seems to approve of. We tell her we love her and our family loves her. We take photographs and she sits smiling.

"She really knows you," says Nebal. "I'm so surprised."

I am flooded with sadness that we can't take her back to Canada or England with us and look after her. Here is the last member of my grandfather's Syrian family of that generation, alone and looked after by strangers, visited only by a woman she doesn't really know. She has no family here. And the family she does have are all abroad and haven't been able to visit her for so many years because of incessant war. All we can do is provide the nursing home for her and pray.

Afterwards, we invite Nebal for lunch and she shows us the newly rebuilt downtown district known as Solidaire. The hairs stand up on my arms as we drive through a pristine reconstruction of the Ottoman and French mandate-period architecture that had been completely destroyed in the civil war. The buildings are all brand new, but there is something familiar about them. When I last drove through these streets in 1993, the roads were completely potholed, the buildings empty ruins, beautiful facades were crumbling into gaping holes full of sandbags; the area had been deserted, and Siham had almost wept over what had been lost.

And yet, I am now driving through streets that Nebal says have been rebuilt according to the original plans; you can look at old photographs of shattered buildings and match them with the exact replicas that now stand on their ruins. It is eerie; the only phoenix I have ever witnessed. Could this ever happen to Baghdad? Can its past be reborn? The streets are lined with open-air cafés that Nebal says bustle at night with Lebanese out for a good time Beirut style. We sit on the terrace of a beautiful restaurant adorned with coloured tiles, and Nebal recounts the story of her life over endless *mezze* dishes. For ten years she nursed her father, who suffered a stroke when her sister was diagnosed with brain cancer around the time of the Gulf War. Then her husband almost died of heart failure, but survived after her church prayed for him. The doctors and nurses said it was a miracle because he had only 30 per cent of his heart left. Nebal believed he had been saved by God.

Her Turkish father, a Syrian Orthodox Christian, had been persecuted by the Turks, much as the Armenians were, in the early part of the twentieth century. He'd lost everything and walked to Iraq over the mountains with his gold wrapped around his body under his clothes. Kurdish bandits captured him and stole the gold, so by the time he got to Baghdad he was penniless, a refugee and alone. But over his lifetime he slowly built up his riches in Iraq. When Nebal was a child, her family would fly to Kuwait for shopping trips. Then the Gulf War came, a terrifying time of houses bombed and civilians killed. They didn't have electricity for six months and had to bake their own bread and buy and make food every day, as they had no way of preserving anything.

The family fled to Lebanon just as the civil war was ending. But now she feels stuck here, lonely and like an animal in a cage, unable to escape the tiny country. One hears stories like hers all over the Middle East, a pained and tragic life cut off from the support of extended family, fleeing wars and never feeling or being truly settled or secure. And yet, she is not difficult company; rather, she is just the opposite. Ever hospitable, ordering more dishes for us to try, offering ways to help us in our travels, and even with her sad stories, she never complains or tries to elicit sympathy; she is merely sharing the tale of her difficult life.

We explain that we are planning to go to northern Lebanon the next day, and discuss how best to get there. Lebanon is a tiny country and anywhere else, the 150-kilometre journey would have been an easy day trip in a rental car. But the roads aren't very good and the maps aren't either, and so she doesn't want us to drive ourselves. The bus could get us to Tripoli, but then it would be impossible to find our way to the small village where Ibrahim lives. We decide to hire a taxi, but she offers to find one of her neighbours to escort us. We resist the offer, but she is insistent. That evening, she calls us full of heartfelt apologies. She had lined up a few people to drive us, but they have all called saying they can't make the journey because a snowstorm is forecast and the roads might be bad and it might take too long to go there and back. We reassure her that we want to hire a taxi, and she apologizes profusely and then lets us go and make our own arrangements.

※

Our taxi driver, Hani, gets us to Tripoli. Rather than look at a map, he leans out of the window, asking people where the village is. One man offers to jump in and help us find it, another waves dismissively up the mountain and a third makes intense gestures of turn right, turn left, until none of us can follow anymore. But Hani is jolly; he has already told us his life story and all about his brothers and sisters. He drove us up the coast from Beirut, pointing out landmarks and beauty spots and ignoring the Hezbollah supporters and refugee encampments by the sides of the road. We had been told that once we got to the village we could just ask for Ibrahim's house, since he had been the mayor until recently.

We head up into the snow-sprinkled northern mountains of Lebanon, and I know that just beyond the distant hills is Syria and my grandfather's hometown. We enter the village where the road narrows to a lane, and the houses are walled in and turned away from the road. We stop the first man we see, and this time he does get in and rides with us through the few turns it takes to find Ibrahim's house. Once there, Hani says he'll wait in the car and rest. It turns out he didn't sleep the night before because he took his brother's shift (they share taxi duties), and so is relishing the promise of a long nap while we visit inside.

The driveway is dominated by a huge lush green orange tree, which still bears a few gleaming oranges shining through the leaves on the grey winter's day. Ripe fallen fruit decorate the grass below. We walk up to the door and it is opened by a young woman who smiles politely and ushers us upstairs without saying a word. We don't know who she is, but assume all will be revealed shortly. We go through another door and into a spacious entry hall where we are greeted by a middle-aged woman with strawberry-blond blow-dried hair and bright lipstick. The other woman disappears, and we realize that she was the maid. The new woman says a friendly hello in English and then starts speaking rapidly in Arabic.

I shake my head, and then a man who has to be Ammu Ibrahim comes into the room. I know he is ninety-two, but he doesn't look older than seventy. He is rather tall, his face is narrow without looking thin, and his cheeks are full and high. His eyes are large and brown behind his glasses, and he is dressed in a brown cardigan over a shirt and tie and long trousers. His hair is thick and truly silver.

"Come in, Come in," he says, his English perfectly clear, to our relief. "So you are Leilah, Ibrahim's daughter, Khalil's granddaughter." He takes my hands and looks into my face, "I am so so pleased to see you. You can never know how much this means to me." We move into a large room with a small black wood-burning stove in the centre. "Stand near this if you are cold. What would you like to drink? Tea? Wine?"

Before I know it, I say, "Wine." I feel that an occasion of this magnitude deserves more than a cup of tea, no matter how delicious Arabic tea is.

"And this is my wife, who has the same name as you, Layla."

A small grey-haired lady with big clear smoky eyes smiles up at me (she doesn't speak English), and we all sit down around the stove. I feel that I am among relatives, as if I am really meeting my grandfather's brother and his family.

"You see," says Ibrahim, reading my thoughts, "your grandfather was more than my best friend, really. He was a brother to me. I loved him very much. And his children, I loved them too."

The last time he'd seen my father was forty-five years earlier, in the summer of 1960, just before he left to study in England. I hand Ibrahim the gift I have brought: a simple box made of Western red cedar from the rainforests of British Columbia—a nod to Lebanon's symbol, the cedar. He carefully puts it on the table without unwrapping it.

As I settle into my seat, I look around and notice that the walls are covered in beautiful modernist oil paintings that look like they were painted in the 1920s or 1930s. Some have a feeling of Edward Hopper; muted melancholy in vibrant colours. Then I realize that they are all done by the same hand.

"Who did these gorgeous paintings?" I ask.

Ammu Ibrahim replies with modest pride, "I am the painter."

Scott and I immediately stand up and start admiring each painting as if we are in a gallery. The largest wall is taken up by a bright green hilly landscape dotted with white and red houses with a great Lebanese cedar in the foreground.

"That is this village. Our village. I was born here. I love this place. But it is the view from the hill over there." He points outside the window across the valley. And then he points out his house, where we now stand, in the painting.

We find out that he studied painting for six months at the American University in Beirut when he was young. His dream had been to study art in Europe, but then World War II broke out and he couldn't go. Later, he'd visited all the major galleries in Europe and had seen many masterpieces of Western art and so was largely self-taught. Above where his wife sits is a portrait of a younger Ammu Ibrahim and Layla sitting on the very same sofa drinking their morning coffee beside the black wood stove, a Christmas cactus in full fuchsia bloom between them. It is a tender scene of quiet intimacy between husband and wife.

"I painted that because those quiet moments of drinking coffee with my lovely wife in the morning are my greatest moments of happiness," he said.

Next to me is a painting of two old men wearing fezzes, talking, one touching the other's knee. Beside that is a large painting of an ancient cedar tree, unlike any Lebanese cedar I'd ever seen. The trunk is knotted and gnarled and painted in shades of orange and pink, and the eye is drawn up towards the tree's canopy, which fills the whole canvas with tapering, swaying branches. It's as if you are looking up from a child's point of view. Ammu Ibrahim explains that he paints for himself, that he has never sold a painting, only given them away as gifts or used them to decorate his own house to remind him of happy memories.

"But now we must eat lunch. Where is the driver?"

"Oh, he's asleep in the car."

"Well, I will go and ask him to join us." Before we can protest, he is putting on his coat and walking slowly, deliberately, downstairs and out to the car.

The rest of us are shown into the dining room. The table is filled with countless plates and dishes, which could have fed the entire village, not just two Canadian travellers and Ibrahim's family. There is typical Lebanese *mezze*, *kofte*, *kibbe*, half-moon pastries filled with ground lamb and pine nuts, roast chicken lemon drumsticks, tabbouleh, hummus, French fries, a rice dish with chicken and pine nuts, pomegranate sauce, mayonnaise and garlic. There is also lasagne, made to cater to our North American tastes. Ibrahim returns with a bleary-eyed Hani who says, reluctantly and in an apologetic tone, "He insisted I come and join you."

"Yes, yes," we all agree. When he sees the table loaded with food, he smiles.

As we sit down, I notice the painting that decorates this room is an arresting *Pietà* done by Ibrahim. The Madonna is dressed in bright red robes with a sky-blue scarf on her head and she holds the body of Jesus after he's been taken down from the cross tenderly in her lap. It is like a modern Renaissance painting.

Over lunch, as we are cajoled into trying something from every single dish on the table, I ask Ibrahim about my grandfather.

"He was the best friend you could have," he said. "People treasured his friendship because he was a scrupulously honest man and he treated everyone the same, whether they were very important and rich or very poor and humble. Everyone respected and loved him for that. And he was a very religious man, very pious. He prayed all the time. If you want to know the parents, look at his children, look at your father and his sisters, if you want to see what kind of man he was."

They had met when they were boys, and as young men he and Khalil had hiked from this village all the way to Bscharre to see the

Khalil Gibran Museum. I had seen some photos of their trip in Khalil's album. It had taken them two days to get there and two days to get back. I asked when they had last seen each other.

"Oh, we lost touch when the Lebanese war started in 1973. Then the Iran–Iraq War. And then . . ." His voice trailed off. "I think he died of grief after your grandmother Victoria died. He loved her and missed her so much."

Ibrahim stops talking and starts eating in earnest and we eat until it is impossible to consume anymore. The rest of us try to communicate with our various levels of English and Arabic. At the end of the lunch, we have Turkish coffee in tiny cups and baklava, and a huge fruit bowl is brought to the table—a cornucopia of peaches, kiwis, strawberries and oranges. We politely take one strawberry each.

Ammu Ibrahim looks tired, so we take our cue and tell him that we have to leave. Hani tactfully announces that we'd better leave soon or we will be late getting back to Beirut. I feel frustrated that the visit has been so brief. Ibrahim could tell me so much more about Khalil that no one else could know. But Ibrahim is old, ninety-two, and he doesn't seem to want to divulge more details about my grandfather's youth.

Ibrahim and his wife insist on walking us to the car, making sure we have everything and are settled in. We embrace and kiss good-bye, and Ibrahim gazes at me and says, "Thank you so much for coming all the way to visit us. You have no idea what it means to me, really. To see the granddaughter of Khalil."

I hug him, my eyes smart with tears. He couldn't know what it meant to me to meet the only friend of my grandfather that I would ever know. As we back out of the driveway, Ibrahim and Layla stand side by side under the orange tree, waving at us. For a moment, it is as if it is my grandfather and grandmother I am saying goodbye to. I wave back and when we turn out of sight, I rest my hands over my eyes and cry.

✣

We take a *servis* (shared) taxi to travel to Damascus. The price is ten US dollars, and it's an extra five if we don't want to share the back seat of the yellow seventies Mustang with a third person. A man in a keffiyeh sits in the front and doesn't look at us once through the journey, though he chats nonstop to the driver. The distance is barely a hundred kilometres, but because the road winds through mountains over two thousand metres high and there is a border to cross, the trip from Beirut to Damascus takes all day. In a raging snowstorm, it takes even longer.

As we head towards the mountain pass near Zahle, all the cars on the road are pulling over to put chains on their tires. I can't believe this is the Middle East; we could be in Canada. The wet snow has been pelting the taxi all the way up the mountain, and now the slush is a foot deep and snow is still falling. The visibility is zero. Our taxi driver is a smiling Syrian who seems to be finding the whole caper as amusing as we do. The chains keep coming off, and we watch through the curtains in the back seat while he puts them on again and again. Blanketed in snow, Lebanon is otherworldly.

When we get to the border, the driver takes our passports and goes into the checkpoint. We stay in the car. He returns and beckons to Scott to follow him. I am nervous alone in the car, waiting. I think of the astonished reactions Canadians had when we said we were visiting Syria. When Scott comes back, he relates how the officials grilled him about my name and my father's name, which you have to write on the entrance card. He was terrified that he would give the wrong answer, but finally he said that my grandfather was Syrian, and that our last name was Syrian. He didn't know if that was the right answer or if he should have said that my father was Iraqi. But his answer pleased the guards immensely and they said "Welcome Syria" with broad smiles. For entrance to a police state, I found this all quite hospitable and rather slack, considering I didn't actually see any border guards myself. Anyone could have been sitting in the car in my place. Once across the border, we descend quickly to the plains and the sun comes out, making the snow shine on the barren desert soil.

Said to be the oldest continuously inhabited city in the world, Damascus feels ancient. A layer of dust covers everything, and the friendly people have a worldly sophistication that seems to say that they have seen everything pass through and cannot—will not—be surprised by anything. The Old City is one immense, labyrinthine *souq* with different areas selling sweets, bread, inlaid woodwork, narghile pipes, sponges, medicines, nuts, clothes. You enter by one of the great stone gates into one of the three quarters, Christian, Muslim or Jewish—one in ten Syrians is Christian and there are still four thousand Jews living there—and one can pass endless days wandering through tiny lanes overhung with the shuttered windows of houses almost blocking out the sky.

We start in the centre at the ancient Umayyad mosque, which is decorated in exquisite gold and green Byzantine mosaics depicting palaces, palm trees, gardens and fruit. Behind the mosque we stop in a small antique shop barely big enough for four people and start chatting to the owner, Samir. He orders his nephew to bring us tea from the café opposite where the last living *hakawati* or professional storyteller is practising his art reading stories animatedly from an old book. From the shop, we can see the packed café full of men drinking tea and smoking the narghile, listening intently. Meanwhile, Samir shows us gorgeous rich silk and cotton tablecloths, cushions, tapestries and old jewellery. He asks us about ourselves.

I tell him my father is Iraqi and my grandfather is Syrian. Since the Iraq War, he says, Iraqis have been arriving daily, driving up the prices. The wealthy who could afford to leave fled immediately, but now, two years later, more and more poorer refugees are arriving. He shows us some camel-hair scarves that are woven in Iraq.

"We call this cloth Najafi because it is made in the Iraqi city of Najaf," he says. "It is hand-woven by the women there. We haven't had this type of cloth in Syria for many many years. We can thank the war for this." He laughs cynically. The fabric is coarse and has a faint animal smell, and it is coloured with natural dyes in earthy tones of pink, blue, green, yellow. "These scarves are very warm, even though they have all these holes."

The cloth is loosely woven and looks rather delicate. I wrap the cloth around me and he is right, it is surprisingly warm. He tells us that the Christian quarter is not far away and that we can find an excellent *hammam* (Turkish bath) that has a woman's hour. He also recommends a restaurant for us to eat in that night; he won't elaborate but says that we should trust him, it will be like a dream.

We follow his directions and wander through the pedestrian lanes full of bustling shapes, women covered all in black, men in brown leather jackets and black scarves and hats. People almost brush up against each other but never touch. The houses along the lanes hang over the street, sometimes even connecting into a house-bridge from one side to another. It reminds me of photographs I have seen and descriptions I have read of Old Baghdad where my grandmother Victoria grew up. There are wooden porticos that probably open onto small courtyards with fountains and gardens. A discreet wooden sign with a carving of a crescent moon alerts us to a café; it is called Evening and Morning. We walk through a small door and enter a crowded dark room made of stone and wood with candles dripping on the tables.

Stylish young Syrians are hanging out with their friends drinking coffee and tea and listening to the wailing Arabic music and smoking the hubble-bubble pipes. We sit down and order tea and a pipe, and in a second an efficient waiter sets a water pipe on the floor beside us and lights the charcoal. Scott puts the pipe to his lips, and soon the cherry tobacco smoke surrounds us like incense. We sit speechless at the unexpectedly modern scene, feeling as if we had walked out of

THE ORANGE TREES OF BAGHDAD

an ancient city into a modern bar, albeit an Eastern one. We watch the people conversing in mixed groups of men and women and wonder what they are discussing so intensely. If my North American friends could magically be transported here, they would not believe they were really in Syria.

Scott pulls a copy of the *Guardian* from his bag; it's a couple of weeks old. I sit sipping tea and flipping through the paper. My eye catches a headline: "Months of War That Ruined Centuries of History." In the article, Maev Kennedy describes the British Museum report by John Curtis on the ancient city of Babylon that has just been handed back to Iraqi authorities from US forces. I read in horror about the damage to the famous Ishtar Gate, about broken bricks inscribed with the name of Nebuchadnezzar lying in spoiled heaps, of the original brick surface of the great processional route through the gate crushed by military vehicles, about acres of the site levelled, covered with gravel and sprayed with chemicals that are seeping into unexcavated buried deposits, and of tons of archaeological material used to fill sandbags. The article continues: "The military camp was established by the American forces in April 2003, and damage was already visible when Dr. Curtis first visited part of the site that June. The same contractors, Kellogg, Brown and Root—a subsidiary of the American civil engineering corporation Halliburton, of which the US vice-president, Dick Cheney, is a former chief executive officer— were used to develop and maintain the site throughout, as it grew to a 150-hectare camp, housing 2,000 soldiers."

I pass the paper to Scott angrily. "Read this. They are using ancient Babylon as a military base. Saddam Hussein was always criticized because he built a monstrous replica of the original on top of the remains. But this is worse; there is no recognition of the immense value to humanity of this place. Why would they choose it as a base? Ignorance or else something more vicious and deliberate?"

After an hour or so, we are starving and go out again through the brightly lit *souq* past men selling nuts and dried fruit out of huge sacks as they have for centuries and arrive at a nondescript wooden door lit by an Oriental lamp. I am completely unprepared for what we find inside; an opulent restaurant unlike anything I've ever seen. We've stepped into a renovated 650-year-old Ottoman villa, lavishly decorated in brilliant tiles. The courtyard is surrounded by open-air dining rooms on three levels, but because it is winter it is covered with a canopy. The walls are painted in typical Oriental style, bright colours, intricate foliage and stylized flowers. The floors comprise thick marble mosaics and huge chandeliers made of metal and coloured glass hang low over the whole scene. In the centre is a gushing fountain, and the waiters wear Ottoman-style costumes. The bustling restaurant is filled with long tables of Syrian families; the atmosphere isn't restrained or snobbish, but warm and full of loud voices and laughter and children playing. Rapidly moving waiters race to your table in response to a mere raised eyebrow or an overzealous hand gesture.

Beside us is a table of about twenty foreigners speaking English. After they have finished their meal, a middle-aged man rises and starts giving a speech. He is Iraqi, and it becomes clear that he has been working as an Iraq election monitor in Syria. His voice is full of passion as he describes what a pleasure it has been to work with the team who are from a mixture of European countries, America, Canada and of course Iraq.

"What a relief it has been," he says, "to work with people who treat you as a fellow worker and human being instead of a slave." He says how proud he is that he has been able to work on these elections for the good of his country. He gives out presents to everyone at the table, and they begin opening them as he speaks.

I feel conflicted about eavesdropping, although it is impossible not to listen as the group is right beside us speaking English in a buzz of Arabic. I listen to the gratitude the Iraqi feels to the international community, and I think that this is how a people would truly express being liberated from the tyranny of a ruthless dictator. And yet, the war has killed so many, destroyed so many lives and undermined the West in the eyes of so many Arabs. Damascus is full of Iraqis fleeing violence and terror. The idea of liberating a people and giving them freedom and democracy was so noble, and yet what was actually happening outside of the Green Zone in Baghdad bore no resemblance to the beautiful ideals being expressed at the next table. Iraqis deserved to live in freedom and democracy, and yet the very invasion that was done in their name was creating anarchy and fear in their society, every day moving it further away from the possibility of a peaceful future.

The next morning I go to the Bakri *hammam*. My aunts had told me how their house in Baghdad had contained a *hammam*-style bathroom where they bathed when they were children. By the seventies their parents had transformed it into a Western-style shower and bath. They always joke about how clean Middle Eastern people are and I'd never understood what they meant. Their grandmother, Samira, had likely gone to the public baths when she was a girl, but my father and aunts never did. I enter a large high-domed room with a fountain in the middle and raised platforms like balconies covered in carpets on three walls. Heavy ancient gilt-framed mirrors hang angled downward on each wall. I remove my watch, and it is put in a locked box and I am given the key.

I sit on one of the platforms and nervously undress, not knowing what to do next. There are three other women, one who has wet hair and has finished bathing and is wrapped in a towel and smoking a cigarette, and two others who have just arrived. The two girls chat quickly, laughing all the time, and receive three cell phone calls while they are undressing. I watch them and follow their lead. I wrap a thin cotton towel around me and wait for someone to show me what to do next. The girls notice me watching them and smile at me and

then say something in Arabic. I shake my head, shrug and say "No
Araby" and they smile and seem to ask where I am from, I say
"Canada" and they point at themselves saying "Iraq." They must be
refugees. I say "Abu Iraqi," which probably sounds funny to them,
but I am trying to tell them my father is Iraqi. They seem to understand and start laughing and pointing. They point at themselves and
say "Baghdad." They put on wooden clogs from a platform on the
wall and I copy them.

Suddenly, a rotund smiling middle-aged woman ushers me into
the steam room. The steam obscures everything in a fog so thick that
I can't see more than two feet all around me and don't know what
is happening or where I am. Women emerge out of the steam like
ghosts. Everything is tiled in black, white and red marble and I sit on
a marble bench while the Iraqi girls giggle and chain-smoke even in
the steam room. I become light-headed with the heat and then the
bath woman approaches me. "Feenish?" I nod and she leads me into
the abrasion room, a slightly less steamy marble room flowing with
water, all the taps are on with water running into the sinks and then
spilling onto the floor and being carried away by drains along the
room's edge. We sit on the cool wet floor and she scrubs my entire
body with a black horsehair mitten. She is rough, but effective at
sloughing off the dirt of my voyage. She shows me how dirty my arm
is and when I look at it through her eyes, I agree. Then she brings a
brass bowl and throws warm water over me again and again to rinse
me. Then she leads me into a small alcove with a massage bed in it.
She rubs me from head to toe with a ghee-like substance that feels
very smooth. After this short massage she takes me back into the sink
room. Rubbing olive oil soap onto a sponge that is made of straw, she
mimes cleaning herself, and I know I am supposed to wash myself
again. I scrub and rinse until I am polished clean. She steers me back
into the steam room and I stay there until I warm up.

Finally, I return to the changing area and sit stunned and relaxed
in my towel until I muster up the energy to change into my clothes

and go and meet Scott. The Iraqi girls are still there, chattering as they get dressed. I long to speak to them.

※

Samir had told us that we had to find this special silk shop housed in an ancient madrassa (Islamic school) if we wanted to see the best-quality silk in Damascus. We are leaving in two days, but the next day, unbelievably, we find the store down a blind alley of the souq. The walls are made of striped black-and-white stone and one room contains a clattering wooden loom worked by one of the last silk weavers in Damascus. The dusty courtyard feels as if it has been untouched for the six hundred years it has been there and the arcades are covered in carpets and antiques. The walls are lined with bolts of dazzling silk in every colour imaginable.

A portly man who speaks impeccable English and French, and wears an old-fashioned suit and tie, approaches us. He tells us that, unlike much of the material for sale in the souq, his Damascene silk is hand-woven and introduces us to the man working the loom. His left leg is churning away as if he is riding a one-pedal bicycle and the wooden slats rattle across the silken threads. The intricate patterns are laid out by punch cards that had been created during the Industrial Revolution and remind us of old computer punch cards.

The supple silk is sold by the metre and is not cheap by Syrian standards. The owner explains that the sophisticated, intricate designs are made in two, three, four or five colours and become more and more iridescent and expensive the more colours they contain. He unfurls bolt after bolt of cloth of every different colour, and I covet them all. But I can't imagine an occasion where I'd be able to wear such luxurious material. On a whim, I ask to see the white silk thinking that I haven't found a wedding dress yet. The man throws down bolts of cloth, one on top of the other, plain white with a paisley pattern, white with gold thread, white with silver thread. None of them are quite right. He senses my hesitation and asks if I'd prefer ivory. Yes, I ask him if he has any plain ivory with no other colours. He throws down a beautiful creamy ivory silk which has the classic paisley design embroidered like a subtle watermark; the silk shines a pale golden sheen in different lights and I know this is the cloth that I want my wedding dress to be made of. I think of Khalil, born in Syria, and how right it is that I will wear Damascene silk on my wedding day. My eyes light on a bunch of brightly coloured ties and I ask to see them. I choose a golden tie for my father to give me away in.

A few days later, back in Vancouver, I unfold the paper covering the silk and wrap the material around my body. The smell of the shop lingers for a moment; I am back in the Middle East, enfolded in it. I am reminded of my grandmother Victoria, and I know if she'd still been alive, she would have insisted on making my wedding dress, as she once sewed my Iraqi costume for the parade.

LINA DRIVES THROUGH BAGHDAD WITH FARAH
PHOTO CREDIT: FARAH NOSH

CHAPTER TWELVE
The Death of Lina

On the second anniversary of the Coalition invasion of Iraq, media-reported civilian deaths are approaching 20,000 and the death-rate is spiralling upwards. —Iraq Body Count Press Release, March 17, 2005

Once again I didn't make it to Baghdad, even though I was in the Middle East, just as I hadn't twelve years earlier on a previous trip to Syria, Lebanon, Jordan and Egypt. Back then, it was for fear of Saddam Hussein and the *mukharabat* (secret police), and the upheaval that followed the Gulf War; this time, it is due to the mayhem of another invasion and war, another threat: I am afraid of American soldiers and the wanton violence of the resistance.

My mother and father are visiting me in Vancouver, and my mother and I go out together. My father wants to stay in my apartment and play bridge on his laptop rather than go out for coffee with us.

"He probably just wants to have a nap," says my mum when we are out.

When we get back, my father is sitting on the sofa, staring into space, his laptop beside him.

"What's wrong?" my mother asks.

"Lina is dead," he blurts out. "I've just spoken to my sisters."

Regret and rage fills me. Regret that I didn't go to Baghdad, that I hadn't ignored the warnings of the family. Rage that somehow the war has won, the war has kept us all from being with her for the last years of her life, the last relative from my grandmother's generation.

And then there is the pain, the hurt I feel because I wasn't able to save her; we weren't able to do anything for her but hope and pray.

I look at my father, my mother's arm around his shoulders, and wonder what he is feeling. It is his aunt, he grew up with her. He is used to hearing about these deaths, I think, but at the same time I know it never gets any easier.

"Don't worry about things you can't do anything about," is his refrain whenever I get upset, outraged or emotional at some injustice. "You can't do anything about it. Why worry? Only worry about things that you have the power to change."

It is precisely the helplessness that makes me so angry and worries me so much. But I realize that he never had that luxury; he'd made decisions in his life based on external situations that were too large and beyond his control to worry about. He had to focus on what he could control. And he did.

I'd encouraged my dad to call Lina when he last saw his sisters in London. I'd been telling him that from the moment I first talked to her. I knew he wanted to speak to her, but he'd put it off. I couldn't understand why. Even though I knew the family joked that my father didn't "like Iraq" because he'd never returned, I knew that they all understood the real reasons that he's stayed away. Eventually, a year after the invasion, the four siblings all called her together, and my dad spoke to her in his rusty Arabic for the first time in fifteen years. Her voice was weak. In fact, he didn't recognize her. They all agreed on that; it was the first time they'd heard her strong voice weaken. I had this sense that Lina wanted to talk to my father, that he meant so much more to her than he could really understand. She'd known him since the day he was born, watched him grow up, seen him leave Iraq and had gone to London to see his new life. But for the last fifteen years, she hadn't known him or spoken to him. She needed to hear his voice, his corroded Arabic. I wondered what she thought about when she stayed alone in the house while the war raged for those twenty-one days.

Auntie Lina is dead. I'd known she was ill, but somehow I thought she would get better. The war might stop, and we'd all be free to go back and see her. Her life had spanned over seven decades, and yet she was born under British occupation and died under American occupation. Was the occupation responsible for her death? Were the sanctions responsible? Sanctions had caused doctors to flee the country, hospitals to become dilapidated and antiquated, and medicines to become scarce. The health system, which had been one of the best in the Middle East, was in tatters by the end of the Gulf War and sanctions. The US invasion and occupation had only exacerbated the situation. The reconstruction of hospitals still had not happened.

My telephone conversation with Lina in June 2004 turned out to be the first and last time I'd ever speak to her as an adult. Everything about our connection to Iraq was vanishing. Her phone had stopped working soon after I'd spoken to her, and then she'd become too ill to stay home alone. She'd moved into Karim's house to live with his wife, their children, her brother Clement and his wife (Maha's parents). The phone hadn't worked in their house since the war, and so I couldn't phone them either.

My father asks us to sit down beside him, and we cry quiet tears while he recounts what his sisters told him. On March 4, 2005, my great-aunt Lina died alone in her room in the early hours of the morning at Karim's house in Baghdad. The muscles around her spine were weakening, and she was unable to stand up without assistance. She was disintegrating, and nothing could stop it. The stage of the war that is known as the insurgency, the armed resistance by diverse groups in Iraq against the Coalition and each other, was raging all around her, and the hope that Iraqis had nurtured at the end of the invasion had disappeared in a morass of bloodshed and fear exacerbated by no electricity, water, jobs or personal security. Karim didn't know exactly what had killed my great-aunt. Before the war had started she was fine, she was strong. When Farah visited her four months after the invasion, she was starting to feel weak and tired, but she was still driving, talking, cooking, alive.

Karim said that when she had moved in with them, Lina had worried about being a burden to her relatives. She was strong and proud, and was used to looking after other people rather than depending on others. She found it hard to accept being cared for by our cousins. When her brother Clement died a few months before from leukemia, my great-aunt said, "It's my turn now." Her health had deteriorated until she was bedridden. She called her body an old machine, until she couldn't speak anymore. Then she was still able to understand what was said to her but couldn't answer back.

From the symptoms described over the telephone to my aunts, and then passed from one relative to another and interpreted by Iraqi doctor friends living in exile, it seemed that she had a neurological disorder or an autoimmune disease. In any event, she was wasting away. Her muscles were melting away. The strength in her body was leaking out of her.

Her death came without warning, despite her illness. The day before she died, Karim's wife, Maha, got Lina out of bed, bathed her, washed her clothes and gave her a cup of coffee. At the time, the electricity in Baghdad was running at two hours on and four hours off. The water was running, but there was no water treatment so it was contaminated. Lina seemed the same, better even, managing to read the paper a little, even though she couldn't speak. She shared a room with Maha's mother, Haifa, who she'd known for decades and had now, in both of their twilights, become her roommate. At 2:00 a.m. she woke up and was uncomfortable, so Haifa soothed her. At 7:00 a.m. Maha went into the room to check on Lina and found that she had died in her sleep. Maha felt that Lina's passing had been peaceful.

Again, my aunts in London were at the other end of a phone line, upset but impotent while Lina's funeral arrangements took on the usual bizarre twists of life in post-invasion Baghdad. At least a prayer was said for her the next day at Karim's reopened Protestant church. But Lina was denied a funeral and burial at the Syrian Catholic Church where her sister, her mother and her aunt were interred because the burial ground was full and the church was too damaged. The city morgue was crammed with bodies, so my great-aunt Lina could not be laid to rest there while our relatives prepared a funeral for her in Baghdad. She had to be buried immediately. The priest at the Syrian Catholic Church advised Karim to take my auntie Lina's body to the plot of land in Baqubah. At least it was the same cemetery where her brother Clement had been buried just a few months earlier.

This time Karim went alone. He tied the coffin to the roof of his little car. It was normally a dangerous drive, and today the road to Baqubah was blocked by American troops, so he had to take side roads. It was raining heavily, which was unusual, and the car kept getting stuck in the mud, almost spinning its wheels to a stop and then gripping again. When he finally got to Baqubah, he paid two gravediggers to dig the hole for Lina's cardboard coffin, and so she was in her grave, not twenty-four hours after she had died. There was no funeral. Seven days later, Ibtisam, Amal and Siham held the customary memorial mass for her in faraway London.

⚜

Forty days later, another service takes place, as is also the Iraqi custom, to have a memorial and reception after forty days of mourning. Instead of being held in Baghdad, the mass is conducted in a church in Acton that holds an Iraqi mass every week by an Iraqi priest who ministers to the Iraqi Catholic community in London.

My parents and my youngest sister, Rose, are in London for the memorial service. I am at home in Vancouver, unable to attend because of work commitments. They arrive at the modern church. The altar stands at the centre and the pews radiate out in a triangular formation, the ceilings are low and the architecture contemporary. An Iraqi priest says the mass in Syriac, and the altar boys are Iraqi and wear cotta, plain white robes draped over their clothes.

Although it isn't a high mass, the solemnity of the occasion is emphasized when the congregation is blessed using a thurible, a metal container containing hot charcoal that is ritually swung on chains to waft burning incense around the church. The aroma of the incense and the rattling of the chain remind my mother of the mystery of going to Sunday mass when she was young, because thuribles aren't used at mass much anymore.

Iraqi Christians fill the church. Rose, who lives in Toronto and is a political activist who doesn't like to dress up, was insistent that she must find a black skirt to wear to the ceremony. Ibrahim and Mary both wear sombre black suits. Mary is comforted hearing the mass in a foreign language, not realizing until afterwards that she is listening to the language of Christ. The hymns are all sung in Syriac without accompaniment, which is hauntingly beautiful to my mother's ears.

Afterwards my aunts host a reception, and the house is jammed with well-dressed exiles. Some guests bring platters of food, and Ibtisam and Siham have cooked as well, so there is a buffet table filled with Iraqi dishes. The mourners are mostly friends of my aunts, but they also include Beatrice, a close friend of their mother's who is staying with them. She, and the mother of one of their friends, are the only two other people of Lina's generation present. Beatrice is in her eighties and was a teacher with my grandmother Victoria. My mother and sister have never been in such a large gathering of Iraqis. They are in the minority, speaking English. Most of the guests are women, and Mary is struck that there are so many doctors and professionals among them. Rose feels incredibly awkward to be around all these Iraqis who she thinks she should feel comfortable with because they are family friends. She realizes that she doesn't know much about the culture or the people, even though she knows all about the politics.

Rose had started as an anti-poverty activist in Toronto at university; she couldn't believe the injustice of poverty and homelessness in the city and wanted to do something about it. My parents worried that this was distracting her from her studies, and our aunts encouraged her to put her education first. They also reminded her that poverty was relative and that worldwide there were many poorer people than those suffering in Toronto. They challenged her, "Why don't you do something for Iraq? Your country? What about the injustice of the sanctions?" She'd never thought of Iraq as her country, but in the lead-up to the war, she too attended protests and demonstrations.

At the beginning of 2004, she helped form a group to protest against Canadian companies that were doing business in Iraq or with the US military, to show Canadians that they too were profiting from the war. On June 30, they held a demonstration called "The Day America Hands Iraq Over to America," on the day that the CPA claimed to be handing power back to the Iraqis. A year later, they campaigned against SNC Lavalin, a Canadian corporation manufacturing bullets for the American military, which could not get the two billion bullets it needed from its regular US suppliers.

The invasion of Iraq had solidified Rose's Iraqi identity and she was now feeling more emotionally connected to her activism. And the politics of my parents, who had once considered her too radical, had suddenly moved closer to Rose's. My father used to feel that the United States and its policies and systems were the best the world had to offer, even if they weren't perfect. After the invasion, my father questioned his earlier faith in the West because he could see that America's actions weren't in the interests of Iraqis. He became proud of Rose's activism.

As the afternoon goes on, Rose bonds with Beatrice, who talks nonstop, and regales her with an anecdote of being picked up by an elderly man on her flight to London and with colourful stories of her life in Iraq. She tells Rose about how she'd fled the country after surviving the Gulf War. In Baghdad Beatrice had found out she had been accepted to go the United States and cried with joy at her luck. When she checked on the map and saw that she and her family were being sent to the Midwest, they were terrified. They thought they were being sent to a refugee camp in the middle of the desert. She arrived in New York City with her daughter and her grandson and begged American authorities to let them go somewhere else. The authorities kindly let the family stay in New York in a hotel for a few days, but then said that they had to go to where they had been assigned. When they finally arrived they were relieved to be in a big city, but it still took them years to assimilate.

Mary goes around the room with Ibrahim, introducing herself and getting to know my aunts' friends. The next day, when we speak on the phone, my mother says, "By the end, I realized that there were Muslims and Christians there. It was a mixture of Kurds, Sunnis and Shia. I'd never known that in Iraq, Muslims spoke in one dialect and Christians another. They both switch effortlessly back and forth between the two, even in a conversation. You know, sometimes it's merely a difference in accent and pronunciation. They shift automatically."

They all translated for Mary, but she often felt that she understood what people were saying through their tone and gestures, even if she didn't know the language. She says that as the atmosphere relaxed, some of the guests started looking up their old classmates from Baghdad on the Internet, laughing as they found their friends and relived those easier days. My mother admits that she's never seen this large gathering of Iraqis in London before. A whole community is forming in Greater London of transplanted educated Iraqis which was not there when she'd lived in the same area twenty years before. She kept thinking about Lina, that the memorial service for her death was taking place in London with a community of exiles, most of whom had not been back to Iraq for decades. And yet, a funeral hadn't been possible in Baghdad, in the city she had lived in all her life.

✠

Karim and Maha are bereft; the house feels empty without Lina. She had been like a second grandmother to their children, showering them with affection and love during childhoods marred with sanctions and war.

Lina was the fifth of six of my relatives to die during the occupation. Later Haifa, Clement's wife and Maha's mother, would follow her. She died in the summer of 2005, of dehydration and a heart attack. She survived two years of war and most of the summer without air conditioning or fans because the occupiers still hadn't got the electricity running. When Karim called, he said that two days before she died there was a bomb attack near their house, and the family believes that the incident hastened her death. The blast was so near, the sound so loud, that the windows shattered and the air conditioner flew out of the wall. (Ironic, seeing that it hardly worked anyway.) The explosion was like an earthquake, and Karim went out to see the dead. At least twenty of his neighbours were killed, and one of the destroyed houses backed onto theirs. His friend's wife, a neighbour, was out in the street, and her husband went to look for her and became hysterical when he couldn't find her. They were all distraught and thought she had died. Eventually, she returned, not knowing what had happened in her absence; her decision to go out was why she had survived.

Uncle Clement, and his brother, Uncle Antoine, and his wife, Harriet, and their daughter, Noor, all died before Haifa. Within two years, they all died one after another. Not from a direct assault because of the war, but because of terror, stress, a lack of adequate nutrition, sanitation, medicine, and access to decent health care and good doctors and nurses. Many doctors who had chosen to stay during sanctions had fled the country after having family members kidnapped for ransom, or seeing their colleagues murdered.

I have never met my father's uncles, but my aunts say that there is one uncle, Antoine, who looked exactly like my father as he aged, fulfilling the Arabic saying *Thil thane al walid allah el Khal*—two-thirds of the boy comes from his mother's brothers.

Great-uncle Antoine suffered from dementia in the years before he died. Throughout his entire life, he had visited my grandparents and my aunts every single day while they still lived in Baghdad. He loved the family. In photographs, it is hard to tell the difference between my father and this uncle. When an old neighbour from Baghdad made it to London and visited Amal, she gasped when she saw my father's photograph, thinking it was Uncle Antoine. He died of a heart attack. His daughter, Noor, who was in her forties, also had a heart attack not long after the 2003 invasion. And not long after that, his wife, Harriet, died of unknown causes. A whole generation, with their stories of my family history, was lost in two years. They are the other casualties of war who will never be counted in the humanitarian reports to be released in the years to come.

Auntie Lina had owned her own house, the house that she had lived in with her mother, Samira, most of her life, but since she was a single woman, she had rented it out while she was taking care of our house. It is situated on a street that also contains a government ministry building, and at the time the entire street was being protected by both Iraqi and American troops. Karim and Maha had not worried about looting because the street was barricaded at either end, but after Lina died, Karim returned to the house to find it ransacked, and the man who was supposed to be renting it was nowhere to be found.

"Everything was gone," he told me. "It was like a plague of locusts had eaten the house clean."

Not only were all the personal effects like carpets and furniture stolen, but he was astounded that "the kitchen counter, the kitchen and bathroom sinks had vanished too. There was no telephone and no appliances, and all the kitchen cabinets had been stripped away.

Even the copper wire from the electricity cables had been stolen. The house was completely empty."

Only the desolate walls of the house remained. All of Lina's furniture, photographs and carpets, some that were meant for presents to her nephew, my father, were gone. And this all occurred on a street in Baghdad that is heavily guarded by both Iraqi and US forces.

Karim is now talking seriously about escaping Iraq, since now there are no elderly relatives who will be left behind. His brother and his family will still be there, but maybe, he says, they can get out as well. Karim feels that his family cannot stay. There is no hope. There is a growing movement against Christians. In Mosul, a city in northern Iraq whose population is a mixture of Arabs, Kurds, Armenians, Assyrians and Turkomans, the Christians are being asked to leave. My grandmother's family came from Mosul. Christians have been leaving Basra, the second-largest city in Iraq located in the south, since the beginning of the war, and many of the Christian intellectuals have fled. Karim isn't working much, and although his son is in a special school for gifted children, it is an hour's drive away.

"It's not safe," Karim writes. "US tanks pass in the street, and to them every Iraqi is a potential suicide bomber, so they have become trigger-happy and you have to stay away."

Now Maha goes to our house to clean it in Lina's stead. She tells Amal that she weeps as she goes from room to room. The house is so empty now, and she remembers that it was once the busiest and liveliest house on the street. She was the youngest of that generation. She asks herself what will become of it now.

FARAH'S FAMILY WATCH THE AFTERMATH OF AN EXPLOSION OUTSIDE
THEIR HOUSE, MARCH 2006

PHOTO CREDIT: FARAH NOSH

CHAPTER THIRTEEN
The Flower of the Pomegranate

"Do you realize how history is repeating itself?" ... He was referring to the British invasion of Iraq in 1917.... And within three years we were losing hundreds of men every year in the guerrilla war against the Iraqis who wanted real liberation not by us from the Ottomans but by them from us, and I think that's what's going to happen with the Americans in Iraq. I think a war of liberation will begin quite soon, which of course will be first referred to as a war by terrorists, by al-Qaeda, by remnants of Saddam's regime, remnants (remember that word), but it will be waged particularly by Shiite Muslims against the Americans and British to get us out of Iraq and that will happen. And our dreams that we can liberate these people will not be fulfilled in this scenario. —Robert Fisk in an interview by Amy Goodman on *Democracy Now!*, posted April 23, 2003

It is February 2006, three years since the invasion began, and it is now more dangerous than ever to go to Iraq. There is talk of civil war as large bombing campaigns that seem religiously motivated are occurring with more and more frequency. But Farah has suddenly been seized with the desire to return. Her last trip was a year and a half ago and she has tried to busy herself with other photography projects since, but the urge to document the lives of her family in Baghdad has overwhelmed her. She has had assignments on Hurricane Katrina, the Northwest coast Haida and Canadian troops getting ready to go to Afghanistan. But Iraq haunts her.

Farah speaks to her family in Baghdad regularly, and they tell her it is very dangerous and that she shouldn't come. One of her aunts even calls Farah's mother begging her not to let Farah come. In the end, one of her male cousins relents and says that if she insists on coming, of course they would be so happy to see her. They are mostly trapped in the house and small courtyard, while the occupation rages around them. For months Farah thinks about going to Iraq, not sleeping as she imagines what she will find there, and then one day, impulsively, she buys a ticket to Dubai but doesn't tell anyone at home because she knows what the reaction will be. All Iraqis are hearing from family in Iraq is "Don't come, things are getting worse and worse, not better." Iraq is disintegrating.

Her plan is to find Iraqi victims of war and photograph them. The occupation has not only taken over a country, but has also occupied Iraqis' bodies, leaving bullets lodged in their flesh or confiscating their arms and legs forever. It has consumed their lives. She knows that there are thousands of Iraqi victims, yet the West doesn't see them depicted in newspapers because it is so dangerous for most journalists to get those photographs and also difficult to get newspapers to publish them. Now the US media is filled with wounded US soldiers. Farah feels that the US audience is only "seeing" part of the story. No editors will help to fund her trip as they don't believe she will be able to get the story of wounded Iraqis.

When she finally tells her family of her decision, they are distraught. Her sisters try to convince her not to go; they worry that she might be tempting fate. She has gone and returned safely so many times, how many times would she be this lucky? On her last trip, she experienced three close calls. The first occurred when she was embedded with the US military. She was flown from the Green Zone in a Blackhawk helicopter, and suddenly she saw the city from the perspective of American soldiers. She was flying so low that she could see Iraqis pulling groceries out of their cars, looking up at the noisy helicopter. She half expected someone to shoot an RPG (rocket-propelled grenade) at it. That night she was on patrol with the soldiers and their convoy was ambushed. The vehicle in front of her caught fire, ironically giving her light to take photographs. Luckily, all the soldiers survived, as did she, but she witnessed fifteen minutes of petrifying heavy fighting.

The next close call happened when she was on assignment for *Maclean's* at the military base in Ramadi. Her driver dropped her off, but when she came out after the photo shoot, he was nowhere to be seen. Suddenly, a group of Iraqis in a car bristling with weapons gestured to her, saying they wanted to talk to her. Alarmed, she went back into the base, but the American soldiers did nothing to help her. Starting to panic, she looked around, and saw her driver coming down the road. He was escorted by Iraqi police, who he'd gone to for protection while she was inside. She leapt into the car, but meanwhile the Iraqis had put on masks and started chasing them in their car. Her driver was going over 200 kilometres an hour on the road between Ramadi and Fallujah, and for fifteen minutes they were pursued by the other car. When they got to Fallujah, they went through the city and tried to go straight out the other side to get to Baghdad.

Suddenly, explosions were going off all around them; they had driven into a battle between American forces and Iraqis. Farah reached for her camera, but her driver said, "If you want to die today, take your camera out." She didn't lift up her camera. Their pursuers stopped chasing them when they got to Fallujah, probably because they were outside their territory. But now Farah and her driver were trapped in Fallujah in the middle of a firefight. By nightfall, the combat finally stopped and they escaped towards Baghdad.

The final incident was the worst. Farah and her driver were going to the Green Zone. They went through the Iraqi army checkpoint, and then drove on, but without realizing it they drove through a second checkpoint without stopping. The soldier on duty wasn't paying attention and hadn't signalled the car to stop. In an instant, six soldiers were pointing their guns at Farah, and a nearby tank had swung its huge gun towards the car. The soldiers put zip cuffs on her driver, took their photographs for intelligence purposes and interviewed them. Finally, the guards realized the couple was harmless and let them go. As they were leaving, one of the soldiers said she was lucky to be a woman, because the same thing had happened the day before and a soldier had summarily shot the driver in the head, killing him instantly.

Once home, Farah realized the next time she went to Iraq she would have to make a conscious choice to risk her life for some photographs. So the photos better be worth it. Eighteen months later, there are suicide bombs and car bombs every day; American soldiers, Iraqi soldiers and civilians are dying, and Westerners are being kidnapped. How will Farah be safe from all this now?

On the flight from Dubai, Farah falls asleep. But when the plane descends over Baghdad, she is jolted awake. She sees the city spread out below her in monochrome; it looks black and white. She rubs her eyes and blinks, trying to see the colours she knows are there—brown, beige, green—but she can only see black and white, maybe sepia, the colours of an old photograph. To her, Baghdad is like a silvery gelatine print, and so she knows she has to shoot only black-and-white film, and not use a digital camera. It is as if she were seeing time turn back, seeing modern Iraq slowly descend into the isolated, provincial, poverty-stricken place it had been at the end of the Ottoman Empire in 1917, just before the first British occupation.

Within fifteen minutes of leaving the airport, Farah is at her aunt's house in Baghdad, hugging her family. She can't believe how this monumentally difficult trip could suddenly feel easy. She hasn't slept much in the weeks leading up to the trip, anticipating every danger, finding a flak jacket to take with her. Despite her friends' and family's protests, she is in Iraq. She's made it. She has promised to stay inside with her family, promised not to be seen or noticed as a Westerner, promised not to bring out her camera in public. Her desire to be in Iraq had overcome all the fears of her loved ones and her own personal fears. She is in Iraq.

A few days later, I come back from a walk on the beach, admiring the snowcapped mountains all around me, to find an e-mail from Farah awaiting me.

"'Welcome to Iraq, the worst country in the world,'" her uncle Ahmed had said to her when she arrived. "But I finally feel like I am at home," she writes to me. Her uncle and his family have fled their Baghdadi neighbourhood to stay with their relatives in another area, just as they had done during the invasion in 2003, three years before. The fighting in their neighbourhood is too intense, and so they will try to rent out their house and find another place to live in a safer area. When her driver brought her to the house from the airport, detouring around roadblocks set up by Iraqi police, he told her, "This neighbourhood has become very bad."

Instead of living in the relative safety of the Green Zone or amongst the few brave journalists still reporting from the city, Farah has chosen to live with her family in Baghdad. She can't tell me which neighbourhood because her family is paranoid that someone might find out where she is by hacking into her computer. When she arrived at the airport, she called ahead to tell her uncle to make sure to keep the children in the house, so that when she arrived, and they jumped all over her screaming in excitement, the neighbours wouldn't see or hear anything. She doesn't want anyone to know she's staying there. She didn't even take out her luggage when she got out of the car; her uncle came later and retrieved it. She is moving between a few of her relatives' houses because she knows that if someone realizes that she is a Westerner, she will probably be abducted for ransom or revenge.

Farah tells me that innocent Iraqi civilians are being inexplicably murdered. A grandfather sitting in a courtyard with his grandson is shot and no one knows why. The man selling falafel on the street is killed. Why? After three days, Farah has already stopped questioning these crimes.

The headline in Western newspapers today is "New Abu Ghraib videos shown." Yesterday's lead story was about a video of British soldiers in Basra beating helpless Iraqi teenagers. Farah hangs laundry in the courtyard, looking over her shoulder at the gates for fear of kidnappers lurking on the street. She has already heard story upon story of masked men barging into homes to murder or kidnap civilians, not just Westerners but Iraqi civilians too.

She is woken early the next morning by an explosion and a brief gunfight. Two hours later, her cousin's wife is dragging her children away from the breakfast table as the battle moves down the street. For the first time since I've known her, Farah admits that she is afraid. She has visited Iraq under Saddam Hussein's regime of terror, during the 2003 invasion and in the wake of the aftermath, but she has never experienced this kind of fear: adrenalin-pumping, paranoid, heart-racing, dry-mouth, animal fear.

Farah is staying with her aunt Lamaan and uncle Ahmed and the families of their two sons: fourteen people living together, including their sons' children. Sima, her cousin's wife, shows Farah her scars from when she was shot in the street a few months ago. One bullet is still lodged in her abdomen while the other went right through her body, leaving a ragged hole that has now healed. The doctor fished inside her for the other bullet but couldn't find it. She spent weeks with a psychiatrist and on medication to deal with her nerves after the shooting.

Farah tells me that if I want to catch my cousin Karim at home, I should call him after 8:00 p.m. when everyone is home because of the curfew. He is still my porthole into occupied Iraq. I've had so much trouble getting him on the computer recently that we haven't communicated in a few months. I get him right away on his mobile, but our conversation is brief. Karim is worried about the call being too expensive and says, "Things are very very bad. Nothing has changed, everything is worse. There is lots of violence in our neighbourhood. Electricity two hours a day, water two hours, it is just worse."

Karim's voice sounds gruffer, angrier and deeper, and he doesn't even try to hide his rage. He is worried about Farah being in Iraq.

"She is too small to be here. It is very dangerous where she is staying," he states.

Suddenly, the line cuts off and I can't get through again. I know that he doesn't understand why I care so much. Later, I learn he sent an e-mail to my aunt Amal, saying, "Why is she so interested in Iraq? Everyone here just wants to leave and never look back. If Leilah came to Iraq, she wouldn't last two hours here, and she would want to leave and never ever return."

In her next e-mail a few days later, Farah tells me that she was out with four of the children and her uncle. Even the upscale Mansour district, one of the most affluent areas in Iraq, is not safe for a family outing. They needed to get the kids out of the house because they were stir-crazy from being inside all the time. On the way back, Iraqi police started shooting and speeding through the streets while they were being shot at from somewhere else. Farah's car was lodged in the traffic jam caused by the crossfire. She saw infrared tracer ammunition fire all around her, arcing up and over the car. The children wanted to look at what was happening, but Farah pushed their heads down, worried that they might be shot. They were finally able to zigzag through the neighbourhood to get away and ended up on a street lined with concrete-walled embassies. All of a sudden the car was surrounded by security forces out in position, Iraqi police and American soldiers. They flashed their AK-47s in the air, yelling, "Turn your inside light on! Turn it on so we can see your faces!" On the way home, the children sobbed, saying they wished they had just stayed at home and never gone out in the first place.

Farah is nonetheless determined to photograph injured Iraqis, and her first subject is a traffic policeman who had his face blown up by the Americans. I picture her sitting in her car in Baghdad traffic being driven by Mohammed, her trusted driver. I wouldn't recognize her if I was spirited there right now. She is wearing a full-length black *abaya* that covers her jeans and T-shirt. She has bought local shoes from the market in Baghdad so that even her feet won't give her away to would-be kidnappers. Before Saddam's regime fell, she didn't need to cover up—such are the freedoms that the invasion has imposed. Some women remain uncovered, but the *abaya* is a good disguise, providing a feeling of security in a violent and unpredictable city.

She has been visiting the hospital where limbless Iraqis are given prosthetics. Her driver speaks to casualties of the anarchy and violence that has gripped Iraq in the wake of the war. They are victims of car bombs, IEDs (improvised explosive devices), suicide bombers, missiles and shootings by American and Coalition troops. The driver packs a 10mm gun that he hoists into the waist of his jeans when they get out of the car. He'll ask the victims (men, women and children) waiting for care in the decrepit hospital if Farah can take their photographs. These tragedies have gone largely unrecorded because of the distrust Iraqis have for Western journalists.

Four days later, I receive a short e-mail from Farah. She tells me that "insurgents" planted an IED right in front of her house. The target was an Iraqi police checkpoint that had been set up a few days earlier. Her family and the neighbours were nervous about the checkpoint, knowing that it would probably attract violence, but they were helpless. The police go home at night, leaving the checkpoint unmanned, and the fighters come and set up their explosives, then wait until the police arrive again in the morning and detonate the bomb.

Farah sends me her cell phone number, so I call her. To my amazement, I get her on the line immediately. It's always a wonder to see what works in the new Iraq. She tells me she woke up to a huge blast and the sound of windows shattering, and ran into the children's room to bring them to the back of the house. The scene became chaotic, with police shooting randomly, yelling things like, "Being here every day, we are asking for it!" and "Yes, but what can we do? This is our job, our life." One policeman was killed, and Farah heard the others say afterward, "He had seven children." Two other people were injured. The police reckoned that the perpetrator had to have been within a hundred metres and seen the policemen arrive, since that was exactly when the explosion occurred.

The bomb was planted just behind a palm tree on the other side of the street, in front of a neighbour's house. The woman who lives there had suspected something, and had actually gone out and looked around before her daughter went to school. She didn't see the bomb though. It went off later, after she had gone back into her house. A crater was left in the road behind the mangled palm tree, and a concrete wall next to the house was damaged, surrounded by shards of broken glass.

The Iraqi police went from house to house searching for suspects and took away all the young men. They put potato sacks on their heads as they led them out of each house and onto the street. An older man yelled that they should take the sacks off, but they didn't. Farah's uncle (who is in his seventies) led the police through their house, but as soon as a policeman saw Farah in her *hijab* and *abaya* he averted his eyes and politely turned away into the next room, not realizing she was an outsider. The children were in shock and kept retelling the story of where they had been when the bomb went off. Farah says it was their grace that the blast wasn't bigger.

She tells me the police set up the checkpoint in the neighbourhood as it is known for heavy insurgent activity. The police gave people in the area a phone number to call if they saw anything suspicious. But the people who live on the street are terrified. They know that if any insurgent suspects that someone has talked to the police, that person will be dead.

Farah admits that the neighbourhood is very dangerous, that she hears explosions and gun battles all the time. I ask her if she will move to a safer area, but she answers, "And leave the rest of the family here?" Her family has been living in the house for forty years, where would they go?

The Iraqi police packed up the checkpoint and moved later in the day, and their only relief is that the insurgents wouldn't hit the same place twice. Farah hasn't seen the Americans much on this trip, a couple of times on the streets, but their helicopters fly low over the city constantly, shaking the house when they pass.

As the danger subsides, the family jokes, "Are they going to come and pay for our broken windows out of Prime Minister Al-Jaafari's salaries?" They send each other text messages that say, "If you are sad, if you are hopeless, broke and in debt, congratulations, you know you are Iraqi."

I ask Farah what has changed since she last visited Iraq. She says that it is strange how normal things can feel: the markets teem with people, women go to work, children go to school, cars drive the streets, the sun blazes down. But the landscape of the city is overlaid with huge concrete security blast walls and razor wire. And yet there are rows and rows of fresh yellow flowers planted in the traffic circles and public squares and gardens.

"Baghdad is unpredictable; it can change at a moment's notice," she tells me.

There is a self-imposed curfew at night; from seven in the evening the streets clear out. Farah has to get off the phone; her uncle wants help with his immigration letter. The bombing has persuaded him that the family should leave Iraq.

I can't believe that I hang up feeling that she is all right; she has almost convinced me of the normality of all that she is experiencing. And then the next day, the headlines shout, "Blast Destroys Shia Shrine." The Al-Askari shrine in Samarra, north of Baghdad, has been bombed, and before long there is news of ninety Sunni mosques being attacked across the country. Huge protests overflowing with frenzied men holding machine guns flood Baghdad's streets, and across the Western world newspaper headlines ask if this is finally the beginning of the civil war that has been anticipated for three years.

The next day, in response to the rush of e-mails from concerned family and friends, Farah e-mails us. The family is at home because there is a daytime curfew, and everyone is cooking or working in the garden. She has learned to make two of her favourite Iraqi dishes: *bamiya* (an okra dish) and *kubbat hamuth* (meatballs in rice flour in a tomato turnip soup). One of her male cousins is singing a song about the flower of the pomegranate, and all the women are trying to figure out who the love song is for. They have had worse days; they are fine.

HAIDAR SAMIR AHMED

CHAPTER FOURTEEN
Portraits of the Wounded

As many as 654,965 more Iraqis may have died since hostilities began in Iraq in March 2003 than would have been expected under pre-war conditions, according to a survey conducted by researchers at the Johns Hopkins Bloomberg School of Public Health and Al Mustansiriya University in Baghdad. The deaths from all causes—violent and non-violent—are over and above the estimated 143,000 deaths per year that occurred from all causes prior to the March 2003 invasion. —"Updated Iraq Survey Affirms Earlier Mortality Estimates," Johns Hopkins Bloomberg School of Public Health, October 11, 2006

The next time I see Farah is in Vancouver, three months later. She invites family and friends to a slide show at her parents' house, to show them the images from Iraq she risked her life to bring back to the West.

When I arrive, I am amazed that she looks the same, beautiful and radiant, not haggard, tired or like someone who has just spent six weeks in a war zone. Immediately, she gives me a handful of gold jewellery.

"I almost got stuck in Iraq because of that gold," she laughs.

I'm mystified. I knew she had been to see Karim but not that his wife, Maha, had asked her to bring back some of my aunt Amal's gold jewellery.

"I was wearing it when I got to the airport," she explains. "At first the officials almost didn't let me leave Iraq because I was supposed to have an exit visa from the Ministry of the Interior in central Baghdad. The rule had just been changed and I didn't know about it. Luckily, there were some other people in the same predicament, and so we persuaded the guard to call the ministry to ask if we were allowed to leave without one. I told him my parents were Iraqi, and he looked at my documents. Finally, after four hours of waiting, we were given permission to leave. I was so relieved. I didn't want to go back into Baghdad. I'd said my goodbyes to the family already, and it was really really hard. I couldn't go through that again."

But that wasn't the end of it. When she went through security, the woman checking her asked if she was wearing any gold. The guard could see the gold plainly around her neck and on her wrists, in her ears.

"Of course I am, I'm Iraqi," Farah answered.

"Only Iraqis are allowed to take gold out of the country," the guard said.

It was the same arbitrary rule as under Saddam. I'm sure now, as then, that women are smuggling their gold out under their *abayas*.

"'Where did you get the gold?'" the guard asked.

"I said it was mine and that I came in with it," Farah says. "The woman went away and got a fellow guard, who said, 'Where did you get this gold? Where is it from?' I told him I came in with it, and I grabbed my earrings and said, 'These are from India, and the ring, an Ottoman gold coin, this is my mother's.' So he asked me, 'Are you Iraqi?' I said 'Yes, both my parents are.' So he said, 'Let me see your passport.' Of course, it's Canadian." Farah handed over her Canadian passport. He said, "'Until you produce your father, either you stay or your gold stays.'" Farah says, "'Produce my father? Listen, I've come all the way here alone, I am really scared, and all I want to do is go home. Can't you hear my accent? Who do you think I am?' He just kept saying that those are the rules. Finally I called over the guard who had called the ministry and begged him to help me. He vouched for me and my Iraqiness and finally they let me go."

Because of Farah's tenacity, I am now holding my aunt Amal's jewellery, the first of her belongings that she will see in sixteen years, since she left Iraq for her holiday to England in 1990 just before Saddam invaded Kuwait. She never moved in the traditional sense of deciding to leave one place and adopt another; rather, she left Iraq on vacation and was never able to go back. The bracelet is heavy, 22-carat gold, with the heads of two lions joining at the clasp—the lions of Babylon twisted together into a circle of gold. The necklace is a simple gold rope. Farah says that they don't have gold like that in Iraq anymore, and when she showed it to her family there, they were impressed with its quality.

She pulls out a small plastic box and presents it to me.

"That is for you, a present from Karim."

"What? He shouldn't have sent me anything. It's ridiculous."

"It's a wedding present. He was really casual when he showed it to me, like it was nothing special," Farah says. My wedding had taken place the summer before. Karim had always teased me about being so old and still not married.

I opened the box and pulled out a gold chain with a heart-shaped pendant on it. As I looked more closely at the pendant, I realized it wasn't a heart but a map of Iraq with two veins running through the centre, the Tigris and the Euphrates. The west of the map was rough, representing the desert sand, while the east was smooth and shiny.

"It's Iraq," I say, not wanting to show my eyes welling up.

When the rest of the guests arrive, we take delicious homemade baklava and strong tea and get seated on cushions on the floor, waiting for the slide show to begin. A hush falls over us as the lights are dimmed and the first photograph of an amputee is projected onto the blank wall in front of us. He is a young man who has lost an arm. With black, slicked-back hair and strong features, his handsome face stares directly at the camera. His sleeve is rolled up and the stump of his arm hangs beside him. His younger sister sits behind him on the couch he has just got up from; her expression is an exact replica of his, serious, defiant, proud. Farah tells us that his father is dead and that he was the eldest son, the breadwinner of the family, and that he has six sisters.

"His name is Haidar Samir Ahmed," Farah says. "He is seventeen, and behind him is his younger sister Athra, who is nine years old. He lives in Karradat Mariam, which is just metres from the Green Zone, Saddam's former presidential palace. It was a district heavily hit during the 2003 war. His mother told me that Haider is 'sick with anger' and jealous of his brother Ahmed because he has two arms. They haven't spoken for two years. His mother sells soda, chips and cigarettes to neighbours from her apartment to make ends meet. Haider says that he wants to commit suicide sometimes, asking, 'Who did my arm go for?'"

That question echoes around the room, "Who did his arm go for?"

"What happened to his arm?" I ask.

"He was injured on April 11, 2003," Farah explains. "He was home alone watching over their apartment. The family was staying with relatives. He didn't have food to eat, so he went out into the streets. He was caught in American gunfire. Someone picked him up after he was hit and took him to hospital. He can't see out of his left eye. He has spent over two million dinars [approximately US$1400, enough money to live on for a year] on surgeries and medical care."

"So he was only fourteen years old when the accident happened?" I ask.

"Yes."

Someone asks how she got the photograph. Farah explains that she persuaded each person that agreed to be photographed to let her take their picture in their own homes. It was risky, but she didn't want to photograph them in the impersonal atmosphere of the hospital where she had initially met them. She and her driver established some ground rules to protect themselves as they went about the project.

"We agreed not to wait for more than fifteen minutes for anyone," Farah says. "I learned that from what happened to Jill Carroll [the American journalist for the *Christian Science Monitor* who was abducted on January 7, 2006, and eventually released on March 30, 2006]. She had been waiting for over an hour to meet someone when she was kidnapped. We also agreed that we would only spend thirty minutes at any house we went to because we were afraid that someone would discover that a Canadian was in the area. Of course, that didn't always happen and sometimes we spent much longer with people." She laughs.

SAIF YUSIF HANOUN
PHOTO CREDIT: FARAH NOSH

The next photograph is of two boys. The eldest is sitting on the edge of a wooden table in a kitchen. He scowls at the photograph, and his prosthetic leg sits severed from his leg in front of his healthy one. The stump is cut off below the knee, and his younger brother leans into the wall, looking up at the camera shyly.

Farah explains, "That is Saif. It was significant to have his brother in this photograph because his mother told me that Saif beats his brother because he is so angry and frustrated." On May 5, 2003, he had a high fever, and his uncle was taking him to hospital. They went up onto a bridge and a man was trying to tell them to stop, but it was too late. The Americans blasted them with gunfire.

"For no reason?" I ask in disbelief.

"I don't know," Farah says. "He doesn't know. He was twelve then. He lost his leg fourteen days later. He is fifteen now. His brother is nine. The family sold their car and some land to pay for his surgery. His father left Baghdad and is now remarried and living in the United Arab Emirates. He won't return until there is security in the country."

The next photograph is of a father standing lopsidedly with his daughter. He is missing his right arm and leans his bandaged stump on a crutch, his right leg missing as well. His daughter holds his prosthetic leg, and her eyes pool up at the camera. She will be literally carrying her father's leg for the rest of his life.

DUYAR SAI FEHAN PHOTOGRAPHED WITH
HIS DAUGHTER, SHAMA
PHOTO CREDIT: FARAH NOSH

Farah tells us that he was injured on May 25, 2003, when his car was run over by an American military vehicle. Two other people in the car died, and he lost his arm immediately and then his leg to gangrene. He spent seven million dinars on medical costs. He sold his car and had nothing in the house where she photographed him. To help him, people gave him gifts, and he borrowed money.

He said to Farah, "You know how a worm walks the earth, little by little? That's me, little by little."

"He is the only provider of the family, all young kids." Farah speaks slowly. "How is he going to work? There is no compensation, there is no organization that is going to give these guys a monthly salary to keep their families going. They need a fund for Iraqi war amputees. Even if they were given a hundred dollars a month it would help. There wasn't even anywhere to photograph them. That is the entrance to the bathroom, and this is the middle of the kitchen," she points out. "It was so small and dark...there was just one window."

She changes the slide. The next photograph is of a man lying on his side in bed. At first glance, he looks normal and is even smiling. Then I notice that part of one leg is missing. Farah tells us that when she approached him, she asked if she could photograph him at home. She called him *ammu* (uncle) in the Arab way of showing respect for one's elders, and he called her *bint* (daughter).

"Daughter! I would not let you enter my neighbourhood to visit me. It is far too dangerous for you," he said to her.

Farah laughs as she says, "When I pressed him to tell me which neighbourhood, we realized that I was living a few doors away from him with my relatives. I told him I could easily just walk over. He was surprised that I was living there!"

She continues, "He was injured by American gunfire just last year. He just got out of his car, and they riddled it with

MUHAMMED ALI ABDEL HADI
PHOTO CREDIT: FARAH NOSH

bullets. After ten minutes of fire, the car had fifty-six bullet holes. He said he didn't even see the American soldiers; he just got out of his car and that was it. He has no idea why he was shot at. Those portraits above him are of his father and his uncle."

I have been reading these stories of daily bombings, and I have never seen a single image of these people. Of normal people in their own homes whose lives have been destroyed by this war, which they were powerless to stop. Everyone in the room is transfixed by what they are seeing and murmur their agreement at the injustice of it all. After three years of war, thanks to Farah's bravery, we are looking at some of the first images of the real price the Iraqi people are paying for their "liberty."

The next photograph is of a man with no legs, praying on a prayer mat on his bed.

"His name is Ali," Farah says. "We really connected. You know, I had this rule that I'd only spend half an hour with each person, but we spent eight hours together. I just love him. He is like my brother. I think about him, and I will definitely visit him if I return. He was

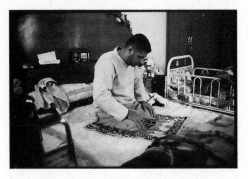

ALI YUSIF KARIM
PHOTO CREDIT: FARAH NOSH

ashamed of being an amputee, and he only agreed to be photographed if I wouldn't publish his photo in Iraq or anywhere else in the Arab world. He said to me, 'I am going to tell you my story but remember, I'm an Iraqi army soldier and I signed up for this. I signed up to die. But what's happened to me has happened to civilians that go out to buy bread for the day. Those are the people you should feel sorry for.' He was so selfless. He had never prayed before, and now he prays five times a day. When he had the accident the first thing he thought was 'Oh my God, I am going to die and I don't pray.' That is why he wanted to live. Then he said that if God gave him a choice to get his legs back, but in exchange he would lose his ability to pray, he wouldn't want them back. He was so sincere."

"Were all of the people here happy to be photographed?" Farah's sister asks.

"Most of them were because no one was listening to their stories. They said things like, 'You are the first person who has ever come to ask me about what happened to me.'"

"Are there enough prosthetic limbs and wheelchairs to go around?" her sister continues.

"Well, many of these people have to pay for their own treatment," Farah explains. "Ali's family had to pull together the money to buy him that wheelchair. When he got out of the hospital he wasn't even given a wheelchair. I mean, he doesn't have legs! He says the Iraqi government looked after him when he was in the army, but now that this has happened they have just forgotten about him. This was six months ago. It was an IED that got him."

Ali fades away and is replaced on the wall by a man with white hair and a beard, standing perfectly balanced on one leg without a crutch. If you only looked at his torso you would think his leg was still there. But it isn't. He was attacked by a suicide bomber.

"He told me he had been an Iraqi police officer for thirty-two years," Farah says. "He was on duty at the main gates of the police station. A green Land Cruiser broke though

RAZAK RASHED ABBAS
PHOTO CREDIT: FARAH NOSH

the barricade, and the man driving was wearing military clothes. He watched the tall young man get out of the car and then their eyes met and the stranger pushed the trigger. Next thing he knew, his stomach was hanging out and he just held it in. His leg had also been blown off. His friend put him and his severed leg into a truck and took him to hospital. That was three years ago. He was given a thousand dollars' compensation, and he receives a third of his salary, on which he supports six children."

Farah reminds us that there are female victims as well, but it was impossible to find any to photograph. Women's lives have been greatly restricted under the occupation, and you don't see as many women in the streets. Farah tried to get permission from some of the female victims in the hospitals, but their families usually didn't want them to be photographed.

The room is silent. The final photograph is the most chilling. A man without legs is lying on an examination table in a hospital. One arm is resting over his heart, and Farah tells us that he lost his other arm as well as his legs. He is a young man in his mid-twenties. All of us want to know what happened to him.

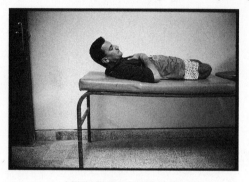

MUUAD IBNAYAN HADI
PHOTO CREDIT: FARAH NOSH

The man was with friends, and they were getting ready for another friend's wedding. They reached the New Baghdad Bridge, and there was an Iraqi police convoy behind them. Suddenly, there was a blast; it was an IED that was intended for the police. They never found his hand," Farah explains. "His family has had to pay for everything, every injection, since the day of his injury. Rehabilitation doctors in Baghdad told him that he wouldn't walk again, that they couldn't do anything for him because he was a triple amputee. They couldn't give him prosthetics for some reason—they just don't have the resources to deal with such a difficult case. He didn't know he could go to the Green Zone to get help from a clinic initiated by the American military. Iraqis can go to the Green Zone if they have three pieces of ID, but it is very intimidating for them. Large groups of soldiers with their guns bristling make approaching the entrance a daunting experience.

When Farah went to see him he had been in despair for three months; without his legs and one arm, he knew he had no future. There was nothing much any of his family or friends could do for him. She told him that she would take him herself to the Green Zone clinic. The next morning, she went into his house and picked him up, and her driver carried him to the car. Farah spread out a towel on the back seat for him to sit on, and was very attentive to

him, asking him how he felt, as she knew what a huge event this trip
was for him. She was on the verge of tears looking at him without
his limbs, sitting beside her.

It was the first time he had been on the streets since his accident
and he was very jumpy and very afraid. He said, "I can't handle
the outside world, I'm broken inside." They passed a car that was
riddled with bullets; the victim of the shooting was still in the car,
his lifeless head lolling to one side. Farah was heartbroken that on his
first day seeing Baghdad again, he had witnessed the aftermath of a
murder. She had to calm him down as they went through the centre
of Baghdad, and when they arrived at the Green Zone, she had to
reassure him that despite being Iraqi they would let him through.
Once inside, the American military doctors were wonderful, and
they immediately began giving him physiotherapy and told him that
there was hope: he would be able to have prosthetics for all his lost
limbs.

A month later, she heard from him. He still hadn't received his
prosthetics, and he kept asking Farah when she was coming to get
him to take him back to Canada with her.

DATE PALMS IN BAGHDAD FROM THE VANTAGE POINT OF AN AMERICAN HELI-
COPTER

PHOTO CREDIT: FARAH NOSH

CHAPTER FIFTEEN
Min Al'Sima,
"From the Heavens"

So yesterday was the burning of books . . . The National Library and Archives—a priceless treasure of Ottoman historical documents, including the old royal archives of Iraq—were turned to ashes in 3,000 degrees of heat. Then the library of Korans at the Ministry of Religious Endowment were set ablaze. . . . And the Americans did nothing. All over the filthy yard they blew, letters of recommendation to the courts of Arabia, demands for ammunition for troops. . . . I was holding in my hands the last Baghdad vestiges of Iraq's written history. . . . Why? Who set these fires? For what insane purpose is this heritage being destroyed? —Robert Fisk, "Library Books, Letters and Priceless Documents are set ablaze in final chapter of the sacking of Baghdad," *The Independent*, April 15, 2003

Before Farah goes back to New York, she comes over to show me some of the photos of her family that were to be published in *Time* magazine the following week. Since she'd visited Karim in Baghdad, I wanted to know how she'd found him and his family. Two years had passed since she'd last visited his house.

"Did your father receive the *min al'Sima?*" Farah asks me.

The name means *from the heavens,* and it refers to a traditional sweet nougat that is covered in white flour and can be found only in Iraq. Once she mentioned it, a memory surfaced. I could feel the dry powder in my mouth, but I struggled to remember the actual taste of the nougat. Slowly, the sweet chewy texture and the taste of the pistachio pieces came back to me. My grandparents used to bring it for us on their visits to England. I'd forgotten about it until now. Karim had sent some for my father through Farah, and she'd mailed it to him when she'd returned to New York.

"Yes, he got it," I confirmed. "He loved it. When the box arrived, he hoarded the nougat all for himself. Like Proust's Madeleine, the first taste brought Iraq flowing back into all his senses."

As we drank tea, we talked about her trip and how strange it was that she was back here in the peace and tranquility of Vancouver. I asked her how she dealt with witnessing the tragedy of Iraq again and again.

She explains that taking photographs and publishing them helped.

"It's my way of shedding it," she tells me. "If these pictures get out, and people see them and read their stories, then I will be relieved. I am worried about the pictures of the Iraqi victims not being published. A part of me thinks now that I could have gone all this way and done all this work only for no one to see the photos. I thought the American publications were going to be all over the story, but . . . who knows? Maybe I haven't found the right place. The family story was easier to sell, but that isn't what I went to Iraq for. These victims need to be seen."

I hadn't received an e-mail from Karim in months. He didn't seem to go to his office very much and even when he did and we tried to talk, the electricity situation was so bad that we kept getting cut off. I hadn't had any direct contact with him for so long. Instead, I was saturated with news of incessant daily bombings and killings. I was constantly imagining the worst. I looked up the Iraq Body Count Website, which kept a database of every reported killing. It was a wonder that anyone was still living: you could be assassinated, die of gunshot wounds, be exploded by a suicide bomber, an IED, an American soldier, a car bomb, an air strike . . . death was especially protean in Iraq.

The last we'd heard, Amal had had a rare opportunity to speak to Maha, who was upset because Baghdad was suddenly closed to all traffic. It was raining, which was unusual, and US Secretary of State Condoleezza Rice and British Foreign Secretary Jack Straw had flown into the airport on a surprise visit. But because of bad weather, they couldn't take a helicopter to the Green Zone. Most officials travelled from the airport to the Green Zone via helicopter because it was simply too dangerous to travel through Baghdad by car. But now, Rice and Straw had to be driven. In order to make their route safe, all the roads were closed and the city was brought to a complete standstill. Karim's wife was afraid that if this lasted until the next day, she'd have to cancel the henna party she was organizing for a relative who was getting married. Celebrations are not easy to arrange when you are living in a war zone. When I told my father this story, he commented, "Just like under Saddam, the whole city stopped when he was moving from place to place. What's the difference?"

Farah's driver had taken her to Karim's house, which is in a mixed Muslim and Christian area. As soon as they'd driven into the neighbourhood, Farah said, "I felt like we were in another world. Most of the houses had front and back gardens and people were working on them, peacefully gardening."

The middle-class neighbourhood was not one of the wealthiest in the city, but was well maintained and cleaner than other residential areas, and it seemed richer and more serene than the rest of Baghdad. It almost appeared to be out of place amid the anarchy, fear and ugliness of much of the city. But Farah's family lives in one of the most dangerous neighbourhoods, a mostly Sunni area where there is intense insurgent activity.

The appearance of tranquility was an illusion; I told her about the huge blast on the street behind Karim's house. A house was blown up, and one of Karim's friends found the arm of a young girl in the street afterwards.

Karim's wife cooked an elaborate meal for Farah. The centrepiece was a biryani, which is a traditionally special spicy rice dish of meat, nuts, raisins, spices, eggs and onion.

"I called them the day before and told them that I didn't want them to go to any trouble, that they shouldn't forget how small I am and how little I eat. Of course, there was way too much delicious food, but it was amazing," she tells me. Iraqi hospitality, at least, has survived the war intact.

Karim and the family were happy to have company from outside the country. Farah's Arabic was now so good that she was not only able to communicate with them in their own language, but also in their own dialect. Mostly the conversation, as in every household in Iraq, was about security and about the dreadful stories people heard daily from their friends and family. Farah was becoming exhausted by all the tragic tales but that was all they could talk about.

"They don't have anything else going on," she says.

I ask her what Karim and Maha were like, having not met them in person myself.

"Karim is the storyteller, more gregarious and outgoing, and Maha is quieter," Farah tells me. "Karim couldn't believe I was in Iraq. He gave me trouble, saying I shouldn't have come, that it was madness."

The area where Karim worked was becoming progressively more perilous. Farah said that a few weeks ago, he'd been in his office and it seemed to be business as usual. Unbeknownst to him, the entire street had been cleared out and everyone had left their offices and cars. The security guard in his building came and knocked on the door and then shouted at him, asking what he was still doing in the building. Apparently, there was an unexploded car bomb on the street, and everyone else had been evacuated. When Karim got down to the street, there were police everywhere. One asked him, "Is that your car?" His little car was parked in the empty street a few metres from the only other car—the one that was packed with explosives.

The policeman shouted at him that he could move it or leave it, it was up to him. Karim had a split second to figure out if he was going to get his car out or not. He was terrified. But he really didn't want to lose his car because it would not be easy to replace.

Once Karim had told me how he'd waited years to get that car. Finally, one day not long before the invasion, he had been called to pick up his new vehicle. But after the invasion he had been afraid to drive it around Baghdad because of the looting and stealing. It was much better to have a beaten-up old car, as you'd be less likely to be a victim of a carjacking or worse, being killed for your car, which happened all the time. So he'd kept the car at home, waiting for things to calm down. When they hadn't got better in three years, he decided to start driving the car anyway.

Farah said that after that car bomb, Karim decided to close his office.

"He's had to tone down his work," Farah tells me. "I think he had a warning from a friend. They are keeping clients they already have, but they have stopped soliciting new business."

Work was very complicated these days in Iraq. If you had work lined up before the war, then you were able to make enough of a living to survive. Men who already had work were lucky, but men looking for work couldn't find any. And there are very few job options. Army and police salaries are good by Iraqi standards, but it is practically suicidal work. The only other options are to sell CDs on the street, or work with the occupiers and risk being murdered as a collaborator.

Karim had pointed out to Farah the couch where Auntie Lina had spent her last days.

"I remember she lay on that couch, and she just kept going down," Karim had said to Farah. He'd said Lina's deterioration had started soon after the last time Farah had visited. Farah was lucky she saw Lina up and driving and talking, although the elderly woman was already tired and not well at the time.

Now that Lina was gone, Karim and his wife looked after our family home for us, my grandparents' house. Farah had said to them it was too bad that they couldn't go to see the house.

"I wanted to take photographs for you," she says, but she knew that it would be impossible. Karim agreed that it was a nice idea, but didn't take it seriously. Farah explained that it wasn't worth moving around in Baghdad unless you absolutely had to. Iraqis rarely go out, and it is not worth venturing outside just to take photographs.

But even without photographs, I know that my father's childhood home now stands on a gradually emptying street as more and more people desert the neighbourhood, flee Baghdad, give up on Iraq. Most end up in Jordan if they have money, or Syria if they have less. Few make it to the West. Canada took only a couple of hundred Iraqis in 2006.

Farah's visit to Karim took place soon after the bombing of the mosque in Samarra and the violent reaction that followed when mosques were burning all over Baghdad.

"Karim was comparing Iraq now to the age of the Mongols of Hugalu [Genghis Khan's son], saying that mosques in Iraq haven't been burnt since that time," Farah explains. "Books were burnt then and thrown in the river. They say the river turned black from the ink of the books. But then he said that if we burn our own mosques and Korans in the very place that Islamic history was born, then how can we criticize Europeans for their cartoons about Islam or an American stepping on a Koran in Guantanamo?" Karim was comparing events now with incidents that had happened eight hundred years ago. Iraqi memories stretch back centuries rather than decades.

Karim also told Farah a story about his time in the military fifteen years earlier. A commander had asked him whether he knew if another soldier was Shia or Sunni. The soldier in question was Karim's really close friend, but in those days you didn't know the difference, so he replied, "Well, I don't know, he's Muslim." Iraqis are always telling me that the difference between Shia and Sunni had not been very important in Iraq under Saddam. Saddam targeted anyone who was against his regime; it didn't matter what religion the person was. Anyone who opposed him was at risk; anyone who didn't was relatively safe.

Karim was tired; he looked shattered compared to the last time that Farah had seen him. But Farah found all Iraqis to be weary, literally worn out.

"You can see the exhaustion on their faces; the tension takes such a toll on them. You'll see though, when I get the photos developed, they look smart and tidy. They are keeping their lives together some-how," she says encouragingly.

She puts her hand up to her face, which lights up suddenly and then darkens.

"Oh yes, they told me that Jill Carroll's driver was Christian and went to the same church as them," Farah said. "Karim went to church the Sunday after the driver was killed and saw his young wife there with her baby. She is the same age as us, and he said it was just so sad seeing her there alone."

No one knew why the killings and kidnappings were happening, she says. Anyone, anywhere, could be a target and people didn't know who might be attacked or by whom.

"For some reason people aren't too afraid to speak on mobile phones, but they are afraid of computers now," Farah says.

I ask her, "How did you feel being able to just drop into Baghdad one day and then walk away and leave the mayhem? Did anyone ever get angry and say it is all okay for you, you can just leave, come and go as you please?"

Farah shakes her head and looks down.

"No one ever said it to me, but I felt so upset when I left this time," she acknowledges. "I felt humiliated, so embarrassed that I could pack up and leave. Saying goodbye to them was so hard; I just wanted to disappear without them noticing. Everyone was being so sad, and in those last few hours, I wished I could disappear. It was so humiliating leaving, especially with the teenage girls. They'd say, 'You are so lucky, I want to come to New York one day.' They ask me about my life all the time, and what it's like. What can I say to them? I'm free. It's easy. What do you do? They met my boyfriend when he was taking photos there, and that is the weird thing because he could never go there now. An American guy? In that neighbourhood? There is no way. They say, 'Tell him we hope that one day he can come back to visit us.' But they know at the same time it is impossible."

Farah's family never spoke about the future when she was living with them, she never heard them say, "When things are better we will do this or that…"

"They think of the future only in a fearful way," Farah says. "My aunt thinks about her son, what she will do if he doesn't come home one day. It's that kind of fear. Not ever about when this is all over. It's just day by day, how to get through each day."

I want to know if her relatives ever talked about the past, if not the future.

"Yeah, they are longing for those days," she tells me. "They say, 'We should have stuck with the regime.' They call them the good old days. And that is significant, because when the invasion was inevitable, they started fantasizing about what life would be like without Saddam Hussein in power. They saw it as an opportunity for a better life, even though of course they didn't want war. Now they are saying, 'What were we ever complaining about? This is so much worse than under Saddam. It just gets worse all the time.'"

Farah pauses before she goes on.

"The worst is that they don't have hope anymore," she says. "It's one thing to be in a conflict zone when you have a sense of hope. It is completely different being in the same situation without hope. The tension is so heavy. The expressions on people's faces are so intense, and you never get a sense of optimism anywhere in Iraq these days."

She looks down and takes another sip of tea.

She then tells me that she went to the Green Zone one day and saw an Iraqi photographer that she used to see before the war. Through the razor wire she asked him, "How are you, how are things?" and he said, "Not good, not good at all." Then he just walked away. Farah hadn't seen him in two years and she was shocked by his demeanour. Usually, Arab warmth and hospitality was proffered no matter what the circumstances, but he gave nothing. Farah guessed that something must have happened to his family or someone close to him because he was clearly in shock; he couldn't even talk to her.

"So if they don't have hope, why are they not putting a gun to their heads?" I was starting to feel despair myself.

"God. Religion," she states simply. "You just believe that God has written all of this for some reason. They say, 'We have to trust in Him and that He will get us through it. We have to take comfort in that it is written. And how can we go against that?' That's the only way they survive psychologically."

Farah found herself turning towards God, especially when she was confronted by terrifying situations on Baghdad's streets.

"I have tendencies towards Islam and get a sense of peace from it. Because it would be really hard at times and I would catch myself asking God to bring peace within me, to make me feel peaceful. I would catch myself saying that sometimes, if I was freaked out that maybe we were being followed. I was so nervous. One of my cousins told me that if I was ever really afraid that I should ask God to put peace inside me. You say it in a particular way, it works. If it can work on a semi-believer like me, then think of how well it works on someone who has a relationship with God and the Prophet and all His prophets."

Farah hadn't really thought about Islam before she started going to Iraq. It had never occurred to her; she was secular. But being around people who believed and experienced living that belief, and her family talking to her about it so much, started to change her.

"They do it in a gentle way. They tell a story, and I am open to it. I am thankful that they have religion because if they didn't have that now they would have nothing to live for. It is the only thing that they have. I am so glad that it has the kind of power to give them a sense of peace."

I interrupted her, saying angrily that it was other human beings who were creating all this horror for Iraqis. It was a human problem, and it should have a human solution. To turn to God almost seemed to be absolving humans of responsibility for the catastrophe.

"Oh yes, they all know that. They'd say, 'What kind of animal would do this?' There are waves of that, but when they try to bring themselves down from that, they pray. You can have both of those feelings, but prayer is a sanctuary for sure. I don't know if it will be enough for my aunt though . . ."

"What do you mean?"

"Didn't I tell you about the twins?"

"No, what happened?"

"Oh God, I can't believe I didn't tell you." Farah looks at me, her eyes big with emotion.

"A few weeks ago when I was back in New York, I got a phone call from Baghdad. My aunt said, 'The twins are missing.' These are my cousin Ehab's wife's sister's boys. Remember, I lived with them for a few days during the war? Her name is Suhad. She has three boys, two are twins in their early twenties. Suhad's husband went missing in 1982 under Saddam. Late one night Iraqi soldiers just came to his house. He was a Shia. He was in his *dishdasha*, his white nightgown, you know. The soldiers were looking for his brother, the twin's uncle, who had a quiet reputation of being in the opposition. They said they wanted to talk to their uncle, just ask him a few questions. The twin's father insisted on going with his brother. So they took him away, and he never came home. No one ever saw him again. The family were afraid, but they thought he'd be back. They had no idea what happened to him, nothing. They never even found his body after the war. Nothing." She paused for a moment, deep in thought. "I slept beside Suhad during the war one night, you know in 2003. She told me that her husband still visits her in her dreams. This is twenty years later. She is still talking about him. He's still whispering to her in her dreams. So her boys are everything to her. She told me it wasn't just marriage, it was love."

The twin boys were in the Iraqi army at age twenty-one just before the invasion began. Suhad made her sons desert because, she said to Farah, "I absolutely cannot tolerate losing them." At the time, Iraqis knew that fighting the Americans would likely mean death for a soldier. They knew that their firepower was unequal and that most Iraqi soldiers would be cannon fodder.

Farah goes on, "She kept saying, 'What would I do if something happened to my boys?'"

She hid them in the house during the invasion and the beginning of the occupation. If the doorbell rang, their younger brother would have to go and get them and tell them to hide on the roof. They never ever left the house. For weeks, they didn't even go out in the garden. They didn't want the neighbours to see them because they knew that they were supposed to be in the army. Under Saddam, anyone could be an informer. But the twins survived the war; miraculously, they weren't discovered.

Farah continues, "So, I call Ehab's wife, Suhad's sister, three weeks ago, and she says her nephews, the twins, are missing. They were working as security guards at a children's hospital. Every building has security guards now, even the children's hospital. When I called, they had been missing for four days. I asked her, 'Has there been a request for ransom?' And she said, 'We have not yet received a phone call.' And I knew that if there was no demand for ransom then they were dead. Two days later I spoke to her again, and she said that they had found the boys. Her brothers had done a round of the hospitals, and found their bodies in one of the hospital morgues. They didn't even recognize one of them because he was so riddled with bullets. They didn't even know it was him. They thought they had found only one, and then they went back to check again and realized it was him. Their bodies had been dumped on the side of the road with twelve others in the same district where Jill Carroll went missing. Just dumped at the side of the road."

"But why?"

"No reason. There is no reason to any of it anymore. I was devastated, I was in shock for a week. Now Suhad has only one son. I know how crazy she is for her twins. So I thought she was just going to commit suicide. There is no way she can survive this. Apparently, she was in the kitchen and she grabbed a knife and tried to stab herself. I think it was out of pure grief after the funeral," she says. "Her younger son grabbed a pistol and threatened to kill himself, too. I know it sounds unbelievable, but he probably knew no one would let him do it. They just couldn't handle it. Then her son said, 'We have to stick together because we are all each other have right now, so you have to stick around and I have to stick around. Because we're all we have.'"

AFTERMATH OF A CAR BOMB

PHOTO CREDIT: FARAH NOSH

CHAPTER SIXTEEN
The Smell of a Car Bomb

I heard a man named Abu Sabah say: "They used these weird bombs that put up smoke like a mushroom cloud. Then small pieces fall from the air with long tails of smoke behind them." I heard him say that pieces of these bombs exploded into large fires and that most people thought it too danger-ous to send their children to school. —Eliot Weinberger, "What I Heard about Iraq," *London Review of Books*, February 3, 2005

After weeks of not being able to reach Karim on the computer, I buy a cheap calling card and phone him on his mobile to thank him for the necklace. I get through right away, amazingly. He always laughs when I am surprised to reach him. It is curfew, and he is at home for the evening. When I thank him for the necklace, he says it is nothing, and that his daughter has the same necklace that she wears every day as well. Sure enough, when Farah sends me the photographs she has taken, there it is, the same necklace on his teenage daughter, Reeta.

He has just returned home from buying food in the market with his wife. The streets were already empty at 8:00 p.m. because it is so dangerous to be out at night. I ask him what he thinks is going on in Iraq now. He tells me that there are many countries that have an interest in Iraq: Iran, Syria, Jordan, Saudi Arabia, Kuwait and of course the United States. He thinks they are all jostling for a position in the future of the country. But it is the Iraqi people who pay on a daily basis while not gaining any share of the wealth. At the moment, his biggest fear is car bombs.

"Imagine how many cars are around you every day, then imagine that each one could be the one that kills you. You can see how terrifying this kind of insecurity and violence is for us," he says. "Every morning when we leave the house, we pray only one prayer, that we are allowed to return safely to our homes, especially the children going to school. My son has to travel across Baghdad to get to his school. The journey is much more dangerous than before."

I tell him that Farah felt his neighbourhood was more peaceful than other Baghdad areas.

"Yes, our neighbourhood is safer than other neighbourhoods, but still we are always afraid. There is a checkpoint on the main road that goes into our neighbourhood that is often attacked. We have heard many bombs explode there. My office is in central Baghdad, but I only go there once a week. My secretary is too afraid to come to work anymore. Many car bombs have exploded there because it's a commercial street; we had three or four bombs in one month. A week ago at 10:00 a.m., just as I was arriving at my office, a bomb exploded right in front of me, a hundred metres away. We are living in a movie." He laughs at the irony. "Luckily, it was a small bomb. No one was hurt. My wife was with me. Of course, she was very afraid."

I ask him whether it was the first bomb he's personally seen detonate.

"Oh no, I myself have witnessed at least five car bombs explode. Imagine how many there must be if I alone have seen five?"

"Yes, Farah told me what happened to your car a couple of months ago."

"She told you about that? Yes. When I came out of my office, I saw that my car was parked right beside the car with the bomb. There were no other cars on the street, just my little car. The police were all waving guns at me and shouting for me to move the car quickly, if I wanted to keep it. Can you imagine how much my hand was shaking as I unlocked my car and got inside to drive it away? Then the police defused the bomb. They have learned how to do this from the Americans."

Karim's anger is rising again as his voice gets louder.

"Nobody can imagine what it is like here," he says. "Everywhere in Baghdad is unsafe. Last night we heard gunfire all night long. And today we saw the aftermath of many explosions, small bombs, car bombs, suicide bombs...we are experts now on all types of bombs." He laughs again.

He and his wife can recognize the various types of explosions by the kind of clouds of dust in the air, the sounds that the explosions give off, even the smells that they exude. As he tells me this, I imagine the explosions that cleaved the limbs from the men in Farah's photographs.

"You know Farah was in Baghdad to photograph victims of the war, innocent people, I've seen the photographs, and she is trying to get them published...so people here will know what is really going on there," I tell him.

Karim is cynical.

"Well, it won't make a difference," he says. "Nothing is going to change here, people will look at them in Europe and America for a moment and then forget about it. I tell you no one can do anything for us now."

I change the subject because I know that a couple of years ago Karim was more optimistic about letting the world know what was really happening in Iraq. Now he has seen the fruits of three years of the world's indifference and inactivity. Instead, I ask him why he's stopped going to work.

"It is safer for me not to be in my office right now," he explains. "The people that are being attacked work for commercial companies that help the Americans on the bases and for their other projects. I wouldn't work for those companies . . . it's far too dangerous. No one can protect me, I would have to protect myself. There are many militias working for every different interested party, and I have no way of protecting myself."

I tell Karim that the main thing most North Americans ask me is why there is a civil war in Iraq. They want to know why the Sunnis and the Shia hate each other and are starting to fight and kill each other. I ask Karim what he would answer to people here.

"Oh yes, there is a civil war in Iraq, but it is very complicated." He sighs. "It's not just one part of the population against another, as it was in Lebanon, for example. Families are intermarried, Shia and Sunni, but then outsiders are coming and telling the Sunnis to move out of one neighbourhood and into another, and then telling the Shias the same. The people are becoming divided, but it is hard to divide families completely. It is so difficult because most people have some uncles that are Shia and some that are Sunni. Are they going to kill their own uncles? But there are death squads operating and people have to obey them because they are terrified for their lives. These differences were never as important in the past."

Karim tells me that many Iraqis think that the Iranians are involved as well.

"We know that Iranian militias have killed over two hundred pilots from the Iraqi army," he says. "I have many friends in the Iraqi army, and they have been targeted. Of course we all remember the Iran–Iraq War, so they don't like us. And you see Iranians have the same appearance as us, so we can only tell they are different by language, but some of them speak Arabic. No one can recognize them in the streets and tell they are Iranian. It's easy for them to be here without anyone knowing."

"What about the Americans? What are they doing now?" I ask him.

"The Americans are only protecting themselves," he says bitterly. "There is no government in Iraq, only in name. Nobody can do anything without the American ambassador giving his approval. They have to take his advice. And they want what is best for them only, we

know that now. We know they are building the biggest US embassy
in the world here, it will be over a hundred acres. Why do they need
this?"

I tell him that every time the US or the UK are criticized for the
war, officials cite free elections and a democratic representative
government as proof of the correctness of the invasion.

"So what do you think of your elected democratic government?"
I ask him.

He sneers, "Iraqis think democracy is a very bad word. There is
no law here. Under Saddam, he would make a law and the next day
it would be enforced and everyone would obey it. Here, our government is powerless to do anything. If you go to the police station with
a problem, they say they are powerless. No one can help Iraqis. No
one can help the people." He then echoes what Farah said: "The situation is hopeless now. If there is hope it is for ten years from now.
But for now, we have nothing."

"Do you think the Americans will stay in Iraq?" I ask.

He scoffs at my question. "Of course the Americans will stay. They
have many bases here; they are working for their interests. For them
it seems it is good for them to be here. Who knows why? No one can
guess what their policy is, but it is a big plan for the whole Middle
East. It has just begun with Iraq. I tell you, Iraq is just the beginning."

"So you don't think anything is better since the fall of Saddam?"

He says I could ask any Iraqi and they would say the same thing:
"Nothing has changed for the better. It is the same as living under
Saddam. Then, every day we had a problem, and it is the same now.
We have no water, no electricity, today it was on for only two hours.
Now it is summer, it is around 40 degrees. We have no fans or air
conditioners. We have to sleep on the roof as we always have, even
with all the war raging around us. Today we found a bullet in our bed
on the roof. It fell down in the night. Every day we hear gunfire in
the streets. Today we heard huge fighting with the Americans. We
can recognize the sounds of the different American equipment now."

Karim's children ae used to the war. It has become habitual for them to witness car bombs and hear explosions, and every day they see dead bodies on television and people being killed. His daughter is now a teenager, and his son is almost twelve. They are growing up in the midst of this war, trying to study, go to school. His daughter dreams of becoming an engineer. She used to think about becoming a doctor, but now she doesn't think that is such a good job.

Karim doesn't think Christians are being singled out. "Not especially targeted, now that everyone is killing each other. Every house has guns. The government sent a policeman to guard our church, but what can the police do if a car pulls up with a bomb inside? And suicide bombers? They want to die, so how can we stop them? And remember that in 2002, a few months before the war, Saddam released thousands of prisoners from his prisons, including Abu Ghraib, as a present to the people of Iraq for giving him one hundred percent support in the elections. Political prisoners were set free as well as real hardened criminals who now terrorize the streets, robbing and killing innocent people. All these criminals are now free to do whatever they want."

"Why is there so much killing in Iraq?" I ask, exasperated.

"Hot weather, hot blooded, hot tempers," he jokes again.

I realize it is a stupid question. It is war.

Then he continues, "All we hope every day is for our house and family to be protected. Even gas is being limited! The price of fuel has gone up. It used to be twenty Iraqi dinars a litre, which is about one cent. And now it is 250 Iraqi dinars, which is ten or twenty cents. To fill our tank used to be one dollar, now it is seven to ten dollars. There is no fuel at the gas station, you have to queue for three to six hours for it. So we have to buy it from the black market. The government has no money . . . where is all Iraq's money going? No one knows."

He reminds me that nothing has been reconstructed. The streets are still rubble. No one has moved one brick to rebuild the city.

American tanks destroy the streets. They drive anywhere they like, in any direction, and they don't care.

"They will kill you if you are walking or driving in the street and you are in their way," he says. "They will drive over your car or shoot you. You might not believe it but it is true! Today there were three American vehicles in the street when we came home from picking up my daughter from her friend's house. Instantly, we stopped and moved to the side; otherwise, we would risk being killed."

I want to know what Iraqis feel about the West now. Of course, they didn't want a war, but once it had happened Karim had hoped that the occupation would give something to the Iraqi people, and that it had to be better than what they lived through under Saddam. I am saddened but not shocked when he says, "Iraqi people hate Americans now because they destroyed our country. My friends say that they are worse off than under Saddam Hussein. We thought it would take a year for everything to get better, but now we are entering the fourth year since the war. Four years. I can't believe it."

"Do you still want to leave the country?" I ask Karim.

Our family has been discussing how to get them out, but to get an Iraqi into a Western country has become extremely difficult. As Iraq has an elected democratic government, the people can't claim to be refugees or persecuted. The fact that they live in a war zone and in a country under foreign occupation isn't considered reason enough for a visa.

"And go where?" Karim answers angrily. "The other day the Iraqi airport was attacked. The US doesn't even know who did it. So they have closed the airport for a few days. The Jordanian border is closed now; they don't let Iraqis in. We can still go to Syria, but the road is extremely dangerous. It would be very hard to leave our house, our car, our family. We would have nothing. Every day my wife and I talk about leaving, but we are always saying, 'But where would we go?'"

As if he realizes how bleak his life sounds, Karim suddenly changes tack.

"You see, life here is very different from in the West. Don't forget there are many good things as well. Family and relationships between people are very good and close. My cousin lives in Scotland and is married to a Scottish woman. At Christmas he told me that they had to send out over one hundred cards. It seems no one visits each other at Christmas in Scotland, they just send cards! Here at Christmas I visit thirty or forty friends, and my wife and children receive the men from the other families. At New Year's I stay in and other people come to us. If we have more than four empty wine bottles we know it has been a good Christmas, if only one or two we say, oh it hasn't been so good."

Most Iraqis don't drink very much, and when they do, they usually just have a small taste.

"And day to day, we have good relationships. Here, my wife drinks coffee with her neighbour every morning at ten o'clock for half an hour, either at her house or ours. My brother lives close by and I see his children every day. I love them, they are young kids, and if I don't see them for a day then I feel very sad and say to myself, 'I must go and see them.'"

The line suddenly gets cut off, and I am left listening to the emptiness. I walk out into my street and suddenly notice how many cars are parked there and how many drive by, one every few seconds. The engines are loud, I can't ignore them. I imagine being afraid of every one of these cars. I pass other people in the street, men, women, children, and I am not afraid. Spring is coming slowly to Vancouver, the cherry trees are starting to blossom, the crocuses are out, orange and purple in the grass, and the snowdrops have almost finished blooming.

IRAQI EXILES IN DAMASCUS

PHOTO CREDIT: FARAH NOSH

CHAPTER SEVENTEEN
New Baghdad in Damascus

Yesterday I lost a country.
I was in a hurry,
and didn't notice when it fell from me
like a broken branch from a forgetful tree.
—Dunya Mikhail, "I Was In A Hurry"

It is July 2006, and Farah is in Damascus to cover the Syrian reaction to another war on their borders, this time to the west. Israel is bombing Lebanon in "retaliation" for the kidnapping of two soldiers by Hezbollah, the Shia political organization, and Lebanese refugees are fleeing to Syria in the thousands. This time I can picture exactly where Farah is, recalling my trip to Damascus just one year ago.

Another country sheltering my Middle Eastern relatives—and the happy childhood memories of my father and aunts—is being bombed. Now Iraq and Lebanon, the two countries that they love, are in ruins. My aunts fear for Syria if the war spreads. Despairing and helpless, one minute they are watching the news constantly, the next they have decided not to watch it at all and are only listening to Arabic music on the Internet.

They called their Iraqi friend Nebal whom I met on my visit to Beirut last year. She fled Iraq after the Gulf War and is now in her fifties. Since I met her, her husband, whom she had been nursing full-time, has passed away. She lives with her mother-in-law whom she

253

now looks after. My aunts have spoken to her every night since the bombing began, and she is terrified. There is an army camp in her Beirut suburb, and tonight the Israelis have been attacking it all night long. She has barely slept. Her son is to be married in Sweden in two weeks, and before all this happened she had her ticket, her visa, her dress, her shoes—she was very excited about going. Now the trip is impossible because the airport has been bombed, and the only ways to leave Beirut are by car to Syria, which is very dangerous because Israeli aircraft fire rockets at "suspicious vehicles," or by ship, which is only available to foreign nationals. Her other son was with her in Beirut when the bombing began, but managed to get evacuated by the Swedish embassy because he has a Swedish passport.

She cries to my aunts, saying the bombing has taken Lebanon back twenty years in just a few days. This year was the first year that tourists were back in droves. I had sensed for myself the tentative beginnings of a new optimism when I was there last year; the Lebanese were dressing up and going to cafés and bars. I felt the resurgence of the Beirut my parents had yearned to return to, when it was famous for being the Riviera of the Middle East. A week after a taxi took us out of Lebanon, in that hair-raising journey through a snowstorm over the mountains to Damascus, a huge bomb killed the ex–prime minister, Rafiq Hariri. After that, the Lebanese were terrified they would be drawn back into another war, and now they have been.

And what of Great-auntie Selma, now ninety-eight and still in the convent with the nuns taking care of her? We haven't been able to find out if she is all right, but as far as we know, the Israelis have not yet bombed northern Beirut.

Nebal says to Siham, "Don't worry, my mother-in-law is so deaf that she hardly notices the bombing. So probably all the old women in the convent don't even know what is happening!"

I find myself thinking of Selma, another great-aunt in a different country, living out her last days too with the sound of aerial bombardment as a kind of dreadful musical accompaniment. I think of all the Lebanese people I met last year: my father's namesake, Ammu Ibrahim, in his village outside Tripoli; Ibrahim's family who cooked Scott and I that huge Lebanese feast and took us on a tour of the mountains around their home. One of his paintings still haunts me. It is of a mother clasping her young adult son in a fierce embrace. Ibrahim had titled it "A son going abroad." He said this was the tragedy of Lebanon—that all the old people are left behind while the young emigrate to the West because there is no future for them at home. This is not just the tragedy of Lebanon, I think. This is the tragedy of the Middle East. I think of the destitute Palestinian refugees I met in Beirut's southern suburbs, which have been bombed to apocalyptic extremes by Israeli warplanes. I think of the selfless women working for the non-profit organization that helps the refugees, and the Syrian taxi drivers and waiters I met along the way. I wonder if the American University of Beirut campus is full of displaced Shia from the south of Beirut, flocking into its beautiful park by the sea for safety, camping out under the palm trees.

Farah is in Damascus to cover the Syrian reaction to this new war, but she is also visiting all her Iraqi relatives who have fled Baghdad for the safety of Syria. So many Iraqis have arrived—some estimates put their number at one million in a city of five million—that there is now an entire suburb in Damascus, Qadissya, that everyone is calling New Baghdad or Little Baghdad. It is not only Sunnis who are fleeing, but Shia and Christians as well, and most of the newly exiled Iraqis are young families.

I call Farah and she is just getting out of a taxi. She says she has just returned from visiting her relatives in Qadissya. She sat in a room full of fifteen young Iraqi men, all of them her cousins or extended family, who are prime targets for assassination back home. Many have first-hand accounts of brutal killings of family members in 2006, and they have all arrived in the last few months. All felt that despite everything they had lived through since the war began, they now had no choice but to flee.

Their anxieties have shifted since they arrived in Syria. The women are relieved; they have stopped having to fear for their husbands' or sons' lives every time they leave the house, but are now facing new realities. It's not easy getting on in a new country, trying to find work and creating stability for their children, but at least the day-to-day terror has been alleviated. However, they are still plagued with worries about family members they had to leave behind.

Suhad, the mother of the twins who were assassinated, and her remaining son, Haider, have moved to Damascus as well. Farah spent two days walking the streets of the old city while Haider told her the whole story of what had happened to his brothers. I imagine them walking through the tiny alleys, talking and talking. Farah only knew the bare outline of the story, and now he was telling her the details. She promises to relate it to me when she got back. His heart is broken, his life over since his brothers were killed, she says. Even though he is in a new country, starting a new life, he is without hope and says that he will never be able to move on.

His mother is in complete denial. She tells Farah that she feels like all the other mothers who have been forced to send their sons away to Jordan or Syria to protect them. She doesn't feel that her twins are dead, but rather that she has sent them away. So many Iraqi mothers are saying goodbye to their sons, the only difference is that once in a while they will hear from their sons. She does not, will not. That is the only difference, she says.

After Farah and I talk, I call my aunts in London. Amal answers the phone, and I ask if she has heard from Karim in Baghdad.

"Karim is deeply depressed, in despair," she says. "The summer heat in Baghdad is always unbearable, but without running water or air conditioning, fans, refrigeration, it is excruciating."

Usually, families sleep on the roof at night, but with all the helicopters flying low over them, they can't even get proper rest. There is no security, and they don't know when they will be touched by the violence that encroaches, ever closer. They say everyone they know is leaving Baghdad; their street is deserted. My aunts tell Karim to take his family to Jordan or Syria, and that they will help and send him money or even come and meet him there, but he is paralyzed. He and his wife are afraid to leave everything and become exiles. It is difficult to take the children away from all that is familiar, their family and friends. They've never left Iraq.

In the last month, there has been growing pressure on both Sunni and Shia in Karim's neighbourhood. Both sides are threatened by militias who want them to move into separate neighbourhoods. They use kidnapping and blackmail as intimidation. This is reminiscent of what happened in Lebanon during the civil war. Karim is worried that they are going to have trouble in their neighbourhood now. More and more bombs have been going off near his house. Thankfully, the Christians have been left alone by both the Shia and the Sunni, but the violence is so random that no one is immune.

Then Amal tells me that they called Ammu Ibrahim in Lebanon to see how he was. His village has escaped Israeli bombing so far, but he said that Lebanon is wrecked. His wife is gravely ill and was in hospital when the war started. His son lives in the United States and was planning to visit his mother before the war began. Now he can't come. Amal told Ibrahim that she and her sisters were thinking of going to Lebanon this September and had wanted to visit him. They haven't seen him for forty-five years. But now that too is impossible. Ibrahim started crying, saying how much he would love to see them. Amal started crying as well.

I hang up the phone and pick up the newspaper, July 24, 2006. Iraqi Prime Minister Nouri al-Malaki is saying that the breakup of Iraq along sectarian lines is now inevitable.

AERIAL VIEW OF BAGHDAD FROM AN AMERICAN HELICOPTER
PHOTO CREDIT: FARAH NOSH

CHAPTER EIGHTEEN
Iraq Comes to Me

Baghdad is an ancient city, and although it has never ceased to be the capital of the Abbasid Caliphate . . . most of its traces have gone, leaving only a famous name. In comparison with its former state, before misfortune struck it and the eyes of adversity turned towards it, it is like an effaced ruin, a remain washed out; or the statue of a ghost. It has no beauty that attracts the eye, or calls him who is restless to depart to neglect his business and to gaze. None but the Tigris which runs between its eastern and its western parts like a mirror shining between two frames. . . . The city drinks from it and does not thirst, and looks into a polished mirror that does not tarnish.
—Ibn Jubayr, *The Travels of Ibn Jubayr*, 1184

A week before I am due to visit my aunts in London in August 2006, Siham telephones me excitedly. I expect that she is calling about the war in Lebanon, which is intensifying by the day, despite calls for a ceasefire.

"Maha and Reeta are going to try and get a visa to visit us. They are in Amman, Jordan." I haven't heard Siham so animated since before the war began over three years ago.

"Jordan? They left Baghdad?" It takes a moment for me to understand what she means.

"I told them they should get out of there. Their street is a ghost street. Empty. All the families, all their neighbours left the minute that school ended for the summer. Left for Syria or Jordan. I told them they needed to leave as well. Now they are applying for a UK visa there."

"Will they be there when I am in London?" I say, alarmed that I might somehow miss them.

"Yes, they'll be here for weeks. I promise you'll see them when you are here," Siham says.

"How did you convince them to leave Baghdad?"

"I don't know," she says. "In summer, the heat is unbearable. Really, you can't imagine it. Without electricity, there is no air conditioning—it is absolutely stifling. They are bored, trapped inside all the time, and now they can't go out because of the violence. I told them that maybe if they went to Amman, I could meet them there. But now they're there, I told them to try and get a visa to come and see us here. It would be nicer for them to come here. But, of course, the whole family can't come."

"Why not?" I say, my voice rising, indignant.

"The British government would never grant a visa for the whole family. They'd be suspected of wanting to emigrate if they did. And of course wouldn't you want to emigrate? Why not? Since this war, their lives are at risk every day," Siham explains.

For so long, Karim and Maha hadn't wanted to leave their house and belongings, or their elderly, dependent, family members. But now no one is left of the older generation, and they are free to leave. They were also anxious about the trip to Amman, as the road is very dangerous. But finally, they decided they couldn't stand their living situation anymore and risked it all and left without even telling us.

"So just Maha and Reeta are coming?"

"Yes, Karim and Samir will have to stay in Jordan. I don't want to get my hopes up that the visa will be granted, I know how difficult it is even to get a holiday visa. We have to pray," Siham says. "Pray!"

When I hang up, I realize that Amal and Ibtisam haven't seen any of their relatives or friends from Iraq since they left in 1990, and Siham hasn't seen anyone since 1980. To see Maha will be like seeing a sister, not merely a cousin. Maha is an only child, but she spent all her childhood at my grandparents' house, so my aunts are like her older sisters. She is almost twenty years younger than they are, so she is also like a daughter or niece. My aunts have only had snatched conversations with Maha in the last three years because her home phone has never worked since the invasion, and conversations on the mobile are very expensive. But nearly all of those telephone calls contained horror stories or bad news about the family.

Within an incredibly swift two days, their visas are granted and Siham buys their flights to London. What had seemed impossible for weeks, months and years before, and improbable mere days ago, is actually going to happen—the aunties will see their cousin again and meet her fifteen-year-old daughter for the first time. I can't believe that I am finally going to meet my Baghdadi relatives.

⌖

We meet in Amal's living room; in all my fantasizing about meeting my family, I'd always imagined it would happen in their home in Baghdad. My aunts' house was the last place I had ever envisioned seeing each other face-to-face for the first time. But now it seems inevitable that we should meet in London, halfway between my life in Canada and theirs in Iraq. I walk into the living room where they are sitting, waiting. I haven't spoken to either of the women directly before since all my communication has been through Karim, and they don't speak English. My youngest sister, Rose, arrived a few days earlier from Toronto. They all watch me as I walk over to my cousin Maha, who stands up, and we hug warmly, giving each other the traditional three Iraqi kisses on alternating cheeks.

I realize we are almost the same age; she is thirty-nine, four years older than me. But she is the mother of two teenagers, has lived through three wars and a decade of sanctions, and has been trapped in Iraq since she last visited Europe as a child. I am told we met during one of her trips to Europe, but I don't remember it.

Maha is my blood cousin; we have the same great-grandmother, Samira, so Reeta is my second cousin. Maha is not very tall, but is round, heavier than she appeared in the first photographs Farah took in 2003. She has a beautiful face, prominent cheekbones and large dark eyes; she wears her hair short and is dressed in brown trousers and a pale cream blouse. She starts speaking to me in Arabic, but we are looking straight at each other in an intimate way that strangers don't usually share. My Arabic is rudimentary and so we depend on Amal to translate. I am wearing my gold Iraqi-map necklace, and when I hold it up and thank her for sending it to me, Maha smiles.

Then Rose says, "I know Palestinians in Toronto who wear necklaces like that of Palestine."

Maha answers, and Amal translates her sarcasm, "Yes, everyone who has lost their country has to wear one of these necklaces. Wear their country around their neck."

Reeta is sitting on another couch, watching us. I walk over to her and she looks up but doesn't move, so I lean down to give her a hug and three kisses. She slowly unfurls herself and quickly hugs me, embarrassed. Her body is soft and limp. She is far more beautiful in real life than the photos show. She has large brown eyes with such thick long black eyelashes that I am convinced she must be wearing mascara, though Amal had told me on the phone that Reeta doesn't wear makeup yet. She has long thick black curly hair and high cheekbones. She is slender with the shy bearing of a teenager innocent of her beauty. She dresses like many other teenagers around the world, in jeans and a pale pink T-shirt and bright pink running shoes with Velcro straps. Apart from her dark colouring, you wouldn't know that she is Arabic and has never been out of Iraq. But Reeta was born in Baghdad in 1991, just after the Gulf War, grew up under sanctions and became a teenager during the 2003 invasion.

Amal asks me how my flight was. That day there had been a massive terror alert in London after police had uncovered an alleged plot to blow up ten aircraft. I tell them it was strangely easy. Arriving wasn't a problem; it was leaving Heathrow that was said to be practically impossible.

"How was your flight from Jordan, Maha?" I ask.

It was Reeta's first flight, and Maha hadn't flown for twenty-five years.

Amal chimes in, "They were nervous that they wouldn't know what to do, but once they got to the airport, they realized that it was easy."

I look at Reeta and say, "Did you like it?"

She looks at Amal and says softly, "Shinoo?" ("What?" in Iraqi Arabic), but Amal insists I say it more slowly in English, and Reeta understands and nods vigorously, yes, she liked flying.

Karim had told me how he'd tried to explain flying to his children before the war, but they hadn't understood. With the war they'd seen thousands of flying machines, almost all military, but this was the first time either of his children had flown. I'm sure he was sad not to be with Reeta on her first-ever flight.

I ask them how they like English life so far; they have already been in London for a few days. They nod and laugh together like sisters. Their laughs are very light and long.

Siham explains that there is an Arabic expression, which roughly translates as, "You are like a deaf man at a wedding who can't hear the music." You say this to someone if they don't understand what you are saying to them. Maha and Reeta feel like that when they hear English.

But then Maha says, "Life here is so easy, there is nothing to do."

Maha opens her palms and explains that in Baghdad they often have no water supply, and so they have to store water in tanks on the roof. She proceeds to explain the details. They don't get hot or cold water anymore from the taps because the pumps can't work without electricity. In the summer, the temperature outside is over 50 degrees Celsius, and the water heats up naturally in the tanks and they have to carry it down from the roof in pans to use in the house. The only time I ever saw this done was in Lebanon when I visited my great-aunt. But without electricity it is difficult to get cold water. They don't have a steady electricity supply, and so they buy it from a generator set up by a man down the street. They don't know when the generator will be turned on or off, and if they plug in too many appliances, then when the generator comes on there is often a power surge and a fuse is blown. They blame each other when the fuse goes, and this causes arguments about who forgot to turn off the appliances, even though no one knows when the electricity will be on or off.

This summer they had no air conditioning, and sometimes it was so hot that they would just throw water on their smooth stone floors and lay in the water to cool down.

Amal stopped her, repeating in disbelief, "You just lay on the floor of the house to stay cool? Fully clothed?"

And for the first time I heard a phrase that would be repeated often throughout their stay: "But what else can we do?"

"Speaking of water," Maha says in Arabic, laughing again, "when Baghdadis dig wells in their back or front gardens to find water, they often strike oil instead." Of course, this makes them very angry since nothing can be done with it, so they just cover the hole again.

"You can't drink or wash in oil," Amal grumbles.

I ask Maha how Karim is. This is the first time they have been apart since they got married. She says he is all right but deeply traumatized. A few weeks ago, since I'd last heard from him, he was sitting in his car at a police checkpoint waiting to go through. A policeman approached the car two cars ahead of him, and as he got to the car it disappeared in fire and smoke right in front of Karim's eyes. They think it was a suicide bomber. There was only one car between Karim's car and the bombers. Karim's window was open and his arm was resting on the car door. In an instant the whole front of his car and his arm were covered in blood and pieces of flesh. He saw body parts everywhere—of the murdered policeman, the bomber and innocent bystanders. It was a miracle that he wasn't killed or injured. He was so horrified that he drove straight to his brother's house, which was nearby, and had to lie down for several hours to get over the shock until he was well enough to go home. Amal shakes her head as she translates. All I can say is, "Oh my God. He must be distraught." Maha just nods her head gravely. I look at Reeta, wondering what she is feeling as we are talking about her father, but her facial expression betrays nothing.

Amal asks Reeta whether she is afraid at school.

Reeta gives her favourite response, "Yani," which means many things in Iraqi Arabic depending on the context, but here means "kind of."

She pauses, and Amal teases her, "She says yani for everything."

Reeta seems intimidated by her new aunts. They treat her intimately like a daughter, but she doesn't know them and they are a strong force when together. Reeta explains that she was terrified when she first went back to school after the war. At first, every time they heard an explosion they would be sent home by the teachers. Often the windows would shatter. Eventually, the bombs were going off every day, and the students wanted to study, so they stayed at school all day despite the danger. Now they leave the windows open so that they don't shatter. Reeta is so used to the blasts that she doesn't even hear them anymore.

Maha adds, "When I took Reeta back to school after the war ended, I mean, it was months after it ended, but finally they opened the schools. We walked into the school and there were no photographs or images of Saddam Hussein in the halls or classrooms. This terrified us. We were so shocked. We didn't know what it meant. So we immediately left the school again."

Siham reminded us that Saddam had not yet been captured, and everyone was still afraid he might come back. They had lived with his image everywhere for their whole lives, thinking about him every day, and the shock of those pictures being gone was petrifying.

Instead of the jubilation and relief one would expect, there was a strange absence and no one could imagine what might fill it.

"Now the Iraqis are saying that life was better under Saddam," Maha laughs.

"Do they really mean it?" I ask.

"Well, probably only because they know he isn't going to come back. But yes, before, our lives were more stable. Life was very hard, but we could go out, leave the house, go to school and work, we had our life. We had security," she says.

"Do you care about Saddam's trial? Do you watch it on television?" She flicks her hand away and tilts her chin up dismissively.

"We don't care what happens to him. It's over. We know he will die in prison."

Amal changes the subject. She insists they show Maha and Reeta a good time and not talk only about the war incessantly.

"Shall we go to the park later?" she says to Reeta. "She loves the park, we had tea there last night, like a picnic, and she wants us to go there again. They don't go out of the house in Baghdad." But when she asks Reeta if she wants to go to the park, she answers *"yani"* and shrugs her shoulders. "This is a democratic household," Amal jokes. "You are allowed to make decisions here. Oh, these women, they don't want to make decisions, they don't want democracy. They want to be told what to do! That's what they are used to." They all laugh.

In the park, I notice that Reeta doesn't seem to have any muscles. She is slim but her body is slack and soft. I realize the reason is that they never walk anywhere. Reeta is driven to and from school, and stays inside the rest of the time. Maha is upset because she herself has gained weight in the last three years.

"All we do is eat. Cook and eat. We are stressed. So we eat," she says.

It isn't easy for them to walk for a long time, they tire much more quickly than we do, but they love being outside. I see the park through their eyes, a park I walked in most days with my mother when I was a girl. It is a typically English mixture of a carefully pruned garden with a wilder aspect of fields and huge chestnut trees. Reeta doesn't speak much unless we ask her a question. I am chatting away, anxious for us to feel natural, despite everything.

As we walk she tells us how much she hates sleeping on the roof at home now. Her little cot bed is left on the roof especially for that purpose and folded up in the day. Since the invasion, the American helicopters fly so low over Baghdad that Reeta can actually see inside them as they pass over her house; the soldiers, often not much older than herself, sit in the helicopter doors, their legs dangling over the side, their boots and their guns pointed at the sleeping people of the city. They are so close that she can see their faces as they fly over her. The helicopters are painfully loud, she says, and I ask how low they come. Reeta points at a nearby tree and says that they would hang as low as the treetop. It's not very tall, just a little higher than a two-storey house. Reeta sits up in her bed, crouched in her nightgown under her blanket, watching them circle. She hates them and feels angry when she sees these men peering at her while she is trying to sleep.

Suddenly, Reeta cowers behind me in fear, clinging to my arm. I imagine she is remembering her fear and anger, when a dog comes bounding up to us. Amal shouts that Reeta is terrified of dogs. In Iraq people don't keep dogs as pets, and so most are wild street dogs that will bite you and can give you rabies. Amal has explained to her that these English dogs are harmless, even nice, and that people keep them as pets because they are cute, but Reeta doesn't care. She is frozen and won't move until they are gone. I try to tease her lightly, saying that I can't believe she is terrified by dogs, she who has lived the last three years in a war zone.

She frowns and says, "I am used to the war, but I am afraid of dogs."

They have another reason to be afraid of the American helicopters. Maha tells us that near their house one day a helicopter came and hovered in the sky, then three car bombs went off in close succession and soon afterwards the helicopter left the area. Nothing else happened after it had gone. In the absence of any accurate or reliable information, quickly, the rumour went round the neighbourhood that there was a connection between the helicopter and the three bombs. Did they set off the bombs by remote? No one knows. No one knows what the meaning is behind any of the violence in Baghdad anymore and what is connected and what isn't. Rumours run rampant and many Iraqis say that the Americans are deliberately stoking the violence, to keep Iraq on its knees. They can't even gauge what to be afraid of and what to run away from. Death can come from anywhere and be caused by anything.

Maha giggles suddenly.

"Did you hear about the time Lina went out and her car broke down?," she asks. "She didn't know what to do, so she went up to a policeman directing traffic at a roundabout and asked him to help her. (They don't have AA service in Baghdad.)" Amal inserts these parenthetical comments whenever she translates, giving me another dimension of simultaneous translation, cultural interpretation. "He offered to fix her car but only if she would direct traffic while he worked on it. So suddenly, there was Lina, a civilian woman in her sixties, directing the flow of traffic in the centre of the city." Maha chuckles as she tells us this, wiping her eyes at the memory.

Amal says, "She was incredible, Lina was. Did you know that she baked us birthday cakes on our birthdays every year, even when we weren't there? Throughout the whole time we were away, fifteen years, she always remembered and celebrated."

That evening, after the visitors have gone up to bed and we are eating our traditional evening snack of a piece of fruit, Amal reveals to me that Reeta didn't want to come to England for this holiday, didn't want to leave her friends and life in Baghdad. Amal is puzzled because Reeta seems unmoved by England, her eyes don't light up with excitement at any of the sights she has seen so far. She is passive and painfully shy. She is also fretting about her weight, even though she is very slim. She and her friends have made a pact not to gain weight in the summer holidays and so she keeps refusing to eat, and then feeling faint and then repeating the pattern the next day.

The next morning, at the breakfast table, after we have finished eating a traditional English breakfast of sausage, bacon and eggs and all insisted that Reeta eat some of it, I give Amal the gold bracelet and necklace that Farah smuggled out of Iraq in the spring. We all laugh at the irony that Maha could have brought it to Amal herself. I tell them of how Farah almost had the gold confiscated on the way out, and they are horrified and worried at all the trouble they caused her. Maha produces other pieces of jewellery she brought with her: my great-grandmother Samira's wedding ring, a large flat gold oval setting filled with irregular-cut diamonds, and another simple diamond ring in a gold setting. Piece by piece, Iraq is coming back to my three aunts.

Maha tells me that Amal drove her past the house I grew up in, which she remembers visiting as a child when she and her parents came to London. She came with my relatives in one of the family convoys through Europe to England. Her parents have both died since the invasion in 2003. Amal asks Maha what happened to her mother, how she died, even though we've heard bits of the story before.

Maha looks down, pausing to collect herself, then she tells us slowly that in July 2005, a political party that was running in the election set up a campaign office on the street directly behind their house. Maha's mother, who was a widow by then, was still living with the family, but Auntie Lina was already dead. In the run-up to the election, a bomb exploded at the office. Maha and the family were at home, and the force of the blast shattered all their windows and caused the air conditioner to fly from its post and across the room to smash against the next wall. All the cupboards flew open and the contents tumbled out onto the floor. The family ran out of the house and over to the next street to see what had happened. Maha saw the severed arm and head of the suicide bomber on the ground. Maha shakes her head sharply, as if she is trying to dislodge the memory from her mind.

They went back home through the fog of dust created by the explosion. The next day Maha's mother took ill. It was summer and very hot, and again nothing was working. Of course, the air conditioner had been broken in the blast, but it was useless anyway because there was no electricity. Maha's mother was too ill to get upstairs to sleep on the roof, and so Maha stayed inside with her, spraying water on her face periodically to cool her down. She died a few days later of unknown causes. They all believe that the shock of the attack was what killed her. In the photographs Farah took in 2003, Maha's mother looks healthy for her age, with no hint of illness.

"This is usual in war," says Amal. "Maha says that the daughter of a friend of theirs got diabetes when a bomb went off at her school."

"Is that possible?" I ask. "Medically, I mean."

Amal shrugs, "It happened."

I am lost in my thoughts as the conversation continues in Arabic, until I notice that Amal has her arm around Maha who is crying into her palms.

"What's wrong?" I ask.

"She is worried because we told her that the whole family thinks she should talk to a lawyer while she is here," Amal explains. "We want to find out if there is any way she can apply for the family to come to England. They have to get out of Iraq. But she doesn't want to move here and become a refugee. She just wants to stay in Baghdad and for everything to get better."

Reeta leaves the room, taking a few plates with her, but I see she's holding back her own tears. Reeta misses Baghdad already; the idea of leaving forever is tormenting her. Every time the subject comes up, and it does every few hours, she bursts into tears. Even though Iraq is in such anarchy, the British government and many other

Western countries regard the country as "free" since it has held democratic elections. It is more difficult now to apply as a refugee than it was during the years of Saddam's dictatorship.

I see their predicament clearly for the first time. Karim is in his mid-forties; it would be extremely complicated for him to leave everything he has built up in Baghdad and move to an English-speaking country and start again. What would he do? Become a cab driver, a cook? His engineering degree would be worthless, and since he doesn't have a huge sum of money to bring into the country, he would be a refugee. He would be dependent on the charity of the country he arrived in. Reeta is top of her class in Baghdad and wants to be an engineer. But for her to leave Baghdad and move to another school system and do as well in English as she has done there would be very difficult. Her brother is a couple of years younger than her, but suffers the same predicament.

"Maybe if we make a list of all the suffering in your family, like the story you just told us about your mother dying as a result of the bomb blast, maybe the lawyer would be able to argue your case better," I suggest.

Maha nods, wiping her eyes.

Siham asks them, "Tell us, did you know that the war was coming in Iraq? You know, at the beginning?"

Maha answers, "No, no, no. Of course not. We didn't have satellite then, or Internet, or mobile phones, we only knew what Saddam told us. We didn't even know about mobile phones really. There is a joke in Iraq about an old man who is offered a mobile phone, but he won't take it, even though it is free, because he says, 'This one doesn't have a wire. I want a phone with a wire to the wall.'" Maha laughs. "Not that those work anyway. We thought it would be like when the US bombed us in 1998, when they bombed some government buildings in Baghdad. No, we didn't know it was going to be war, invasion and occupation. We knew nothing about what was coming."

I explain that we knew for six months before that the US government was building a case to go to war with Iraq, arguing it at the
UN, and that we knew how massive the bombardment would be,
how they'd been building up the military for the attack, that we all
went to demonstrations to stop the war. I tell them that there was
a huge worldwide demonstration against the war on February 15,
2003, when millions of people around the world took to the streets
to show that they were against this war.

Maha shakes her head. "We knew nothing about this. We didn't
expect anything," she says. "Twenty nights we sat by the walls away
from the windows." Maha moves her chair against the wall and sits in
it, demonstrating and re-enacting what she had done. "Twenty nights
we sat against the walls so we might be safer if the ceiling caved in,
rocking and praying to the Virgin Mary to spare our lives. The plates
on the tables shook as the bombs came over. We could hear the
missiles flying by our house. We were terrified. We thought we
were going to die."

I picture all the houses in Iraq, mud-brick homes in small villages,
concrete apartment blocks, the slums of Sadr City, the suburban
houses of Baghdad, and I realize that for those twenty nights, every
human being was doing the same thing, praying not to be killed,
praying to be saved. Some had their prayers answered, others did not.

"When we went out after the war, the city was unrecognizable—
they bombed so many buildings," Maha adds.

"Like which ones?" Amal wants to know, so she can imagine it.

Maha starts to list all the buildings that were destroyed and how
the corniche along the river which used to be lined with fish restaurants serving *masgouf* is now completely inaccessible.

"You can't walk by the river?" Amal exclaims.

Maha tells her that they don't go out, that you don't go anywhere
anymore.

"You can't cross the city anymore anyway because of the Green
Zone.... We never go to Mansour district anymore," she says. "It is

America," Maha answers when I ask her what she thinks of the Green Zone (now trying to be renamed the International Zone by friendly US media).

"Do you remember there used to be a very nice restaurant in Mansour where they sold the best shwarma in the city?" Siham asks.

"We never go there now," Maha says. "We can't get there. You know the bridge you cross to get there, to get to the area where Saddam's palace was, we cannot even cross that bridge, it has a huge blast wall up. To be honest we can't even see the bridge anymore. To get to the other side of Baghdad would take all day and it would be far too dangerous."

"So you didn't see the statue of Saddam coming down in the square?" I knew it was a stupid question, but the image was iconic in the West.

"What? No, of course not. We didn't have electricity, television or telephone! We saw it much later," Maha responds.

"So how did you know the Americans had entered Baghdad?"

"We saw them." Reeta says quietly.

"You saw some soldiers?" I ask Reeta. She nods.

Maha answers for her, "Our neighbours came to the house and told us that there were American tanks nearby. We live near the street that you have to take to get into the centre of the city. We saw the colossal convoy of tanks and black army cars and soldiers entering the city. They came right near our street. Everyone went into the streets to watch them enter. They were waving at the people; people were just standing, watching them. A few tanks were stationed in our neighbourhood. The people were angry, not happy. The Americans tried to throw people chocolate."

"Soldiers threw chocolate to all of you who had been through all that?" I say in disbelief. "How long were you there watching?"

"All day. They had so many tanks and cars and guns. It took all day for the convoy to pass us," Reeta adds.

I realize that I hadn't seen that image of the American army taking the city. What did the convoy look like? What did the endless

American military machine sound like when it was roaring into the city?

"There were fires burning all around Baghdad. Saddam had started fires with oil. He thought that the US missiles wouldn't be able to see the targets through the smoke," Maha says.

"These were Iraq's famous weapons of mass destruction, our sophisticated technology. Smoke from oil fires," Amal states.

"And to think that we thought it would be heaven the day we got rid of Saddam Hussein. We'd dreamed of it for so long," Maha says bitterly. "Reeta was sad, she cried but she had only known sanctions and Saddam Hussein. But it was so painful living under sanctions for anyone who knew life before." She pauses. "Karim told you about the family we know who were shot as the Americans entered the city?"

"Yes."

"That was so terrible," says Siham after Maha tells her the story, since she hadn't heard it before.

"Yes, we were so lucky that we weren't one of the people who were killed," Maha says. "A few days after the Americans entered Baghdad, we all went to Karim's parents' house. We had to make sure they were all right. Just as we were turning the key into their front door, a house two doors down was struck with a bomb. It was a cluster bomb. Shrapnel flew out and whizzed past my head." Maha touches her head, and you can tell that she still hears the sound of the shrapnel escaping past her skull. It shattered all the windows in Karim's parents' house. "We hadn't even entered the house yet. We ran into the streets crying and ended up running to your house, where Lina was staying." They stayed there for a whole day, too traumatized and terrified to risk going home.

"Oh, we are so lucky no one was killed that day," she continues. "You know, during the war, when elderly people died, no one could take them anywhere to be buried; it was too dangerous. So they buried them in their own gardens. And when the war was over they went and dug them up and reburied them in the proper way.

Imagine, their own parents or grandparents."

We sit in silence. Reeta and Maha remembering, Amal and I imagining.

"And you know, when they invaded, they should have thought about security," Maha says angrily. "They just destroyed government ministries and didn't stop people looting, even at the university. We heard that the Americans came with their tanks and destroyed the front doors and encouraged people to come in, saying, 'Go and take everything, it was all Saddam's. . . . Now it is yours.' That's what they said."

"They saw it as giving it back to the people," I offer tentatively.

"But it belonged to Iraq as a whole, not just to be taken by anyone. It was robbery."

We all sit silent.

Then I ask, "Has anything been rebuilt? Have you seen anything new?"

She laughs. "No, nothing has been rebuilt. You know before, we had no suicide bombers, no problems between Sunni and Shia. Ambassador Paul Bremer was the one who talked about the Sunni triangle. What's the Sunni triangle? I've never heard of it. And we had security."

Maha adds, "You know, they say that American soldiers who are killed in Iraq, who don't have American citizenship, are buried out in the desert. They don't want to bother sending their bodies back home. Too expensive."

No one knows if this is true or not, but after everything that has happened, it seems a plausible rumour.

⚜

The next day, we take Maha and Reeta into central London for the first time. Once settled on the train to Victoria, Reeta says matter-of-factly, "This is the first time I have been on a train."

"A lot of firsts on this trip for Reeta," says Amal. "First time on a plane, a train, and what about buses?"

"No, I've never been on a bus either," she says.

"How did you sleep, Leilah?" Amal asks. I tell them I had hardly slept thinking about all the stories they'd been telling me about the war. Rose and I had stayed up very late, talking about all their tales, and how hard it was to comprehend that Maha and Reeta had experienced all that they had.

Amal translates, giggling, "Oh, they slept so soundly, like logs. It's funny that you were feeling stressed about their stories. They forgot all about them when they went to bed."

I look out the window, the familiar route into London, showing the backs of houses and straggly gardens, and I wonder how it looks to Reeta. I imagine the landscape she is used to experiencing in Baghdad—a ruined city, blackened buildings, poverty, beggars, street children, markets, noise, music blaring from dented old cars, tension on people's faces, fear. Once we arrive at Victoria Station, we get straight onto a double-decker bus and clamber to the top deck, seating Reeta and Maha in the front so they can watch London unfolding below them.

The bus goes past all of London's landmarks. We point out Westminster Abbey, the Parliament Buildings where Blair and the British government decided to go to war, Downing Street where Blair and his family live, Trafalgar Square and Leicester Square. We find ourselves getting off at Oxford Street. Even though Baghdad is a populous capital city, London's population is overwhelming. I see all the shoppers through my cousins' eyes, and the prices, when compared to those in Iraq, are astronomical.

"You can get everything in Baghdad; jeans are only about five pounds," Amal tells me.

We duck into a bookstore when it starts to drizzle, and while we are browsing, Maha says, "You know, Uncle Daoud wrote a book."

We all turn and stare at her.

"What about?" I ask.

"When he died, he was writing a book, he hadn't finished it. It was a book about everything America had done in Iraq. It's a history book. His second wife has the manuscript. But it is written by hand in Arabic script," Maha says.

"Did she keep it? His wife?" I hadn't even known he had remarried to, it turns out, one of his first wife's cousins.

"I don't know, I think she still might have it."

"I wonder if we could get a hold of it," I say.

"It's in Arabic though," Maha repeats.

"I'd love to read it. I'm sure my father would too."

"We'll see if we can find it."

For Reeta and Maha, seeing such a swarm of people out in the streets is a novelty.

"That is the biggest difference," Maha says, "between here and Iraq. Here, everyone is going about their business without fear. Unless people are at home in Baghdad, they are afraid. They can't go anywhere, nowhere, without fear. And, of course, Baghdad is in ruins compared to London, but we are used to that now."

We stop in a trendy pub that serves food. Maha asks Rose and I if we've ever worked in a restaurant.

"Of course," I respond.

They think it is very funny that we have worked. Maha went straight from school to being a wife and mother. Many Iraqi women have careers but they go straight into university and don't take part-time jobs in restaurants while studying. We explain that many women in the West get jobs when they are young, sometimes to pay for their tuition. An Iraqi friend of Amal's has a son close to Reeta's age who is working at a Salvation Army shop in order to make his application for medical school more appealing. He's asked if Reeta wants to come with him for the day. Maha is trying to decide if she should let Reeta go. Reeta really wants to work in the shop, and no one seems to notice the irony of a young Iraqi girl working at a charity shop in Britain.

Then they start to quiz us about whether we drink alcohol.

I say, "Yes, we like drinking wine but not really beer."

They had seen the pubs closing in a town near my aunt's house where they'd gone out for dinner before we arrived.

"The girls were wearing such short skirts and high heels," Maha remarks. "One girl was falling over in the street, right beside a policeman. But he didn't do anything. In Iraq, he would have slapped her face and sent her home to her family. But he just ignored her. It was disgusting. Everyone was so drunk. We saw two people being sick in the street. Why do they do it?"

Rose and I look at each other.

Rose answers, "Well, I guess they think it is fun."

"Fun? Would you do that for fun?" Maha asks.

All the women are looking at us.

"No, not like that. But that is what people do," I say.

"They should see what it is like to live with suicide bombs going off all the time. Then they might know what life is really about." Maha just shakes her head.

Luckily, our food is served and, distracted, we stop the discussion.

Over coffee, the conversation turns to the Gulf War.

"What did you think the reason for that war was then?" Rose asks Maha.

Maha says, "I remember, we woke up one morning, and they told us on the news that there was a coup in Kuwait. No one was to leave Iraq, and the popular army was being called up to get ready to help the Kuwaiti people. That's what they said. On television they showed a group of men wearing *dishdashas* who were said to be responsible for the coup. Remember, this was in 1990, only two years after the disastrous war with Iran ended. The next day we realized that they had actually invaded Kuwait."

"Did you know why they did it?" I ask.

"Kuwait was stealing our oil, apparently," Maha says. "They said the Kuwaitis were provoking our Iraqi honour saying things like, they can buy an Iraqi girl for one dinar. Because Iraq was so poor after the war with Iran. They say that the American embassy gave the green light. Of course, Iraqis didn't want another war. Exhausted soldiers who had finally been released from army duty after ten or fifteen years were called up again. The sanctions began on August 3, 1990."

"Did you know that the UN was preparing for war against Iraq?" Rose wanted to know.

"We knew that the UN was telling Saddam to leave Kuwait," Maha confirms. "People were withdrawing money beforehand and buying as much as they could because they knew that there would be shortages. On January 16, the Iraqi news announced that the UN had given an ultimatum that the Iraqi army had to leave Kuwait, but they didn't. At 4:00 a.m. the bombardment started and went on for forty days, until February 28. Until the 2003 war, it was the worst days of my life. Each night we went down into the shelter, about twenty of us . . . it was in a private hospital near our house that was owned by our neighbours. There were no windows. We prayed in the shelter mostly. One night there was a massive noise, and we were suddenly thrown aside. The whole building was shaking, falling apart; we thought that the building was collapsing on us. I was pregnant with Reeta. We were terrified, but we had to go out because we were afraid that the building would fall in on us. When we got out we saw that they had hit the telephone exchange next door. The policeman came and asked us where the bomb was. That was the first thing the Americans did; they cut communications. There was no telephone, no bridges. The bombing was less intense during the day. It would start at around seven at night and go until seven in the morning. There were no shops open. Once in a while a little shop would open, and we could get bread. We had our rations; the rationing had started before the war. We got black flour, rice, sugar, tea, oil and soap. No fruit or vegetables. By the second day of the war, white bread began to look brown; they were mixing something else into it. We think it was ground date stones."

I remembered the stall on Denman Street in Vancouver that I had stopped at in 2000; they had had a sample of the small rations that Iraqis received because of the UN-imposed sanctions. At the time I couldn't believe that this was how my own relatives were living on the other side of the world.

"From 1990 to 1997, we got the same rations every month," Maha continues. "The food usually lasted for about ten days. Everything else you had to pay for, but it was very expensive. You couldn't afford a kilo of rice or half a kilo of sugar. Before we used to buy it in huge sacks, but we couldn't anymore. After 1997 when the UN started the Food for Oil program, we got enough food to last a month, dry beans, lentils, powdered milk. We made our own bread, pita bread on the Aladdin stove, you know the one?" I knew from my time in Beirut about these stoves on which many people in the Middle East cooked and made tea, and sat around for heat in the winter. "So you know the Aladdin. I love it. But fruit and vegetables were very difficult to find then."

"What did you do all day when the Gulf War was happening?" I ask her.

"Lina was living with us, and we stayed inside mostly. We went to your house once a week; we'd take an oil lamp and make sure everything was all right. It was winter, and we didn't have oil or petrol. We had no heating. It was very cold," Maha explains. "You know, one of our cousins had to go and fight in this war. He was the kind of gracious young man that everyone wants in their family. He'd be the first to put up a curtain rail, fetch watermelons from the market or fix the roof. He was conscripted into the army. He had been doing a business studies diploma and he was sent to the front line without any history of being in the army, near the border between Saudi Arabia and Kuwait. After a few days of training he came back to visit his parents and brothers. They begged him not to go back to the front because they knew it would be a disaster for him. But he was afraid that if he deserted the army Saddam's men would bring him back to the house and kill him in front of his parents. So he went back, and on the second day of fighting he was killed anyway. His body was brought back to the house in a cardboard coffin on the roof of a car. His father, your great-uncle Edward, had a heart attack at the same time, but maybe you know this story. He knew he wouldn't survive anyway."

His brother Nusrat was already a cripple because of a wound he received as a conscript in the Iran–Iraq War. Then he'd spent five years as a prisoner of war in Iran and finally returned to Iraq a changed man. His life was over, his youth shattered.

"What did you think of the Americans at that time?" I ask Maha.

"We didn't know anything about America," Maha says. "We thought that it was the United Nations who made war on us. But now Iraqis are thinking back to the first war, now that we have had this second war, and they are wondering whether the Americans tricked Saddam so they could have an excuse for a base in Saudi Arabia. We are starting to notice a pattern, connections."

TWO SCHOOLGIRLS WALK PAST AMERICAN TROOPS

PHOTO CREDIT: FARAH NOSH

Chapter Nineteen

A Letter from
the City of Peace

*Iraq is in the throes of the largest refugee crisis in the Middle East since the
Palestinian exodus from Israel in 1948, a mass flight out of and within the
country that is ravaging basic services and commerce, swamping neighbour-
ing nations with nearly 2 million refugees, according to the United Nations
and refugee experts. The UN High Commissioner for Refugees, which
appealed for $60 million in emergency aid last week, believes 1.7 million
Iraqis are displaced inside Iraq, whose prewar population was 21 million.
About 50,000 Iraqis are fleeing inside Iraq each month, the United Nations
said. Roughly 40 percent of Iraq's middle class is believed to have fled....*
—Carolyn Lochhead, "Iraq Refugee Crisis Exploding," *San Francisco
Chronicle*, January 16, 2007

Now that the six of us women have been living together for a few
weeks, we have developed a morning routine. Siham and Amal get
up early and go to work. The remaining four of us wake up, Ibtisam
and Maha usually first, then me and finally Reeta. Rose has gone
back to Toronto. We have breakfast together: strong English tea,
pita bread and *lebne*, sliced tomato and cucumber dressed in olive oil,
clotted cream and jam and toast. The clotted cream reminds Ibtisam
of the buffalo cream they ate in Baghdad. They'd take their own
plate to the farmer who would boil the water buffalo milk and then
skim the cream off the top.

Today, we sit outside in the garden. The September sun is bright and warm for England, and the pears fall off the trees with an occasional thud. The fruit is collecting in various stages of rotting at the foot of the tree, so we pick a pear or two to have with our breakfast and find that they are small and ugly but taste fresh and sweet. We clear the dishes from the table and tidy everything away in the kitchen. We have spent weeks discussing Maha and Reeta's fate: What countries could they apply to? How could they leave Iraq? Would England or Canada take them? To Ibtisam and me, the situation is urgent, but to them, it feels as if they think they have time to spare. They are paralyzed by the dilemma.

Reeta makes Turkish coffee and brings it out to us in tiny coloured cups decorated with butterflies. By now I am used to hearing Arabic. I recognize many of the words, and translating has become more natural. I know that someone will translate if there is something I need to hear. Otherwise, I am free to observe and be in my own thoughts.

Maha looks around the garden. "If I lived here, the only thing I would miss about Iraq would be my house."

Ibtisam translates. "She says, 'If I could pick up my house and bring it to England, with everything still inside it, then I would be happy, I wouldn't miss anything else about Iraq.'"

"What about people? Her friends, her culture? Language?" I ask.

Maha laughs her tinkly laugh. "No, just the house and everything in it."

Ibtisam continues, "She loves her house. She doesn't like the houses here. To her, they aren't...homey. They don't feel like home to her; she can't explain it. But I know what she means; I felt the same way when I first moved here. The houses are so different in Baghdad; it was hard to feel really comfortable in an English house. The style is different. I didn't want to live here when I first came."

"And now?" I ask.

"I feel better, I am used to it. I don't know if I could go back. I've changed," Ibtisam says softly.

"So, if you could stay in Iraq, if it wasn't for the war and lack of security, would you want to stay even with everything you've been through?" I ask Maha and Reeta.

By now Maha can understand my statements or questions in English if I speak slowly. "Yes, of course, but we have to leave somehow. We don't have a choice, there is no future there. It is over."

Ibtisam has tears in her eyes; she didn't choose to leave Baghdad either, fifteen years ago. She hesitates before she says anything, and I look at Maha and Reeta. They have both started to weep.

Ibtisam continues, "It isn't easy to leave your country behind. I miss people there still. I miss our house. Even if it is a ruin now. And the garden? How is it?" Maha doesn't answer her. "You see, it is different there. People don't move house easily, they don't buy and sell property and move around. Your house is your house, and if you have children you build an annex and you hope that your son will live with you and his family too. So a house is really important to us. Your house is your life."

I try to lighten the mood. "I guess you should never have left Maha in charge of looking after our house then, if she's let it become a ruin."

Ibtisam manages a smile. It was actually Lina who was taking care of it until she died.

Reeta is weeping hard into her palms. I want to know what she is crying for.

Ibtisam says, "She misses Iraq so much. You have to remember she has never left Iraq before, everything she knows is Iraq. She likes being here on holiday, but if you suggest that she could stay here, go to school here, and not go back, she starts to cry."

"Even though she is free to do everything here that she can't do there? She still wants to go back there?" It seems impossible to me that they would go back to that horror. We catch glimpses of what is happening there on the news every evening. Every time we talk about it, Maha simply shrugs. "I know, but what can we do? This is our life."

"But you could come to Iraq, Ibtisam. You could come and see your house," Reeta says, wiping her eyes. "You have an Iraqi passport, you could come back with us."

"Yes, but we couldn't be responsible for you if you came," Maha adds. "If you were killed, we couldn't be responsible for your decision to return to Baghdad."

Then Reeta turns and looks at me with a cheeky glow in her eyes, and sweeping her finger across her neck says, "You couldn't come. If you came to Baghdad, they would cut off your head." She giggles.

"Are you serious?" She looks at me with big dark eyes, repressing her mischievous smile and nodding hard.

"Yes, she is," Maha agrees. "You couldn't come. They would know you were a foreigner. You don't speak Arabic. They'd know right away and you'd be targeted."

"I would not speak while I am there." I wink at Reeta, covering my mouth with my palm.

Ibtisam smiles a little. "No, it is impossible, it is too dangerous. Impossible. They would kidnap you for ransom if they found out about you."

Ibtisam starts crying again. I touch her arm. "What is it?"

She doesn't say anything but continues to cry. She doesn't even try to control it, and it is the first time I've seen her break down over everything. I wait. Finally, she stops and says, "I don't think I will ever go back. I want to, I thought maybe we could. But we can't go back now, and things are getting worse. I think we have to realize that we have to sell the house. We should get rid of everything and sell it. Even now we wouldn't get anything for the house. Who would buy a house now? But we have to accept that we aren't going back. Now is the time to sell everything, give the new things to the poor, and get back the valuable sentimental things. It is time. We are never going back."

I am shocked to hear Ibtisam say this. I have never heard her speak about the house so decisively. Our whole family has waited for so long for stability in Iraq so that we could go back.

Then she adds, "Of course, it is your father's decision."

"Reeta is afraid of your house. She used to go and stay the night with Lina. To her, it is an old house with high ceilings and full of ghosts. Lina kept it exactly the way it was when you left. Exactly. We don't like visiting old houses, even museums here, they are creepy," Maha says. "It's sad, there were ten or twelve beautiful old carpets all rolled up with mothballs inside. But the moths got them, ate away at them. Now they are ruined."

My father's inheritance had disintegrated before he'd had a chance to claim it.

Reeta nods, and says to Ibtisam, "I used to stay in the house, and sleep in your beds, a different one each time, and look in your drawers and cupboards. Sometimes I would try on your clothes, playing dress-up, and as I got older, your jewellery. I wasn't supposed to touch anything because Lina was looking after everything for you. Leaving it as it was. But I couldn't help playing with it, and I didn't know you." She says this by way of apology.

I'd always imagined the house as slowly decaying as only an unlived-in house can do. I never pictured my aunts' clothes still hanging in the closets, their jewellery on the dressing table or in their jewellery boxes. I'd never pictured the physical remnants of the life Ibtisam left to go on holiday in 1990 and never returned to. Now I added the picture of Reeta, who had not been born when she left, going through her aunts' clothes and jewellery. She even went so far as borrowing some clothes for this trip, without knowing Aunt Ibtisam, never having met her. It must have felt like going through someone's belongings after a funeral. Except it was more like looking through a used-clothing store; she didn't know the person who had once worn them. They were mere objects again. And yet, she did know that they belonged to Ibtisam and so she felt strangely responsible while she rummaged through her things. But Ibtisam could hardly remember what she had left behind.

"Do you know there is a painting of Safita there? Painted by Ammu Ibrahim," Ibtisam says to me.

"Really, he painted Safita?" I thought of all the paintings surrounding Ammu Ibrahim in his house in northern Lebanon. "We wouldn't want to lose that painting, would we?"

"No, no, we wouldn't," Ibtisam says slowly. "It's very important."

How could we decide to give it all up? After all that waiting, would we just abandon it all, decide that we couldn't wait anymore? It was the same for Maha and Reeta. When would they know that living in Baghdad was too dangerous, that they had to save their lives by leaving everything behind and becoming refugees? I didn't realize until then that for many refugees leaving home was a deliberate choice. One day it is necessary to depart with nothing rather than stay with everything, because all you have is worthless. We were watching the value being drained from Iraq, the oil, the people, the culture, the heritage, the educated, and it was happening so quickly.

"Do you know what else we found there? Did your father ever tell you about the newspaper he wrote?" Maha asks.

I didn't know what she was talking about.

"We found a newspaper that your father must have created when he was a boy, maybe eleven or twelve years old. It has stories about all the people in the house, mostly what the women were doing, what they were cooking, eating, who was there and who wasn't, who was visiting. He must have done it every day one summer. Did he ever tell you about this?" Maha asks me again.

My father is someone who hardly writes notes, never mind letters, and so a newspaper was completely out of character. I had imagined him as a boy who played backgammon and chess, collected stamps, never as a writer. When I asked him about this later, he laughed.

"I don't remember doing that at all. I'd completely forgotten about it. I must have been so bored!" he said.

I picture my father as a boy in a house full of women. Their activity centres on domestic duties, and perhaps his friends in the neighbourhood aren't around for the summer. I imagine a young man observing all the goings-on of a busy household, recording all these seemingly trivial details of life. A life that is now lost and gone.

"Don't throw that away!" I say to Maha, "I want that newspaper!" It was a direct record of a time that my father hardly remembers and finds difficult to describe, something that would give me the essence of life in his boyhood household. This is what I'd wanted from him. My father echoes me when I tell him about it.

"We should get that. It would be funny to read it now!" he says.

We finish our coffee and as no one remembers how to read the meaning of the future in the coffee grounds as many Arabs like to, we go back inside. We discuss what we will cook together for dinner. Ibtisam wants Maha to show her a simple zucchini dish that she's forgotten how to make, and I want them to teach me how to make some Arabic meals. Soon the garlic is frying and the tomato paste is added and I watch while Maha scrapes the wooden spoon back and forth along the bottom of the pan. The smells fill the kitchen. Ibtisam has an electric stove, but Maha is used to cooking with gas or on the Aladdin.

When Siham and I were out buying the vegetables at the Iraqi store nearby the day before, Siham reminded me that Reeta's entire childhood had been spent under sanctions. We stood filling plastic bags with tomatoes, cucumbers, zucchini, fresh parsley, lettuce, figs and apples.

"They didn't have fruit and vegetables then," Siham explains. "You should ask Maha about it. You know, they couldn't get chocolate under sanctions. So the children had no sweets. So you know what Aunt Lina used to do? She had some sugar cubes from before, who knows how old they were, because you couldn't get sugar cubes in the shops under sanctions, but somehow she had them. And she would give them to the children, Reeta and her brother, after meals as their sweets. One sugar cube each."

While I watch Maha cooking, I am prompted to ask her how they lived under sanctions. She looks at the fridge.

"We didn't have a fridge; it didn't work without electricity, so we just bought things day to day. We had little to no electricity until 1998 since there were no parts for power stations," Maha says. "And we kept everything, we never threw any food away and we always ate the leftovers. Our bread was made with a mixture of flour and wood chips ground down, to make the flour go further. If anyone did go to Jordan for any reason, everyone would beg them to bring back bread. People became very poor very quickly; they were selling things like their doors and windows just to live. We didn't have any new material for clothes, so we had to take old clothes and cut them up and remake them. Nothing was imported. Now we can buy anything in Iraq. But it is so expensive."

Maha sighs, lost in thought.

"We had no planes, so no one went anywhere," she continues. "And if you could get an exit visa somehow, no one would give you an entry visa to come into another country. We were totally isolated from the world. When Reeta was a few months old, we had no electricity and so we had to call around to our friends and family to find out who had electricity for heat. It was so cold at our house in the winter, and I was worried about Reeta. Finally, one of my uncles said he had electricity and we went there to get warm. After 1998 we had power, but it was two hours on and two hours off."

The zucchini pieces sizzle and splatter as Maha drops them expertly into the pan.

"So is anything easier now?" I ask her.

"Shall I tell you what my day is like these days? A normal day for me now?"

I hand her the can of tomatoes and she tips the contents into the pan.

"I wake up and if I have heard bombing in the night, the first thing I do is call all my friends and relatives on my mobile to make sure everyone is all right. We don't have electricity, and sometimes we can't get gas for the cooker."

"So it's difficult to make tea and breakfast?"

"Since we don't have water in the tap, we need a motor to pump water into the taps," Maha says. "When there isn't electricity we can't do that. We have to get the water from the tanks. Some people have generators to supply them with electricity. There is one in our neighbourhood that supplies everyone on the street. When the electricity comes on later in the day, we might have five hours with none and then an hour on from the government. But electricity from the generator is very expensive. So no, no hot water. In winter we heat it on the Aladdin stove if we have gas. But in the summer, like I said before, the water in the tanks on the roof is boiling hot, so we fill pans and wait until it cools to use it in the evening."

"Is there a school bus to take the children to school every day?" I ask.

"No, no. They go with ten other children with their driver who has been driving them for years," she explains. "The car is an old station wagon. My son used to sit at the back because he was one of the youngest, but he is moving closer to the front as he grows up." She laughs. "No one uses public transport, it's far too dangerous."

She continues stirring the tomato sauce, sprinkling dry mint on the surface and whirling it through the sauce.

Once they have left for school, Maha has to dust the house. "There is so much dust everywhere, and on our clothes."

"Do you have a washing machine?"

"We have four."

"Four?" I ask, surprised.

Ibtisam pipes up, "It's because before, under Saddam, you never knew what would be in the government shops day to day, and whether what was there today would ever come back for sale. So we used to go shopping every day and just buy multiples of whatever was being sold that day. One day they would bring in dishwashers and everyone would buy three or four because if they broke down, you didn't know when you'd be able to find a new one. The next day would be fridges or washing machines, and so on."

"Lots of people sold these extra machines under sanctions," Maha adds, then reminds Ibtisam, "Did you know you have a whole wardrobe at your house full of brand-new towels, never used. And sets of dishes, all still in the boxes. And a suitcase full of new nightgowns. Never used."

Ibtisam nods, a little ashamed.

"Did you have to sell things under sanctions?" I ask.

"Well, my husband had a job, so not really," Maha says. "But my mother had to sell some of her gold because her pension wasn't enough to survive on and the price of living was going up and up all the time."

I ask her whether they had air conditioners.

"We have an air cooler. The air conditioner was broken in that bomb blast I told you about. Really you need one in every room in Baghdad. We only have one air cooler which uses less electricity, and we do everything in one room in the summer, sleeping, eating, we all live in one room. The rest of the house isn't usable in the heat."

By now Maha's put the lid on the pot, and the zucchini is simmering in the tomato and mint sauce. She turns the heat down.

"Now we just leave it to bubble for a while," she says to me.

"What about the rest of your day?" I ask.

She brings her hands together, almost into a prayer position.

"I just spend my time worrying. When the children are at school and my husband at work, I just worry until they come home. I usually hear two or three bombs close by every day. I call them when I hear explosions to make sure they are alive. I only go out to the neighbourhood shops. I don't drive anymore. I am too afraid."

I ask her why she stopped driving.

"There is no petrol sometimes, and so people have to queue up, sometimes all night, to get it. This in a country we know is swimming in oil," she says sarcastically. "There is a queue for men and one for women, and the women's queue is shorter. So often I was the one to go and fill up the car. One day I went to fill up the car and I didn't see the American tanks coming and I just passed them. It was very dangerous, and they could have opened fire. If you go in front of an American tank, they can kill you. There is a new law that you have to leave a hundred metres between you and the American convoy. All the streets and pavements are destroyed because of the tanks. They go anywhere they want. Anyway, now the people can't queue all night."

"Why not?"

"Curfew. Everyone is at home by seven. The curfew is from 9:00 p.m. to 6:00 a.m. And on Friday the curfew is in the day too, from 11:00 a.m. to 3:00 p.m. You are afraid all the time; afraid of policemen, American soldiers, kidnappings, bombs, militias, check-points. Now they stop you and ask you if you are Sunni or Shia and they decide whether to kill you. I never go out alone now."

"Do you have guards on your street?" I'd heard of local check-points being set up in different neighbourhoods.

"Yes, we employ guards, as we did in Saddam's time, as we had many people stealing cars then. At that time, the guards just walked in the street, and if they saw a stranger in the car they would stop him and see who it was. After the war, they bought some guns. It is more like a deterrent," she says.

"So what do you do in the evenings?" I ask her.

"We just watch television if there is electricity. We used to go out to social clubs, swimming pools on days off, now, nothing," Maha states.

"What do you hope for the future?"

She laughs. "I just want everything to go back to normal, normal life, as it is here in England. In Iraq, there is always something. Like under Saddam, they forced you into a job and you had no choice; you couldn't leave your job. Everything was forbidden. You could be hung if you left your job. And now everything is forbidden because there is no security. I just want things to go back to normal."

☒

Later that evening we gather around the computer. Maha speaks to Karim and Samir in Jordan every day via Yahoo Messenger. She has never been separated from them, so these weeks have been hard on the whole family. Ibtisam has bought a webcam so that the family can see each other. Tonight, we are all there when Karim calls. Everyone adjusts their hair and clothes because we can see ourselves onscreen, and then we answer the phone. There is a webcam on the computer that Karim is using, and we see him wearing a headset. He is there with his other relatives who have also escaped Baghdad to Amman for the summer. We all greet one another, and I say hello to him. We are seeing each other for the first time.

"Hello, Leilah," he replies.

His voice is familiar but he looks different than in the photographs I'd seen of him. He is saying the same thing to Ibtisam and Maha in Arabic, that I look different from the photographs he's seen of me. Then Ibtisam and I leave the family to speak in private.

After the call, we all congregate in the study and chat, while Siham plays on the computer. Siham decides to try to find her house in Baghdad on Google Earth. This site uses satellite photographs to guide you in aerial views of cities all over the world; you can "fly from space to your neighbourhood." The images are three-dimensional, so not only can we "fly" like a helicopter over the city, but we can also swoop down and almost see the city from the angle of a pedestrian. We can zoom up and down like Peter Pan.

In the box labelled "fly to," Siham types "Baghdad, Iraq," and the earth turns and we soar through a cloud until that clears and we see the centre of the city in detail. Quickly, we are gliding over the prairie flatness of Baghdad, the sand-coloured buildings laid out in a grid around the green river, which you feel moving sluggishly through the city. We keep falling closer and closer through the sky, and we zero in on the neighbourhood where our house stands and where Karim and Maha still live. We can see the flat roofs of the houses and the green of the trees; the city looks open and peaceful. But then the detail gets blurry again and we can't get any closer, can't see the checkpoints or the blast walls or the fortifications around the Green Zone. Suddenly, we are hovering over the house, looking down on the roof.

"This is our house," says Ibtisam.

"Which one?" I lean in. I see a beige square shape and a green square behind it, and then a bigger square of green. "Is that your garden?"

"No, that is the neighbour's garden. She has two gardens, they are very large. That is our garden," Ibtisam says, pointing to the screen.

"It's not very far from the river," I remark.

"No, but we can't go near the river anymore." Maha sighs wistfully.

I watch Ibtisam closely; this is as near to her house as she has come in fifteen years. I can see Ibtisam mentally filling in the gaps between what she can see and what she remembers. I don't point out that there are areas on the map where there are the traces of buildings—they look like watermarks—in the centre of the city; faint lines where government buildings or army buildings that have been destroyed used to be. I don't know if Ibtisam notices them. My mind strains to see the house. I have seen old photographs and now I know where it is situated in the city. But I have a bird's-eye view, not a human view. I can't get any closer.

"Let's drive to your house," Ibtisam says playfully to Maha.

"Do you remember how to get there?" I ask.

"Of course." Ibtisam moves the cursor down the street, turning left and right a few times until we are hovering over Maha's street. "It isn't far."

"Oh no, we live close to your house," Maha says.

Now we hover over their roof.

"That's where you sleep?" I say to Reeta. "That's where you see the helicopters?"

"Yes, they fly lower than this," Reeta says.

"Is it every night?" I ask her.

"Yes, usually one, two or three fly around each night," she explains.

"Do you know what they are doing?"

"Sometimes they are protecting high-ranking Americans in the streets below, and so they are watching for anyone behaving suspiciously. Or they are just checking on the neighbourhood," Reeta replies quietly.

Now that I had this view, I could imagine it vividly.

"Tomorrow we'll fly to Vancouver," says Siham, closing down the program. "And see your house."

I want to keep looking; I want to see the Green Zone, Fardis Square, Saddam's palaces, the huge embassy the Americans are building, Sadr City, the Palestine Hotel, the mosques, the bridges, the churches.

"You can't see the Palestine Hotel from the outside anymore," Maha says. "The road is closed to the Palestine and the Sheraton. It's a dead-end street with a huge blast wall at the front; you can only go in if you are staying there . . . mostly Americans and foreigners stay now."

"Isn't that where you had your wedding reception, Maha?" I remembered Amal saying that. At the time, all I knew about the Palestine Hotel was that it was where all the foreign reporters stayed before and during the war.

"Yes, I got married there. In 1988, after the Iran–Iraq War and before the Gulf War," Maha says.

Reeta is very shy and hardly opens any conversation. When we are alone, I can talk to her and she understands enough English to reply with a soft yes or no, but she can't expand on anything I say. I invite her for walks in the park with me, and her face lights up in excitement, but she is silent. As we walk through the lush summer greenery, I speak to her, chatting away about our lives, the differences, the similarities and when we might see each other again, and she nods or shakes her head. I am never sure what she is getting so it is a strange, one-sided conversation. I find it hard to just walk in silence. I feel that there is too much I want to talk to her about.

But during our time in London, we've built up an older sister, younger sister relationship. When I come back to my aunts' house from meetings in London, I phone and tell the women which train I will be on. Reeta insists that they come and meet me at the local station. I get off the train, she and Amal or Maha are there too, and Reeta rushes up and gives me a hug, giggling shyly at my surprise since they never tell me if they are going to be there or not.

We take them to the seaside because Reeta has never seen the sea before. She loves it, and again, we have a silent walk along the water, almost an hour long. I am full of emotion, thinking that she'd never enjoyed the simple pleasure of going to the beach with her brother when she was little. We dip our feet in the sea and look out over the water. All I can think is that they have to go back to Baghdad.

At my aunt's house one evening, I say, "Ibtisam, ask Reeta if she looks forward to anything, does she think about the future?" She was only twelve when this last war started and now she is fifteen.

Reeta shakes her head, speaking in Arabic, she understands me.

Ibtisam translates. "She is saying, 'No, I don't think about the future, we don't know what will happen, maybe the universities won't even be open by the time I finish school. We just have to live day by day. I think about the past, before the war, when life was normal and there was no killing. Not the future.'"

"So what do you think of war? Is there ever a good reason for war?" I ask Reeta.

She shakes her head emphatically. "No, never a good reason. The Americans are far away from us . . . why did they attack us?" Ibtisam responds in English.

"Did you understand what the war was for?" I press.

"She remembers the UN inspection teams, but she never believed the Americans would invade her country," Ibtisam says after listening to Reeta's response.

"What do you remember most about the war?"

Reeta speaks for a long time, then stops suddenly.

Ibtisam translates. "It was the last day of the war. Reeta and her brother went with her parents to take back her aunt, Karim's sister, to her uncle's house. When they got there, a bomb exploded. A missile had been fired on the house behind her aunt's house. The explosion was massive; fire, shrapnel fell on them. Windows shattered. Everyone ran in different directions. It destroyed the whole house. In a second, the house was gone, flattened."

"Did she know why they hit that house?" I ask.

"No, they don't know why the Americans hit this normal house in a normal neighbourhood."

Reeta continues and Ibtisam listens, shaking her head, tsk-tsking in shock.

"They ran from house to house. She went into the neighbour's house. Maha was still in the car, but she jumped out and started running after them, crying, 'Wait for me, wait for me.' They stayed at the neighbours' until everything had stopped. Then they went back home, and when they reached the end of their own street, they heard a strange noise. It was an American tank, and then another bomb fell. It fell into their neighbour's garden. Luckily, the house was empty, and so only one person, a passerby, was injured."

"Why did they hit that house?" I repeat.

But Reeta is on to another story, and Ibtisam follows her. "During the last days of the war, there was a heavy bombardment of an army base near their house. Rashid Base. The noise of the bombing was different, the family hadn't heard it before. It went on for one day and one night. Then Saddam Hussein decided to put the army tanks into the streets near the base, hiding the tanks in our street. We saw them when we woke up, and we were terrified that the Americans would bomb these tanks. So everyone on the street left, and we all went to your house and Lina was there."

Now Ibtisam is speaking for herself: "You know, at the end of the invasion, at the end of those twenty-one days, Lina cried on the phone when we finally spoke to her. It was the first time she'd cried, everything she'd been through. It was scary to hear her crying, out of everyone."

Reeta understands her. "Lina stayed at your house by herself during the whole invasion," Ibtisam translates. "But sometimes she would drive to us during the day. There were seven of us altogether then, our family of four, Lina and my grandmother and grandfather. We went out, short distances, to check on other people, other families. We had to because we didn't have phones; we had to check that everyone was all right. Lina used to go to her bed at night and sleep during the bombing. 'They don't bother me,' she'd say. When the bed shook, she'd just swear at them. But she started to get a bit weak by the end."

Now that Reeta's started telling stories, she can't stop: "We knew when the bombing would come. We had dinner at 7:00 p.m. because we knew that at 8:00 p.m. the attack would start. We would stay up all night through the barrage. At around six in the morning we would fall asleep until about 10:00 a.m., as that was when the bombing was not as intense. But we didn't really sleep."

"So what about school?"

"There was no school during the war. We went back in May. All the photos of Saddam had been taken out of the books. And we used to have one subject called Patriotic, about how you behave in society, and it was all about Saddam and the Baath Party and what he did. But when we came back, that subject was gone."

"So what do you think of England?"

"Yani, I like it but . . . I don't want to live here."

✥

Amal wants us to eat out at a local Turkish restaurant that features a belly dancer performing on the weekends. Maha loves to go out, but in Baghdad she never does. Amal wants Reeta to have some fun. A group of ten Iraqi women, some Muslim, some Christian, including me, all dress up and go out for a night together. The other invited family friends have an aunt visiting from Baghdad, and so our party consists half of exiles and half of Iraqis who still live in Baghdad. Dining in a restaurant reminds Maha of a story.

"You know my husband's favourite dish is *tishrib leban*. It's a very delicious dish. Leilah, you have to try it, lamb with yogurt and pita bread. Amal, do you remember there was a nice restaurant on Abu Nuwwas Street that served this dish? Well, one night the restaurant was bombed and many people were killed. The owner moved to Jordan and opened a restaurant there instead. So it's gone now. Very sad. My husband loved that place," she says.

After we finish our appetizers, five different dips, the belly dancer begins her show. She is an English girl, but a bold dancer, who comes up close to all the tables as she dances. The English customers don't know where to look as she shakes her belly and her sparkly costume in front of their plates and wineglasses. But our table is clapping along and ululating and cheering, and the atmosphere starts to warm up. We are all dancing in our seats and commenting on the music, which songs we like and which we don't. Maha tells us that the only time they go out in Baghdad now is to a family social club to eat. On Fridays there is a curfew between 11:00 a.m. and 3:00 p.m., and sometimes it is extended if there is trouble, so if they happen to be at the club on Fridays they have to stay there. There used to be a swimming pool there before the war that the children could play in, but not since the war. No water. The only pools now are in the Green Zone.

Soon the waitress comes over and encourages us to get up and join the dancer. I am hesitant, but Amal and her friend get up to dance immediately, and Maha follows them. They are completely uninhibited even though they haven't had a drop of wine. Maha dances with grace, moving her hips in time with the music and the belly dancer. The hired dancer gets up and starts dancing on Maha's chair, and Maha and Amal dance around the room. Now the other customers are clapping along as the women at our table get up and down. Reeta is blushing and won't dance.

"She says she doesn't know how to!" shouts Ibtisam. "She says she has never seen her mother dance either, in her whole life!"

Reeta looks embarrassed, the way fifteen-year-old girls always look when their mothers draw attention to themselves. At the same time, she can't help grinning while she watches her mother dance. Then she looks down at her plate again. Amal pulls me up and I swirl my hips in time with my wrists, hoping that I'm doing a fair imitation of belly dancing. We are all smiling and moving, clapping and shrieking. But we can't convince Reeta to dance with us. After forty-five minutes, the dancer finishes her show, and Amal calls her over to the table and she sits down with a glass of wine and chats to us. She admits she was totally intimidated when she heard that a group of Iraqi women were in the audience.

I ask Maha about covering up when she is out in public, because I see how much they are enjoying being dressed up for an occasion. Maha tells me, mostly through mime, that they don't have to cover their hair yet in Baghdad. Since their neighbourhood is very mixed, they haven't been under pressure to change the way they dress. I ask her if she thinks there is a civil war now.

"Yes, there is a war between the different militias that are working for different political parties," she says. "But not between the people. The people themselves have always lived together and have mixed families. You would be asking people to hate members of their own families."

I ask her about freedom of speech.

"Oh yes, we talk politics all the time. Iraqis love politics. We can't think about anything else, it's our life. Under Saddam we couldn't speak openly of anything. But now we can. But we don't believe anything the politicians say."

"Why not?" I explain to her that while we in the West are skeptical of our politicians and their motives, we still have remarkable faith in the fairness of our political system.

"Well, we see what the politicians say and then we watch and see what the results are. See what they say and then what they do. And then we can see clearly that they lie. It's all lies," she concludes.

When we get home, we have tea in the kitchen. Amal gets out her reading glasses and opens a letter she had received from Beatrice earlier that day. Beatrice is my grandmother Victoria's old friend, another Iraqi refugee now living in the United States. She has become paranoid about speaking on the phone in the US because Iraqis have been given to understand that their lines may be tapped and that they are being eavesdropped upon. She is now in her eighties and left Iraq ten years ago, after the Gulf War. Ironically, she lived for fifteen years under Saddam never being able to say anything on the phone, and now she is in the United States experiencing the same fate. A few weeks earlier Ibtisam spoke to her about her recent trip to Jordan. Usually, Beatrice is extremely talkative and can tell stories one after another without stopping for breath. She hinted that she had other things to tell Ibtisam about her trip, but wouldn't elaborate further.

"I'll write you a letter," Beatrice said. "I'll tell you everything in the letter. I can't say anything now."

Ibtisam reads out the letter in Arabic. "I will translate it afterwards," she says. She starts reading, then says, "Ooh, ohh my God."

I can't restrain myself. "What? What? I can't wait, tell me."

"She went to Baghdad!" Amal exclaims.

Everyone is talking at once in Arabic. Amal keeps reading aloud, peering down her nose, then up at her listeners, then after the first page she says, "She was in Amman, and her nephew's wife in Baghdad was having a baby, so her nephew begged her to come to help her in labour. They said they would buy her a plane ticket. She waited for a month before deciding to go ... Oh, but they shouldn't have done it, they weren't thinking ... She took the flight to Baghdad. She was terrified in the taxi from the airport to her house. She says she can only describe one percent of what happened to her in those weeks. As she drove through Baghdad, she was crying, crying, crying all the way. She says, 'It is in ruins, all the buildings, the streets, and the people. Life in Baghdad is nothing but terror, terror, terror. Fear. Panic. I can't tell you about the terror, my whole stay whenever anyone went out of the house, I was just terrified until they came back. It would take a book to tell you what happened to me in those weeks. I cannot describe Baghdad to you. It is destroyed.'"

I look around at the faces sitting at the table hearing this. "Is it true? Or is she exaggerating a little bit?" Despite all that I know I just can't believe that Reeta and Maha are living in such terrible fear all the time.

Maha and Reeta look stony. "Yes, it is true."

Reeta says, "But I am not scared. I am used to it. Unless I see someone with a beard next to us in the car. Then I feel scared. I would expect the car to blow up. But usually I don't think about it."

"Oh dear, she says that the family received a ransom note saying that unless they give them fifty thousand dollars, the whole family would be killed. Oh, they will kill them anyway, she says. So that dark night, the whole family fled to Jordan." Amal repeats Beatrice's final words: "'I wish I had never gone back. Never go back.'"

Ibtisam says, "They shouldn't have asked her to come. She is an old lady, why did they do that? What good has it done her to see Baghdad like that? Her memories will be gone."

Ruined, like the city.

❊

Ibtisam, Maha, Reeta and Amal cram into the car to drive me to the airport. I'm leaving a few days earlier than Maha and Reeta. We get out at the airport drop-off lane, and I hug Ibtisam and Amal and thank them for their hospitality, which they shake away, saying, "You know, you never have to ask if you want to come and stay here. You just say you are coming. Our house is your house. In our culture, if you are family, you don't have to ask if you can come. You are welcome. Even our friends don't ask. Remember, just tell us you are coming." Then I embrace Maha and Reeta. I don't know where or when, or even if, I'll see them again. They feel closer than cousins, more like sisters, and I wonder what is going to happen to them. Will we next meet in Australia? The United States? Or will they move to Canada? Britain? Or will I have to go to Baghdad to see them again? We don't allude to any of that. We just say brightly, "God willing, *en shallah*, we'll see each other again soon." And they get back into the car, waving through the windows until we can't see each other anymore. They are gone.

AN IRAQI CHRISTIAN CLEANS UP AFTER AN ATTACK ON HER HOME
PHOTO CREDIT: FARAH NOSH

CHAPTER TWENTY
Christmas in Baghdad

Gianni Magazzeni, the chief of the UN assistance mission for Iraq, said 34,452 civilians were killed and 36,685 wounded [in Iraq last year.]. . . . Figures show that almost 100 civilians are killed on a typical day, while dozens of bodies, many showing signs of torture, are found daily on the streets of Baghdad, . . . The UN report also said 30,842 people were detained in the country as of December 31, including 14,534 in detention facilities run by US-led forces. —"Many killed in Baghdad blasts," Staff and Agencies at *The Guardian*, January 16, 2007

It's the week between Christmas and New Year 2007. I'm walking in Kananaskis Country with my father, trudging through the pristine snowy landscape of the majestic Rocky Mountains, about as far from the desert he was brought up in as you can possibly get. The snow is falling in thick flakes around us, the sky is pale blue and the dark pine trees glisten with their frosty decorations.

"So I guess there weren't many Christmas trees in Baghdad when you were a boy?"

"Not many, but we had one. On Christmas Eve, my father and I went to a huge house with large grounds and a walled garden that was on the river near Grandma Samira's house. We'd take an axe and go and choose a fir from the grounds, often six feet high, and cut it down for our Christmas tree. Then we'd carry it home and decorate it with the family that night. I think my sisters have the Christmas decorations in London. Or maybe they are still at home."

"I guess there wasn't any snow though!" I say.

"No no. But it was sometimes chilly," he says. "The shops sold lots of Christmas decorations because there were so many Westerners there at the time, and even the Muslim families often had Christmas trees and gave presents. It was nice to have a feast in the middle of winter, and they'd just enjoy the celebration and the socializing and ignore the Christian element."

He said the children woke in the morning and, like all children on Christmas morning around the world, got presents from Santa Claus who had come in the night. The family went to church and then the men would go from house to house giving Christmas greetings to family, friends and neighbours. The women stayed at home and received the men.

"My uncles used to come to us," my father continues. "Since I was a young boy I'd have to stay with the women, who offered the guests some food. Sometimes we had tabbouleh, after my aunt Miriam came from Syria to live with us. No one had heard of tabbouleh in our family until she came. Apart from my father, of course. They'd joke that she brought tabbouleh to Iraq, and they'd make so much of it, chopping the parsley was endless."

"So you didn't have turkey for dinner in Baghdad, right?" I joked.

"Oh yes, we did," he chuckles. "We bought one a couple of months before Christmas and it lived on the roof. We'd feed the bird our leftovers. Sometimes it flew off, but we kids would chase the turkey and get it back. We'd fatten the turkey up and then the uncles would kill it. The killing was a bit gruesome, but when you live with animals around like that, you aren't really bothered when they die. My mother plucked off the feathers, then boiled the carcass until it was so well done the meat fell off the bone. And then she'd make special rice with the broth. That rice was delicious. You know, the one we make with nuts and raisins."

"I wonder what Christmas was like in Baghdad this year. How are the family?" I ask.

"Well, they are still alive. Not dead yet, so that is good. Actually I wanted to talk to you about the house."

"What's happened?"

"Maha and Karim have been approached by a family, not known by us, who lives down the street from our house. They had noticed that it was empty. Nowadays an empty house is a cause of deep concern. The neighbours are worried that insurgents, a gang, or a militia will take it over and live in it and use it as a base from which to launch attacks, as they have done in many other houses. Then the whole street would be drawn even further into the war. They wondered if our family would rent the house to the wife's sister. This sister and her family had been forced to leave her house in a dangerous neighbourhood where there has been intense fighting and were now living in their house with them."

The last time I talked to Karim was over the Internet. The family had returned to Baghdad. Karim said that Maha and Reeta saw Baghdad with new eyes when they returned from their six weeks in England. It is hard for them to be there, knowing what life is like in the rest of the world. They'd had a taste of freedom, and it was hard to go back to their caged existence.

Karim finally closed his business for fear of kidnapping. A man from a store near his office was snatched by some armed men a few weeks before. He was released after two days without a ransom; no one knows who did it or why. But that incident was enough to scare everyone on the street. Karim has retreated to the safety of his home and now has his computer there. The curfew is enforced every day, and Iraqi civilians rarely leave the house; their home is their only safety, but has become their prison as well.

Now all that the family hopes for is to escape Iraq. The situation in Baghdad is far worse, more dangerous, and security has worsened precipitously since the summer. Day after day, things get steadily worse. They are still not yet ready to flee to Syria, they don't want to leave their house, family and friends and run away. They want to get visas, leave with the right papers.

I ask him if he is afraid for his life, if he thinks their house will be bombed. He replies, "Yes, sometimes the helicopters throw something that gets into the garden."

"What do you mean?"

"The garden is full of these thin pieces of metal, about two inches by two inches, that have been dropped from the sky."

I don't understand what he means. "How many pieces?"

"Hundreds. Maybe more. We clear them up and throw them away."

"Is it debris from a cluster bomb?" He doesn't understand my question.

"We have seen so many things here. You would not believe the things we have seen. I think the Americans have many things to do here. For four days, it has been like the war again. Airplanes and bombs, day and night. No one knows what their plan is, but they have one. Maybe they want Iraq to be three countries." I ask him if he thinks that could happen. "Yes, but it might take ten or fifteen years. As long as it is a weak country, that's what they want." I ask him if he thinks the American plan will succeed. "Of course. The future of this country is over."

I repeat to my father what Karim had said. He nods saying, "I talked to my sisters about the house. On the one hand, if the house is left empty then it probably will be squatted in eventually anyway, and then we might lose the place forever. But renting it is difficult emotionally." It is hard for them to imagine their parents' home, the house they grew up in, being occupied by strangers, it would never be the same. "On the other hand, if they do rent the house perhaps Karim won't be able to get the rent money or much worse, we would never get the family to leave if we ever wanted the house back."

He explained that since there is no rule of law in Iraq now everything is based on a code of honour. They could only hope that the people are honest. The house is in my father's name, and he could choose to sell it. Of course he'd get next to nothing for it because no one is buying houses in Baghdad while there is still war. But my father wants to keep the house.

"It's the family house," he explains. "It was built by my parents, and it's been in the family for fifty years. My logic is, the situation in Iraq can only go two ways. Either it will get worse, and then everyone will be displaced, and we wouldn't need to move the renters out as we wouldn't want to go back anyway. If there is a civil war and it ends eventually, then these people will have to leave. It might take twenty years, but it would still be our house."

He told my aunts to ask Maha to find out if the renter wants any of the furniture or the appliances and to sell her whatever she wants. Maha and Karim will take what they can use and move the personal stuff out of the house. Since Maha's parents died, they have extra rooms where they can store things. But all the belongings that had been left in situ, looked after during the sanctions, guarded by Lina through the war and cleaned since by Maha, will be finally moved out. Maha has already cleaned out one closet, which was full of new sheets. She'd taken the sheets to nuns who run an old peoples' home, who were happy to receive them. They said they'd tear them up to make dressings for wounds.

This year, Maha decorated a tree, but because she was scared, they had to put it at the very back of the house, out of sight so that no one would see it from the street. Iraqi children were very worried this Christmas that Santa would be kidnapped and that he wouldn't make it down the chimney to give them their presents. Of course, when he did come, they were all deeply thankful.

The family went to church on Christmas morning and were given presents from a charity in the West. I remember making similar packages as a schoolgirl, putting a box together to send to less fortunate people on the other side of the world. Now our relatives were the destitute, living in the most perilous city on earth. They received different things in each box. Reeta was unimpressed by hers, which held a toothbrush and toothpaste.

Maha said, "I mean, we know it's useful, but she didn't find it very Christmasy."

And her brother got a dollar in his box.

"Do they use dollars in Baghdad?" I ask my father.

"Of course they do, but one dollar?"

"Pray for us and our country," Karim said in his e-mailed Christmas greeting. That was all we could do.

⌘

A few hours before our walk, at 6:00 a.m. on December 29, 2006, Baghdad time, Saddam Hussein was executed. The electricity didn't come on until 11:00 a.m., and then Reeta and her brother watched the execution on television along with most Iraqis. They'd witnessed so much violence already, their parents didn't think to shield them from this. But the children couldn't sleep that night, and their parents had to go into their rooms and sleep with them. They both had nightmares. Reeta dreamt that she saw Saddam emerging from a river flowing entirely with blood. Karim and Maha thought that Saddam had been killed to cover up everything he knew about American complicity in his crimes. Amal didn't feel anything for him; she considers him an evil man, but she considers George W. Bush just as much of a criminal. It is zero degrees centigrade in Baghdad, and there is no power. The family is freezing cold without heat.

I ask my father, "What do you feel about Saddam Hussein's death?"

"Nothing."

I thought that showing him moments before his death with the noose around his neck was medieval in its barbarity. It felt like the end to a Shakespearean tragedy; Elizabethan in its raw violence.

"But he ruined your life? Your country?"

"I knew this day would come. This always happens to dictators eventually. They all have to die one day. I just didn't expect it would come like this." Then he says, "You know, people often forget that everyone suffered under Saddam. Not just Shia or Kurds. Saddam was indiscriminate in his ruthlessness. He even killed family members and trusted friends. And he could just change his mind on a whim and you were dead."

"Do you worry about Iraq?" I ask him.

"Not really. We've always had war and invasion. Remember, over the centuries we've been invaded by the Persians, the Turks, the Mongols, the Arabians. Iraq is used to it. If you knew the history you'd see. This time is especially bad, but it has always been like this. I wanted to leave. It wasn't accidental, it was by design." He is quiet for a moment, lost in thought. Then he says, "I know a Sunni Iraqi who fled for Canada in the 1990s; he was just as horrified by Saddam Hussein as I was. Anyway, this man went back to Baghdad right after the invasion and he was stunned by what he saw. When he came back he said, 'Never ever go back, Ibrahim. Just forget Iraq. Forget it.'"

I look at my father, bundled up in his ski jacket, toque and gloves, braving the cold temperatures that I know he struggles against, and I know that he will heed this warning.

We stand looking out over the frozen forests with the beautiful jagged stone peaks ringed around us, the snow glistening in the bright sun. In the peaceful silence, I picture the flat expanse of the landscape around Baghdad, the date palms, the river, the relentless heat, the sandstorms, and I hear the clamour of explosions, shiver at the thought of the tension and fear brought on by the presence of violence and death lurking everywhere at every moment.

For now, all I can do is imagine, in ten or twenty years, with my children perhaps, opening up the old house and going inside. Perhaps the photographs will still be framed on the mantelpiece, my aunts' clothes in the closets, my father's newspaper in a drawer. I walk up on to the roof. I look everywhere, but the house is empty. I go back downstairs and out onto the terrace facing the neglected garden, shrivelled and wild. There I am greeted by the ghosts of my grandparents, my great-aunt, my great-uncles, all saying at once, "Welcome, welcome. You've come to visit us. Sit down, sit down, we'll drink tea. We knew you'd come one day. We knew you'd be back."

MY GRANDFATHER KHALIL TEACHING
ENGLISH IN BAGHDAD IN 1962

Epilogue

Mesopotamia or Iraq retained a powerful Christian culture at least through the thirteenth century. In terms of the number and splendour of its churches and monasteries, its vast scholarship and dazzling spirituality, Iraq was through the late Middle Ages at least as much a cultural and spiritual heartland of Christianity as was France or Germany, or indeed Ireland.... Middle Eastern Christianity will not become extinct in the same way that animal or plant species vanish, with no representatives left to carry on the line and no hope of revival.... For practical purposes, however, Middle Eastern Christianity has, within living memory, all but disappeared as a living force.

— Philip Jenkins, *The Lost History of Christianity*

This book was first published in Canada in September 2007, the same week when George W. Bush made a surprise visit to Iraq to announce that security was improving and life was stabilizing for ordinary Iraqis. A few days before my book launch, my father called me.

"We've heard from Karim. They are fleeing Baghdad."

"Where will they go?" I asked, knowing only two countries are admitting Iraqi refugees.

"Syria, they just decided yesterday." He went on to explain that a car had rammed into theirs and when they got out, the driver demanded a large sum of money in dollars. Karim and Maha were so shocked by the audacity of these men that they ignored their threats and quickly got back in their car. The men pursued them as they drove home. At the checkpoint at the entrance to their neighbourhood, Karim asked the guards (who are paid for by the residents) what they should do. They replied, "Just give them what they want. Now that they know where you live, they could do anything."

With no police or justice system to turn to, Karim and Maha handed over the cash, and immediately decided they could not live another day in a country where people could extort money from you on the street in broad daylight. This was true anarchy. The Syrian government had just announced that it was going to close the border to Iraqi refugees; in one week's time, they would need a visa to get into Syria. It was now or never.

Karim and Maha would leave behind not only everything they'd ever known but also four houses: their own, that of Maha's recently deceased parents, a third belonging to my great-aunt Lina and finally my father's house, with all the contents still inside. Everyone knew that once they left, it was unlikely that anyone in the family would return to Baghdad for many years, if ever.

My father asked Karim if he would mind filling a small suitcase with any of my grandfather Khalil's memorabilia that was still in the house. In the forty-nine years since he left Iraq, my father had never made such a request. He was thinking of letters, photographs and documents: birth certificates, wills, house deeds, anything. He knew without asking that it was impossible for Karim to bring anything of monetary value.

Karim replied that he was deeply sorry, but it was impossible for him to take anything at all into Syria. They could only leave with a few clothes and personal effects. He thought Syrian officials were especially suspicious of any documents that could contain coded messages from the resistance or other fighters. Documents could detain the family at the border for hours or even days and could ultimately even stop them from getting into Syria.

As I was reading aloud from my book at the launch, the last members of my father's family were fleeing the city of his birth, becoming what they had most feared: refugees. That morning, Maha had sat in her garden crying, saying goodbye to her beloved house which, despite all the terror and hardship of the last four years, she had not wanted to leave. That night, their taxi broke down in the desert on the dangerous road to the border and they had to wait, terrified of being ambushed by fighters or renegade soldiers, while the driver did the repairs.

The next day, I called my aunts in London and asked Siham if the family had got to Syria. She said yes, they had made it through the border and registered with the UN as refugees. I wanted to know how she felt about finally losing her house in Baghdad. "Of course, I am very upset about losing my house," she replied. "But I am far more angry that I have lost my country."

After a moment's silence she said, "You know the other day I was thinking of something I forgot to tell you about. When we were girls, my mother would make her own rose water. She cooked rice dishes and baklava with it, and splashed it on the linens to make them smell nice. We used to help her make it, pick the petals from the bushes in the garden, press the water and scent from them. I'll explain to you one day in detail how we did it. We used to think it was work at the time. We resented it. But now you realize it was a nice thing to do. It's something we haven't done since we left Iraq. I'll always think of her when I use rose water. You can buy it now in the Arabic shops here. It's not really the same though."

※

Six months later my father came to visit me in Vancouver. "I have something to show you," he said. He pulled out a blue plastic bag with an elongated rectangular picture frame inside. "Do you recognize it?" Inside the cracked gilded-wood frame was a painting, a very simple silhouette of a black hillside with low houses and a tower on it, with a muted brown sky.

"No, I've never seen this before."

"It's Safita," my father said. "The view from my grandfather's house. Ammu Ibrahim painted it when he was just starting to paint. You see it has something written on the back?" In my grandfather's elegant handwriting, I read, "Safita, Syria, Summer 1935. By my life-long friend Ibrahim; drawn from our roof at sunset. The side facing us was shady because the sun sets behind."

"Where did you find this?" I asked.

"It is one of the few things that Karim managed to recover from the house in Baghdad. He thought he could risk it. No one could accuse him of anything sinister for being in possession of a landscape painting, could they?" He chuckled. "My sisters brought it back from Syria when they visited the family at Easter. It's funny that the only thing we have from our Baghdadi house is a painting of Khalil's childhood home, which is also lost to us."

Karim, Maha, Reeta and Samir have now been living in Syria for sixteen months. They cannot work or earn money but the children are allowed to go to school. They have found an apartment to rent in a town full of Iraqi Christians who have also fled the violence. They live on UN rations and what is left of their savings and are applying to any country on Earth that might take them in. They say they cannot stay in Syria indefinitely as refugees, and there is no future there for their children. There are an estimated 1.5 million Iraqi refugees in Syria who are all trying to survive. Unemployment is high among Syrians themselves, and middle-class Iraqis now live hand to mouth or on scant savings, while the poor are forced into crime or prostitution.

Maha says that despite now having the freedom to go out and socialize in the evenings without fearing for her life, Reeta still misses Baghdad. When she walks past Iraqi falafel shops, which have mushroomed all over Damascus, she breaks down and cries at the sounds of Iraqi music and people speaking Arabic in the Iraqi dialect.

Meanwhile, Farah has just returned to Baghdad for the first time in almost three years. She emails me her first impressions; the famous "highway of death" from the airport into the city is now lined with massive concrete blast walls on either side that are painted with colourful murals of Iraqi historical scenes. She says she can't travel that road without thinking of how many people have been killed on it. She wonders if anyone knows the number of deaths that have occurred on that highway.

She tells me that the oranges are ripening now, dusty fruit weighing down the trees. Sitting in traffic makes her anxious because there are many unreported explosions and she hears them in the distance sometimes. Nobody else flinches at the sounds of gunfire or bombs exploding. The other huge difference is what she dubs "the landscape of fear"; Baghdad is now a concrete jungle criss-crossed with blast walls and checkpoints. There were some walls up on her last visit, but now the whole city has been dissected into fragments like honeycomb so you can no longer travel freely.

On my recent book tour in Australia, an Iraqi woman approached me after one of my readings in Brisbane. Light hair framed her relatively unlined face; she surprised me when she told me she was in her seventies. Her name was Noor, which means "light" in Arabic. She'd been living in Australia for decades, but her memories of her life in Baghdad were still intact. Her green eyes shone with the remembrance of her happy childhood. When she was a young woman she picked orange blossoms, drying them in the sun to make orange-blossom tea. No doubt my grandparents did the same, she said. I agreed that they might have.

⚙

I really hate to say this but it is the truth—there is no Iraq now.
—Manal Al Sheikh

I stand behind a podium looking out at scores of Iraqi faces. "I'm here today by happy coincidence," I begin. "My newfound cousin

Natalie contacted me after she read my book." I am breathless with nerves and excitement, I move my hands too much as I talk, as I'm not sure I'm entitled to speak to Iraqis about their own country.

I'd walked into a nondescript building in an industrial area of Mississauga, a Toronto suburb, and been instantly surrounded by warmth and friendliness. Natalie had found me by way of my book a few months earlier. She had been attracted to it because she too was Iraqi but did not speak Arabic and had never been to Iraq. She passed my book on to her father and he recognized the story of my great-uncle, who camped out in a *jerdah* on a sand island in the Tigris during the summers. A family conversation ensued to figure out if we were related. They invited me to give my very first reading for a Middle Eastern group at their Iraqi social club, a reincarnation of the social clubs popular with families in Baghdad. In the audience sit my second cousins and their families, friends and acquaintances, ranging from teenagers to seniors.

I'd never heard of this side of the family. When pressed my father said he had forgotten to mention it, but that yes, he'd known of an older family member who had immigrated to Montreal in the '60s. Finally, Natalie sent me photographs of my father, aunts and grandparents at her parents' wedding in Beirut in the '50s. I was shocked. Who was this woman? From our correspondence, I discovered that I had over two hundred relatives, Iraqis who now lived all over the world, in the United States, Canada, Australia, the UK, France, Syria, Jordan and Lebanon, many of whom had left Baghdad in the last ten years. Here was my lost family, not in Iraq but scattered all over the globe. And now I am meeting dozens of them for the first time, we are united, not in Baghdad but in Toronto.

After the reading, people line up to get their books signed and finally a couple arrives at the front. The man, in his fifties, neatly dressed, has my book in his hand, open to the last chapter, "Christmas in Baghdad." On the facing page is a photograph of an Iraqi woman cleaning up her home. Her living room is wrecked and in disarray but directly behind her is a decorated Christmas tree. "That is my wife," he says and gestures beside him, and I immediately recognize the woman from the photograph, standing in front of me like an old friend. "She doesn't speak much English," her husband adds. "But I lived in England for ten years."

My mind is reeling; I am trying to figure out how this woman's picture got into my book. I ask her if she knows Farah Nosh, but they've never met. She has short wavy reddish-brown hair and large eyes full of emotion. Behind her is another woman, her face bearing identical features but looking much younger. She says, "I am her twin sister, but I've lived in Canada for thirty years." In the flash of comparing their matching faces, I see the toll the last three decades has taken on Iraqis. The sister from the photograph wears her pain in her tired expression and lined face. Obviously a foreigner to Canada, her clothes are drab and old-fashioned. Her twin sister gives off a shinier air, and even though she must have suffered the pain of exile that many Iraqis endured over the Saddam era, her eyes still light up when she speaks.

The man clutches a sheaf of dog-eared papers, enlarged and photocopied photographs. "Our house was destroyed by a massive, 300-kilogram car bomb full of TNT explosives," he says, pointing at the pictures. "Flames shot into the sky from the explosion, windows were blown out, whole walls collapsed and the roof caved in. It was all destroyed." I imagine he's shown these photographs again and again to many officials in Iraq, Syria and Canada, to prove his stories.

He speaks with confidence and anger. "It was New Year's Eve 2003, in the first year of the American occupation. The target was a restaurant next door where some Americans were having a New Year's Eve party. We were at home trying to welcome in the New Year with the lights dim, as we ran everything off a generator in those days. Neighbours saw a car circling unable to find a parking spot directly in front of the restaurant. So it blew up in front of our house instead. It happened at 9.28 p.m." Six people were at home, but they all made it out alive, crawling out of a window. "If it had happened an hour later, I would have been killed in my bed, as our whole bedroom collapsed. I was all cut up from shards of glass from the windows blowing out. I only remember being out on the street and taken to hospital. Five people in the restaurant were killed. Three people on the street died as well, one who had been guarding the cars for the restaurant, and thirty-six people were injured."

He spent three days in hospital: "When the three American journalists who had been injured in the restaurant saw me being stitched up without anesthetic, they decided to go to a private hospital. But in those days the hospitals were still good and I left with a nylon bag with penicillin, cotton, bandages and everything to help me heal. A year later, you had to bring your own supplies." He smoothes out the wrinkled and worn photocopies in his hand and points at a framed picture on the only wall still standing; the entire front wall looks as if it has been knocked in by a wrecking ball, leaving the living room open to the street.

"Ave Maria, that image of the Virgin Mary has been on my bedroom wall since I was little, it is the only thing that survived intact, including me. Everything else was broken or destroyed. Our Lady got us out of the house alive that night."

I ask if he knows who was responsible for the bombing, if there was an investigation. He replies, "No. We have no idea. The police came, the journalists came, the Americans came and they looked around. But no investigation, we never knew who was responsible. This happens with all the bombs."

For the next two years, the family was forced to move from one friend or relative's house to another. "We never thought of leaving Baghdad, our life was there, my job, all our assets, our family. We wanted to stay. But then the foreign car company I worked for pulled out. Letters sent to the head office and to the secretary—a foreigner married to an Iraqi—threatened that everyone in the company would be killed if they didn't close. There were bullets in the envelopes. They shut down right away."

"I tell you under Saddam not a shot was fired in the streets, except for shooting in the air after soccer matches. But after the invasion, anyone could buy a machine gun or a Kalashnikov. It was like Texas! You just went to the American army station, registered your name and got a license, and suddenly there were guns everywhere. It was chaos. It was never like this before." He shakes his head, sighing.

"So you left because of losing your job?"

"No, not even that made me want to leave. It was after two incidents where people threw themselves in front of our car! When they were taken to hospital they claimed they had been hit and demanded compensation. They'd have 'witnesses,' so what could you do? You had to pay up. After the second time, I felt that the country was finished, the people had changed. Society had collapsed, the sewage, electric, telephone and medical systems had been targeted in the invasion and none had been repaired. Nothing had been done. How could you live in a country like that? So we fled to Damascus and then Aleppo and we are only here because of the UN sponsorship program."

"And what do Iraqis who are still there think?"

"When I was in Syria I went back and forth to Iraq once a year to check on our house and people would say, 'We are praying to bring Saddam back.' He was a tyrant, yes, but if you didn't touch him, he left you alone. Now you can't live at all."

By now, everyone is sitting at crowded tables, their plates piled with rice and kebabs. I am propelled to a nearby table and sit down beside the twin sister who lives in Toronto. She explains that she'd not seen her sister for two decades. After the war started she watched it on CNN obsessively. Then, during the day on New Year's

Eve 2003, there suddenly in front of her she saw her twin, crying and wringing her hands in front of their bombed-out house. She leapt out of her seat in shock, crying out to her sister as if she could hear her. Her sister was openly suffering on CNN and she was helpless, she felt her sister's emotions as if they were her own and began crying uncontrollably. As the house was destroyed, there was no way she could contact her sister directly. But at least she knew that the family was alive, though now she also knew that her sister's husband was badly injured. She was in shock; she couldn't go out to a New Year's Eve party after that.

The family became refugees in Syria, and it took them four years to get to Toronto. When they arrived in Canada they were taken to the COSTI reception centre run by the Canadian government. That night the twins were finally reunited after twenty years. They clung to each other and cried for an hour before managing to start speaking. Visitors weren't allowed at the centre, but the workers relaxed the rules when they saw the bond between the sisters. They talked all night long. The family had only just left the centre the week before my event and so coincidence brought us together at the reading. They could have been a mere statistic, another Iraqi family killed by a bomb blast, but instead they were beginning a new life in Canada.

Having the woman in the photograph come to life was as astounding as if I'd written a novel and the characters I'd invented had walked into the room. I knew, of course, that the woman in the photograph was "real," but although I believed in her as a human being, she was still a symbol of something larger, the war in general, Christians in Baghdad in particular. But now that she has walked off the page and stood in front of me, and I've heard her whole story, I know how numb to the reality of the news I am. If only we could hear the explosions, feel the fear, smell the burning flesh, see the dead bodies, touch the blood stains on the streets, look through the cavernous holes of emptied buildings, only then would we really know the utter despair and devastation that our war has made.

✠

Ten years ago, on April 9, 2003, Baghdad fell to the invading armies from the US and the UK, ending the 24-year-old regime of Saddam Hussein. On December 18, 2011, almost nine years later, the Iraq war "ended" as President Barack Obama fulfilled his election promise to withdraw his troops. It was the end of another horrendous period of Iraqi history, an end that came too late for millions of Iraqis, including my father's family.

And the violence has not stopped. According to Iraq Body Count, there have been 122,438 documented civilian deaths since the war began. In the last year alone, more than 4,250 Iraqis have been killed by the conflicts brought on by the invasion. The anniversary of the start of the war, March 20, 2013, was marked by Iraq's worst day of violence this year with over a dozen bombings, including at a bank, a vegetable market and a restaurant, that killed 65 people and injured more than 200. And the bloodshed continues daily.

In a Damascus street, my cousins Karim and Maha bumped into an acquaintance from Baghdad who urged them to seek out a distant relative in Montreal who they'd heard was able to help Iraqi Christians emigrate to Canada. He helped run a sponsorship program through a church. The program has helped Iraqis escape since the early years of Saddam's regime, and the flow of refugees has not slowed in the decade since his overthrow. The distant relative turned out to be Natalie's grandfather, the same man whose wedding my father and his family had attended all those decades ago in Beirut. And so a process began to help Karim and Maha leave Syria; they landed in Montreal in 2009. I will finally meet Karim and his son this year for the first time, and see Maha and Reeta again.

Christians are leaving Iraq in droves. Recent estimates put the Christian population at under 300,000, about 1 percent of the total, compared to 5 percent in 1980. This is a massive, forgotten exodus, a tragedy hurried on by the war. What an irony that George W. Bush, a proclaimed Christian, has hastened the demise of Christianity in Iraq by his ill-conceived and illegal war. Now we watch as Syria has been enfolded in bloody conflict for two years, and the Iraqi refugees that fled Iraq for Syria are often in the surreal position of fleeing Syria for Iraq, hardly a haven.

In May 2011, a friend of my aunt Amal went back to Baghdad after twenty years. He was from the same neighbourhood as our family and went to university in England with my aunt. He took photographs of our house that my aunt forwarded to me with a note saying how sad she felt at how rundown it looks. At first glance, to me, who has seen countless images of rubble-filled Iraqi streets on the news, it didn't look that bad. But as I looked with her eyes, I saw the countless electrical wires draped like a lace web spun all over the house, the graffiti on the pillars, the cracked and blackened walls, the warped gates and the corrugated iron roof on the garage next door. The sidewalks were coming apart. It was a scene of slow decay and dereliction. It looked nothing like the smart new photographs of the earlier days when my grandparents had first built the house.

She also forwarded a photograph of Al Rasheed Street, the commercial hub that connects the north and south of Baghdad. My aunts remember a lively street full of small boutiques, cinemas and restaurants. It had Baghdad's only department store, and as young women they frequented the coffee shop there that overlooked the Tigris. Both Auntie Lina and Ibtisam worked in offices nearby. They bought fabric in the nearby souk that their mother and aunt would make into dresses for them.

The photograph is a shock. Everything the eye lights on is broken down, blackened by explosions. The dilapidated two-storey buildings have porticoes in front of recessed shops; the second floor is now uninhabitable. All the windows have been blown out, leaving only empty frames. Bomb blasts, pollution and age have left black stains on the once cream exterior. Broken benches and chairs lean outside what remains of a juice bar below a massive crack in one of the portico's pillars. What should be a bustling market scene is largely bereft of people, but then I notice a few men in the shadows of the portico, garbage littered at their feet, one caught with his hands up on both sides of his head, in a gesture of despair.

Because of the devastating contrast between these images and my aunts' memories, the photographs are the catalyst for severing the final connection and selling the family home. My aunts looked into the pictures and knew they could never live in the house again, on that street, in that neighbourhood, that they were never going back to Iraq, that the idea was pure fantasy. In ten years, they had lost all their relatives and friends, either to death or emigration. They had once known most of their neighbours, but now only one family remained on the street, everyone else had fled. There was no one to take care of the house and the country was too terrifying to return to. Why would they ever go back?

After years of hand-wringing my father and his sisters had to face the fact that their home in Iraq was gone. They sold it in September 2011, a decade after the attacks of September 11 unwittingly spun the events that led to the American invasion. They think the new owners are going to divide the house up into apartments.

I ask my aunts if they finally feel their house in England is now their true home, but Amal says categorically, "No, I will always feel that our house in Baghdad is our house. Nothing can replace it." Her sisters nod in agreement. "You know when we signed the papers to sell it, we couldn't keep back our tears. We were so emotional, we all cried together. It was very hard."

The last thing that Maha and Karim got out of the house was an icon that had hung on the wall for as long as anyone could remember. Framed in heavy dark wood, it is a faded illustration of the Virgin Mary praying with a large serpent coiled at her feet. It is yellowing, stained, torn and damaged by water. My aunts recalled that it had once been in a church in Baghdad that was torn down and the priest gave it to the family. They thought it was about a century old. Thirteen gold crowns topped with crosses are stuck around the Virgin's head and body; one has fallen down in between the glass and the frame. Each time a prayer was answered, a golden crown was added.

My aunts said that sometimes women in the family had prayed to the icon when they were infertile, asking Mary to bless them with children. Maha's grandmother had spoken angrily to Mary and told her that she couldn't call herself the true Virgin if she didn't answer her prayer and grant her a child. She became pregnant that same month, so she named her daughter Mary. I looked at these crowns symbolizing answered prayers of long-gone family members. We don't know who added them but they are in different styles and must have been added at different times. I happened to be newly pregnant when I first saw the icon, and felt compelled to pray for a healthy child. The following year I gave birth to a daughter.

The suitcase full of documents that my father had asked Karim to bring when he fled is now housed with distant family members living in Baghdad. One suitcase is all that is left in Iraq of a family whose roots in that landscape, culture and language go back thousands of years, an ancient connection that likely reaches back to the earliest Christians, perhaps earlier. A suitcase bereft of even a person to carry it to the next homeland.

My five-year-old son—born just weeks after this book was first published—is currently obsessed with outer space. We are following Chris Hadfield, the Canadian commander of the International Space Station, who is posting photographs of Earth from space via his Twitter account. He takes one of Baghdad with the caption, "Once the largest city on Earth, millions of us call this city home." I send it to my father. He writes back, "Our house was in that teardrop shape bend in the river; to think you can see it from orbit. The river flows on both sides of this part of the city." When anyone from our family next goes to that teardrop shape bend in the river, it will be as a visitor, a stranger in a strange land.

Now I imagine walking down our street in Karrada, peering at the numbers in Arabic on the houses, stopping at "our house," seeing the palm fronds beckoning from the garden behind it, and never being able to go inside, never seeing whether the orange trees recovered and bore fruit. I'll go and find that suitcase, open it and see what artefacts of a life long gone are left behind. I'd like to liberate them.

Vancouver, Canada
May 21, 2013

ℬIBLIOGRAPHY

Al-Radi, Nuha. *Baghdad Diaries*. New York: Vintage, 2003.

Ajami, Fouad. *The Dream Palace of the Arabs: A Generation's Odyssey*, Vintage Books: New York, 1999.

Dabrowska, Karen. *Iraq: The Bradt Travel Guide*. Bucks, UK: Bradt Travel Guides, Ltd, 2002.

Hiro, Dilip. *The Essential Middle East*. London: Macmillan Press Ltd, 1996.

Kattan, Naim. *Farewell, Babylon: Coming of Age in Jewish Baghdad*. Vancouver: Raincoast Books, 2005.

Kramer, Samuel Noah, and The Editors of Life Books. *Cradle of Civilization*. New York: Time-Life Books, 1987

Mansfield, Peter. *A History of the Middle East*. London: Penguin, 1992.

Miller, Janet. *Camel-bells of Baghdad*. London: G.P. Putnam's Sons, 1935.

Munier, Gilles. *Iraq: An Illustrated History and Guide*. Northampton, MA: Interlink Publishing Group, Inc, 2004.

Pax, Salam. *The Baghdad Blog*. Toronto: McArthur & Company, 2003.

Polk, William R. *Understanding Iraq*. London: I B Tauris, 2006.

Ranelagh, E.L. *The Past We Share*. London: Quartet Books, 1979.

Rassam, Suha. *Christianity in Iraq*. Herefordshire, UK: Gracewing, 2005.

Reade, Julian. *Mesopotamia*. London: British Museum Press, 1991.

Riverbend. *Baghdad Burning: Girl Blog from Iraq*. New York: The Feminist Press at CUNY, 2005.

Roberts, Paul William. *A War Against Truth*. Vancouver, BC: Raincoast Books, 2004.

Shadid, Anthony. *Night Draws Near*. New York: Picador, 2005.

Stark, Freya. *Baghdad Sketches*. Evanston, IL: The Marlboro Press/Northwestern Edition, 1996. Originally published in 1938.

Stark, Freya. *Beyond Euphrates*. London: Century Publishing, 1983. Originally published in 1951.

Tripp, Charles. *A History of Iraq*. Cambridge: Cambridge University Press, 2002.

$\mathcal{A}$CKNOWLEDGEMENTS

I could never have written this book without my father's assent and co-operation, and I thank him for entrusting me with his story and giving me the freedom to tell it in my own way. My mother's resolute support and love gave me confidence.

I thank my family, in Canada, England and Iraq, with all my heart for telling me their stories and giving me permission to transmit them to a wider audience. I admire Farah Nosh for her bravery and thank her for being the conduit between me and my Iraqi family. She has permitted me to use quotations and paraphrase stories from her journal, which I am grateful for. If you'd like to see more of Farah's incredible award-winning photography, please visit www.farahnosh.com.

Natasha was my constant nurturer, who helped me discover the drama in the everyday. A special thanks to Serena and Daniel for their detailed and encouraging thoughts on the manuscript.

George Elliott Clarke gave me the initial idea for the book: "You should write a family memoir about Iraq." His ongoing belief in my story made it easier to write the truth. I thank Rosemary Sullivan and Moira Farr for their support at the Cultural Journalism program at the Banff Centre. Thanks to Irving Finkel for agreeing to be interviewed for this book. Thank you to my agent, Denise Bukowski, for believing in this book from the outset and being resolutely committed to its publication. Janie Yoon, my editor, encouraged me to pen the book that I originally envisioned, and I thank her for this trust and her deft editorial hand. I thank Marijke Friesen for her beautiful cover design. Andrea Skinner read early drafts and gave me vital sustenance, and Tristan Hughes gave me counsel and conversation about writing. Jesse Finkelstein walked with me through the last years, insisting I could write this book.

My friends are my lifeline: Yaseen Al-Salam, Gaelle Beauclair, Jennifer Benyon, Thea Boyanowsky, Marianne Brooks, Dianne Carruthers, Andrea Egan, Dara Frere, Amber Houssian, Julia Iriarte, Paula Iriarte, Ameen Merchant, Vincent Marchand, Mark Macarthur, Gillian Guilmant-Smith, Yasmeen Strang, Mark Rowe, Judith Wolff. You have all tended this book.

The Orange Trees of Baghdad was not only written in Vancouver, but at other people's houses in France, England, Spain and Canada. I thank those people for their hospitality: my aunts in London; Andrea Egan in Barcelona; Jennifer and Edward Benyon at Lovegrove Farm; Claire Taylor on Salt Spring Island; Jocelyn and Alan Steedman in Victoria; and Janice Beley at Blue Cat Lane on the Sunshine Coast.

My thanks extend to the Canada Council for the Arts, the Banff Centre for the Arts and the MacDowell Colony in New Hampshire for supporting me at various stages of my writing career. I'm grateful to the editors at *Brick* magazine for publishing the article "The Fruits of War," on which this book is based. Selections from "Finding Family in Lebanon" were first published in the *Tyee* on August 2, 2006, and the article "A Church Rocked to its Ancient Foundations," first appeared on August 6, 2004 in *The Globe and Mail*. "One Year Later, Iraq in Chaos" appeared in the *Georgia Straight* on March 17, 2004. The opening section of the epilogue first appeared in a slightly different form in the 2009 French edition of this book published by Editions Payot.

The sources for the chapter opening quotes are as follows: Chapter Three's opening quote is taken from Robert Fisk's *The Great War for Civilization*, Fourth Estate, 2005; the quote from Chapter Seventeen is taken from *The War Works Hard* by Dunya Mikhail, New Directions Publishing Corp., 2005; the quote from Chapter Eighteen is taken from "Remembrance of Things Past: On the City of Peace, Baghdad," *Al-Ahram Weekly*, Baghdad Supplement, Issue. No 634, April 17–23 2003.

Websites cited include www.iraqbodycount.org, www.democracy now.org, and www.jhsph.edu/publichealthnews/press_releases/2006/burnham_iraq_2006.html (Johns Hopkins Bloomberg School of Public Health).

Additional thanks to Dimiter Savoff of Read Leaf for giving this book another life. I want to acknowledge the generosity of Bob and Joan Mair for their gifts of Iraqi carpets and art. And thank you to my newfound family in Canada for reaching out to me with their wonderful hospitality—and for providing a glimmer of hope, an ending I could not have dreamed of when I began writing. I won't name names here to protect your privacy, but thanks to all of you, I am very lucky in family.

Lastly, I want to thank my husband, Scott, who has, with characteristic passion and unwavering steadfastness, supported me and my writing life daily; without him I could not have written this book.

*I*NDEX

LEILAH NADIR has a master's degree in English Literature from Edinburgh University. Her memoir *The Orange Trees of Baghdad* won the 2008 George Ryga Award and has been published in Canada, Australia and New Zealand, Italy, Turkey and France. Her fiction has appeared in *Descant* and on CBC radio. She has written and broadcast commentaries for the CBC, *The Globe and Mail*, *The Georgia Straight*, *Brick* and the anthology *How They See Us: Meditations on America*, edited by James Atlas.

www.leilahnadir.com